Rights After Wrongs

Stanford Studies in Human Rights

Rights After Wrongs

Local Knowledge and
Human Rights in Zimbabwe

Shannon Morreira

Stanford University Press
Stanford, California

Stanford University Press
Stanford, California

Printed on acid-free, archival-quality paper

Printed and bound in Great Britain by
Marston Book Services Ltd, Oxfordshire

Library of Congress Cataloging-in-Publication Data

Names: Morreira, Shannon, author.
Title: Rights after wrongs : local knowledge and human rights in Zimbabwe / Shannon Morreira.
Description: Stanford, California : Stanford University Press, 2016. | © 2016 | Series: Stanford studies in human rights | Includes bibliographical references and index.
Identifiers: LCCN 2015034992 | ISBN 9780804798372 (cloth : alk. paper) | ISBN 9780804799089 (pbk : alk. paper)
Subjects: LCSH: Human rights—Anthropological aspects—Zimbabwe. | International law and human rights—Zimbabwe. | Zimbabweans—Civil rights—South Africa.
Classification: LCC KTZ209.5.M67 2016 | DDC 342.689108—dc23
LC record available at http://lccn.loc.gov/2015034992

ISBN 9780804799096 (electronic)

Typeset by Thompson Type in 10/14 Minion

Contents

Foreword

SHANNON MORREIRA'S *Rights After Wrongs: Local Knowledge and Human Rights in Zimbabwe* is a profound mediation on the ways in which multiple entanglements complicate even the most critical theories of human rights as a pervasive mode of contemporary world making and world representing. These include Morreira's own entanglements as an anthropologist, social advocate, and a member of the "first postindependence urban generation of Zimbabweans," someone who finds herself among the Zimbabwean diaspora in South Africa. Throughout the book, Morreira draws on this complicated situationality to argue for an approach to understanding the practice of human rights that extends concepts like vernacularization and localization to apprehend what she describes as the "sites of rich polyvalence and cultural ingenuity" at which Zimbabweans come to terms with state violence, economic decline, and chronic hopelessness.

As Morreira's ethnography demonstrates, there is a certain recursivity to the way in which global and transnational human rights discourses get appropriated within specific social, political, and legal processes at specific moments that make up the Oakeshottian "world of present experience." In her analysis, it is important to draw distinctions among the abstract universalist claims (and pretentions) of human rights, the equally abstract assumptions about how these claims should be adopted in practice, and how they are, in fact, actually adopted. It is this last step with which Morreira's study is largely concerned, that is, what might be thought of as the actually existing practice of human rights beyond abstractions of all kinds. Nevertheless, as she points out, these real practices of human rights are never completely separate from the abstractions that to a large extent prefigure them. As Morreira's research on the prevalence of "rights talk" in Zimbabwe reveals, the boundaries of human right ideology form limits to the extent to which the connotative power of human rights discourse can be pushed.

At the same time, Morreira's study of the practices of human rights in Zimbabwe is deeply embedded in the broader arc of history through which Zimbabwe emerged quite late from its contested and violent colonial past with a postcolonial euphoria that by the early 1990s had disappeared in the face of internal political repression and the macroeconomic impact of external International Monetary Fund structural adjustment policies. As she acknowledges, her study unfolded long after Zimbabwe's manifold problems had become markers for a kind of postcolonial trajectory that was on its way to total state failure. These were challenging conditions indeed in which to track the potential of human rights discourse in a country in which independence from a colonial regime did not mean the transition from despair to possibility but rather, as Morreira puts it (quoting Stuart Hall), the "passage from one [set of] historical power configurations or conjunctures to another."

The fraught relationship between postcolonial disenchantment and the utopian limits of human rights discourse is perhaps no better illustrated than in Morreira's discussion of the debates leading up the writing and passage of a new constitution in Zimbabwe in 2013. Although this new social contract was meant to "shine like chrome, as captivating as beads," as a promotional guide put it, in fact, as Morreira discovered, what resulted was the product of a complicated process of normative laundering through which the entrenched "power configurations" of the ruling party were legitimated in the language of democracy, freedom, and empowerment.

And yet, despite the sobering sense of restraint that runs through Morreira's study, she concludes on a note of possibility. For as she argues, human rights discourse is never the only resource for people trying to craft meaning and purpose in the face of violence and suffering. As her research among the Tree of Life movement showed, it was important to keep in mind that human rights were "drawn in . . . as a single set of possibilities amongst many" because even though the language of human rights had become conflated with state power, "it is not possible to shut down all alternative ways of knowing and being in the world."

Mark Goodale
Series Editor
Stanford Studies in Human Rights

Acknowledgments

THE FINANCIAL ASSISTANCE of the National Research Foundation (Grant Number 82098) and the David and Elaine Potter Foundation toward this research is hereby acknowledged. The opinions expressed and conclusions arrived at are those of the author and are not necessarily to be attributed to the NRF or the David and Elaine Potter Foundation. I wish to express my appreciation of this support to both organizations. I wish to thank Munashe Mkaronda for permission to print her poem "Because of You" in this book.

This research would not have been possible without the assistance of several organizations and individuals. I wish to thank all participants who gave of their time and their stories; without these organizations and individuals I would have no book to present here and a much less rich set of life experiences and friendships.

Professor Fiona Ross, from the Department of Social Anthropology at the University of Cape Town, has given deeply and generously of her thoughts, time, and empathy over the course of this project. Fiona, I cannot thank you enough for all of it.

For their support at various points during the long processes of fieldwork and writing this book I wish to thank Jess Auerbach, Tendai Bhiza, David Burgsdorff, Richard Calland, Gillian Charles, Rebecca Chennells, Bertha Chiguvare, Kuda Chitsike, Sally Frankental, Imke Gooskens, Braam Hanekom, Daniel Hargrove, Mohamed Hassan, Patricia Henderson, Ellen Hurst, Robyn Human, Ginny, Peter and Andrew Iliff (Harare still does not feel quite like home without you, Pete), Rita Kesselring, Kathy Luckett, Fungai Maisva, Jacob Matakanye, Langton Miriyoga, Anthony Muteti, Barnabas Muvhuti, Rory Pilossof, Efua Prah, Tony, Bev and Kate Reeler, Mariam Suliman, Anna Versfeld, and Rodwell White.

And, of course, I want to thank James, who has borne the brunt of field-work absences, predawn writing sessions, and other erratic behavior with kindness, generosity, and love and who stimulates my thinking every day, and I have such love for Sam, whose impending arrival ensured that I finally wrapped up my research and whose good cheer kept me smiling as I turned this work into a book.

List of Abbreviations and Acronyms

ACHPR	African Charter on Human and People's Rights (also called the Banjul Charter)
ANC	African National Congress, South Africa's leading political party
CCJP	Catholic Commission for Justice and Peace
CEDAW	Convention on the Elimination of All Forms of Discrimination Against Women
COPAC	The Constitutional Parliamentary Committee, set up under Article VI of the GPA.
GNU	Government of National Unity
GPA	Global Political Agreement, also known as the Interparty Political Agreement, signed by ZANU-PF and the two MDCs in September 2008.
ICCPR	International Covenant on Civil and Political Rights
ICESCR	International Covenant on Economic, Social and Cultural Rights
ICTJ	International Centre for Transitional Justice
IDASA	Institute for Democracy in Africa
IOM	International Organisation for Migration
LOMA	Law and Order Maintenance Act
MDC-M	Movement for Democratic Change (Mutambara faction).
MDC-T	Movement for Democratic Change (Tsvangirai faction).
MSF	Médicins Sans Frontierès, or Doctors without Borders
NCA	National Constitutional Assembly
NGO	Nongovernmental organization
OAU	Organisation of African Unity

ONHRI	Organ on National Healing, Reconciliation and Integration
PASSOP	People Against Suffering, Oppression and Poverty
POSA	Public Order and Security Act (2002)
RAU	The Research and Advocacy Unit
RSDO	Refugee Status Determination Officer
SADC	Southern African Development Community
STOPVAW	Stop Violence Against Women
TRC	Truth and Reconciliation Commission (South Africa)
UCT	The University of Cape Town
UDHR	Universal Declaration of Human Rights
UNHCR	United Nations High Commission for Refugees
UN OHCHR	United Nations Office for the High Commission of Human Rights
USAID	United States Agency for International Development
WCoZ	Women's Coalition of Zimbabwe
WOZA	Women of Zimbabwe Arise
ZANU-PF	Zimbabwe African National Union – Patriotic Front
ZBC	Zimbabwe Broadcasting Commission
ZCC	Zimbabwe Council of Churches
ZDP	Zimbabwean Dispensation Project
ZLHR	Zimbabwe Lawyers for Human Rights

Rights After Wrongs

The Rise of Rights Talk in Zimbabwe

There are no "neutral" words and forms—words and forms that belong to "no one";
language [is] shot through with intentions and accents . . . All words have the "taste"
of a profession, a genre, a tendency, a party, a particular work, a particular person,
a generation, an age group, the day and hour. Each word tastes of the context
and contexts in which it has lived its socially charged life; all words and forms are
populated by intentions.

Mikhael Bakhtin (1981: 293)

Globalisation has two sides: that of the narrative of modernity and that of the logic of
coloniality.

W. Mignolo (2012: 5)

"Rights, Not Wrongs": An Introduction

In 2007, I attended a protest held at the Home Affairs Refugee Centre in central Cape Town in South Africa. My research at the time was focused on Zimbabwean undocumented migration to South Africa—as a Zimbabwean living in South Africa myself, I had a personal and political interest in the topic and in taking part in the protest that day. As an anthropologist and a member of the activist group that organized the protest, I was present when a group of Zimbabweans began the process of writing on banners provided by the organizers before the event. A group of ten interlocutors, comprised of black men and women ranging in age from their early twenties to late fifties, clustered around an old sheet that was placed on the pavement outside the gates of the Centre, with one man brandishing a paintbrush and a tin of red paint. He squatted down, dipped the brush in paint, held it over the sheet . . . and then hesitated. "What do I write?" he asked. "What are we saying to these people?"

There was a moment of silence, followed by a plethora of answers—"We are tired of waiting for an appointment"; "We are not animals that must wait in the rain for them to let us inside"; "We want to be allowed to stay here because things are so bad at home"; "We are tired of being illegal when we have done nothing wrong"; "We want to say that we are suffering, here and at home"; "We have had enough of Mugabe and Mbeki";[1] and "We would not be here if we could make a living at home." The man looked at his companions and said, "But I can't write all those things on a banner. It must be catchy, quick—but it must say why we are here." There was a pause while people tried to think of something catchy, something "quick"—and then one man said, "Just write, 'We want human rights, not human wrongs,' or 'No rights in Zimbabwe, no rights in South Africa.'" Everyone in the group nodded approvingly, and the two banners were made. A language of human rights, it seemed, was able to speak across disparate intentions—to provide a summarizing symbol (Ortner, 1973) that could encompass suffering, tiredness, illegality, personhood, politics, economics, and morality (both "here" and "at home") and "quickly" transpose these to the powerful realm of legal language.

That brief moment outside Home Affairs in Cape Town seemed to provide a window into the entanglements (Mbembe, 2001; Nuttall, 2009) at play when the notion of human rights is called on. Throughout my fieldwork as an anthropologist studying the Zimbabwean political and economic situation in the post-2000 era—working originally with Zimbabweans in South Africa in 2007 and 2008 and then moving on to detailed ethnographic work in Zimbabwe itself from 2008 to 2011—"human rights" (or just "rights"[2]) were invoked again and again, in contexts as diverse as the christening of a child or the personal recounting of a life history marred by political violence. For interlocutors, the phrase "human rights" came to take on a tangible force and seemed to carry enormous symbolic capital (Bourdieu, 1986, 1992). This is not unusual in postcolonial Southern Africa: Englund and Nyamnjoh (2004: 31) argue that the "rhetoric of rights" has become common to the postcolonial African lexicon.[3] The conversation between protesters reproduced in this vignette is a good starting point for this book as it locates the Zimbabwean individuals present at a protest that day within a wider world of academic and political discourse. The vignette raises issues of local and transnational politics and economics, evokes the domains of citizenship and personhood, points to academic debates around human rights as legal practice and as popular discourse, and highlights the (contemporary) primacy of the law as a means to resist marginality (Comaroff and Comaroff, 2007; Robins, 2008b).

Why examine the ways in which Zimbabweans have been using ideas of rights? In the course of the anthropological fieldwork I conducted in South Africa in 2007 and 2008, it became clear that discourses of human rights were central to Zimbabwean migrants' experiences of movement—or at least to the ways in which they recounted those experiences to an audience, be that audience comprised of anthropologist, neighbor, family member, journalist, Home Affairs official, or a mixture of all of the above (Morreira, 2010b). The language of rights carries power: To recount a difficult migration history in its terms means it is more likely to be heard than it is if told in another way. However, it became clear that migrants' notions of what constituted their human rights, or an infringement of those rights, differed from those fixed in legal categories. The contradiction between the comparatively "fixed"[4] definitions of human rights within a legal framework, and the malleable use of human and civil rights talk as discourse and practice within varied local contexts was apparent. In legal terms, rights and human rights are usually conceptually distinct and carry different political and social claims. That Zimbabwean interlocutors moved between both terms without much reflection seemed worth exploring. "Human rights," far from representing a fixed set of laws that outline the basic rights of individuals, was an extremely malleable concept and one that, for migrants, shifted daily according to circumstance. I was led to question in what ways, if any, ideas of human rights were being used by Zimbabweans who were still "at home"—did rights discourse become relevant only on movement across borders, or was it just as relevant within the politico-economic context of contemporary Zimbabwe? And what could the use of rights-based language and ideology tell us about local articulations of so-called Western epistemologies or ways of knowing the world? What forms of knowledge get called on, and what kinds of hierarchies are created in the process? Such questions led me to embark on the detailed fieldwork within Zimbabwe that has led to this book.

The work presented here is based on ethnographic fieldwork conducted in Zimbabwe and, to a lesser degree, with Zimbabweans resident in South Africa, over a period from 2007 to 2011. I argue that although the international legal framework of human rights may present itself as universal, rights are enacted, practiced, and debated in local contexts that influence how, and for what purposes, ideas of rights are used. Narrow legal categories of human rights and civil rights get expanded in popular talk such that human rights and rights come to be used interchangeably: When trying to export such malleable popular uses of rights into the less immediately malleable legal domain of human rights, however, people run into difficulties. Anthropological approaches to the study of human rights by theorists such as Englund (2006), Goodale (2006a, 2006b, 2009a), Merry (2005, 2006), Wilson and Mitchell (2003), and Wilson (2006) assert the need to study rights in practice, arguing that detailed ethnographic examination of local contexts can show the ways in which supposedly universal ideals become localized. In this book I use the contemporary political and economic context of Zimbabwe as a case study to explore the ways in which a global framework of human rights has been locally interpreted, constituted, and contested. I argue that although localization can be seen to occur, it happens within a set of unequal power relations. This furthers anthropological debates around human rights by considering the ways in which the forms that localizations are able to take are the result of the ways in which knowledge is organized and prioritized globally, such that certain ways of representing experience—such as through a lens of individualized human rights—are accorded greater legitimacy than other ways of representing experience—such as through a lens of shared personhood and communal obligations. The politics of human rights discourses, then, can be seen through this case to be part and parcel of the globalized politics of knowledge and power, which carry colonial histories into the postcolonial present (Mignolo, 2012).

The ethnography presented here is multisited, as a key effect of the Zimbabwean crisis has been the movement of people across Southern Africa and beyond, and as the ideas that inform local manifestations of rights talk are global products. Although the assumed universality of rights is important to its global and local legitimacy (the fact that it purportedly applies to everyone, regardless, gives it moral capital), it is also because ideas of rights are flexible enough to be able to incorporate local ideas of morality and personhood that they are able to be considered valid in very disparate contexts. Nonetheless, such localization occurs within the terms of a framework of rights (which itself stems from the organizing logic of modernity) and is therefore limited.

A Brief Historicization: Zimbabwe in Context

The opening vignette showed rights talk to be the mode of expression chosen by Zimbabwean protestors in South Africa, as a means of speaking about political and economic conditions within both Zimbabwe *and* South Africa. How did so many Zimbabweans come to be seeking asylum in South Africa that they were using a language of human rights to critique the conditions in their home country that brought them there and to critique the inability of the South African refugee system to deal with their applications? The Southern African state of Zimbabwe has been in existence since 1980; prior to that, the colonized country was named Rhodesia—a British colony until 1965, it maintained white minority rule until the advent of independence in 1980. Zimbabwe's contemporary situation has its roots in intricate colonial and postcolonial histories and events, and the emergence of rights talk as a mode of expression in Zimbabwe has its underpinnings in this long history, which encompasses precolonial political systems (Bhebhe and Ranger, 2001; Ndlovu-Gatsheni, 2008), colonization and British settlement in the 1880s (Raftopoulos and Mlambo, 2009), and a period of colonial rule until 1980 that saw the introduction and violent maintenance of British (and subsequently Rhodesian) political and legal structures (Ncube, 2001; Ranger, 2001; Ndlovu-Gatsheni, 2008; Raftopoulos and Mlambo, 2009).

In the 1970s the country underwent a violent struggle against Rhodesian rule; termed the Second *Chimurenga* (with the first *Chimurenga* being an unsuccessful uprising by both Shona and Ndebele people against the British South Africa Company in the 1890s), this nationalist liberation struggle eventuated in independence in 1980. The country's first election to include the majority of the population was won in 1980 by one of the two major nationalist parties, the (predominantly Shona) Zimbabwe African National Union (ZANU) led by Robert Mugabe, which had fought the war against the Rhodesians alongside the (predominantly Ndebele) Zimbabwe African People's Union (ZAPU).[5] Independence was followed by a period of postcolonial nation building and economic successes that occurred in the 1980s under President Robert Mugabe's rule (Raftopoulos, 2004). For all its successes, however, the decade of the 1980s was also a period of internal political violence, with the advent of *Gukurahundi*, a state-based systematic program of violence against the Ndebele population, ostensibly in response to the actions of dissidents but in reality an operation that targeted civilians and ex-soldiers alike

(CCJP, 1997). Thus, although Raftopoulos (2004: 2) rightly categorizes the 1980s as "the years of restoration and hope" across some parts of the country, in others they were years of violence and dissatisfaction with the ruling party.

In the 1990s dissatisfaction with the ZANU-PF government grew more widespread: The 1990s saw a period of increasing economic decline, the implementation of an International Monetary Fund (IMF)–directed structural adjustment program and the beginnings of widespread frustration with the postcolonial system of governance (Bhebhe and Ranger, 2001). Varied kinds of civil society rose in Zimbabwe, with some liberal forms advocating mainly for democratic rights and the basic security of persons, whereas more radical forms such as trade unions and student movements advocated for socioeconomic rights (Helliker, 2013). Rights discourses (in the plural) gained prevalence.[6] I will return to this in the following chapter, but for now it is enough to note that the institutional terrain of the country saw a rise in rights talk in the 1990s but that "civil society" was not homogenous and was thoroughly contextually specific. In other words, supposedly "Western" rights were not imported wholesale but were picked up and used in various ways by variously situated political actors.

By the late 1990s economic and political conditions had worsened considerably, and in 1999 Zimbabwe entered a period of severe economic collapse, which occurred hand in hand with a decline in democratic freedoms and a corresponding increase in political violence against citizens (Hammar and Raftopoulos, 2003; Kamete, 2008; Orner and Holmes, 2010; Murithi and Mawadza, 2011; Morreira, 2015a). An opposition party to the ZANU-PF government,[7] the Movement for Democratic Change (MDC) emerged out of the country's trade unions in 1999, with limited electoral success but a wide urban support base. In light of this political threat, violations of the political rights of citizens became increasingly common under the Mugabe government—flawed electoral processes, state control of the judiciary and the media, and frequent violence against the opposition party members and supporters are just some of the critiques that have been leveled by rights organizations at the Mugabe regime (for example, see Human Rights Watch, 2006). Further, the increase in violence included a deepening of structural violence[8] (see Morreira, 2010b; cf. Farmer, 1996, and Kleinman, 1997) to the point that, in 2007 and 2008, the undocumented migrants with whom I worked were trying (largely unsuccessfully) to use human rights discourse to argue that the economic situation was dire enough to warrant refugee status for Zimbabweans in South Africa (Morreira, 2010a). State institutions and infrastructure deteriorated to the extent that in 2004 Hough and Du Plessis categorized Zimbabwe as a failed state. Although such an epithet seems excessive given the state's continued existence (and given the ways in which the state functioned extremely efficiently at some levels, such as the security sector), there is no doubt that life changed radically for most Zimbabweans in a very short space of time (Morreira, 2015a). The invocation of rights discourses by the Zimbabwean migrants present at that protest in 2007, then, occurred in response to the political and economic decline of the post-2000 period but also reflected a much longer history of shifting political institutions and the transnational flow of people and ideas. As Hall (2001a: 213) notes, a series of complex temporal connections are at play in what we characterize as the "postcolony," such that "the 'post-colonial' does not signal a simple before/after chronological succession . . . rather [it] marks the passage from one [set of] historical power configurations or conjunctures to another."

Many things have changed in Zimbabwe and South Africa since that windy afternoon in 2007 with which I opened this chapter. South Africa has seen the inauguration of a new president, Jacob Zuma, and the previous incumbent, Thabo Mbeki, largely disappeared from the South African (but not the wider African) political scene. Mbeki was integral to the development and implementation of South Africa's policy of "quiet diplomacy" toward the Zimbabwean government (see Hough and Du Plessis, 2004), which had angered many Zimbabweans for its seeming ineffectuality at creating any positive change for Zimbabwe—hence the earlier comment that "we have had enough of Mugabe *and* Mbeki." Zimbabwe's main opposition party to ZANU-PF, the MDC, fractured into two factions in 2005,[9] following political infighting, which complicated quiet diplomacy negotiations and weakened the opposition's political position. In addition to changes at the level of party politics in both countries, the social landscape of South Africa was altered by the advent of countrywide episodes of xenophobic violence in 2008 (see Hassim et al., 2008, and Steinberg, 2008), which left sixty-two people dead, hundreds injured, and tens of thousands displaced from their homes (Worby et al., 2008).

Xenophobic violence resurfaced, albeit on a smaller scale, across the country again in 2015. The violence was directed at *amakwerekwere*, a derogatory term for "people who were identified as not properly belonging to the South African nation" (Worby et al., 2008: 7).

Shortly after the outbreaks of violence in 2008, while many of those affected were still residing in temporary camps and shelters across South Africa, neighboring Zimbabwe held both parliamentary and presidential elections, leading to a hope among the Zimbabweans with whom I worked in South Africa that they would be able to leave the uncertain place that South Africa had become to return to a safer and more economically stable Zimbabwe. This was not to be: Although the MDC gained a majority in parliament for the first time, Mugabe regained the presidency following a runoff election from which MDC leader Morgan Tsvangirai withdrew because of violence against his supporters. The 2008 elections were locally, and to some extent internationally, perceived to be the most deeply flawed Zimbabwean elections up to that point in time[10] (International Crisis Group, 2008; Masunungure, 2009). Despite fears of xenophobic violence, most of my interlocutors[11] remained in South Africa.

In early 2009, a power-sharing deal was brokered between ZANU-PF and the MDC with the signing of the Global Political Agreement (GPA), which saw Mugabe retain the presidency and control of the National Security Council, while Tsvangirai assumed the post of prime minister and control over the Council of Ministers. Few of my interlocutors, however, felt the situation changed enough at this point to warrant a return to Zimbabwe. Rather, they feared that the only impact of power sharing would be the loss of a viable opposition to ZANU-PF as the MDC "sold out" to the ZANU-PF dispensation. Even though the signing of the GPA lead to improved economic stability over time, the majority of these interlocutors remained in South Africa. At the time I began field research in 2010, MDC-T leader Morgan Tsvangirai had just "disengaged" from the unity government following the (re)arrest of an MDC MP (New African, 2009), belying fears of the loss of MDC "morality" but effectively showing that, even under the new dispensation, power still lay with ZANU-PF. Tsvangirai subsequently "reengaged," but throughout the period of my fieldwork in Zimbabwe the three parties coexisted in fraught and frosty conditions, with frequent incidences of political infighting that showed the Government of National Unity (GNU) to be largely a misnomer.

Writing in 2012, journalist Mary Ndlovu characterized the situation as one of "political paralysis" that "has brought economic stagnation and a continuation of social desperation" (Ndlovu, 2012); Iliff (2012) characterized Zimbabwe under the GNU as undergoing an "existential crisis beneath [a] thin veneer of normality." In a similar vein, but drawing on a different cosmological foundation, the Zimbabwe Council of Churches (ZCC) deemed the situation serious enough to be categorized as a "moral crisis bedeviling Zimbabwe" (ZCC, 2009).[12] Throughout my research, structural and physical violence remained common, both for Zimbabweans at home and for Zimbabwean migrants in South Africa. In July 2013, Zimbabwe went back to the ballot stations: The country held an election in which Robert Mugabe was reelected as president, and ZANU-PF won a two-thirds majority, effectively ousting the MDC from their (already limited) position in government. As with the previous election, the results were greeted with deep suspicion across the country, with accusations of rigging surfacing as soon as the results became known.

Theoretical Points of Departure: Rights in Context

The protest gathering with which I opened this chapter serves to illustrate the malleability of human rights within popular discourse. What, then, *are* "human rights"? On one level, the answer, although not simple, is at least easily definable—human rights constitute the minimum set of conditions in which people, by the simple virtue of *being* people, are entitled to live their lives. As much of human life is composed of relationships, these rights include guidelines for how people should treat one another and how states should treat their citizens. As such, human rights also constitute a normative moral guide for social behavior (albeit one based in a particular Western philosophical and ethical tradition) that has been encoded in national and international law. In Africa, for example, "human rights" are those things that have been written, in legal terminology or "legalese," into the African Charter on Human and People's Rights (ACHPR) as adopted by the Organisation of African Unity (OAU) in 1981 (Akokpari and Zimbler, 2008) and to which, as African Union members, Zimbabwe and South Africa are signatory. South Africa and Zimbabwe also each have a constitutionally encoded Bill of Rights. How many people, however, are well versed in such legal documents? Legal charters reflect a domain of a specific sector of the elite—yet "human rights" as a phrase is one that is drawn on by many more diverse sectors of the populace, from other elites to, as the preceding example shows, the deeply marginalized. Notions of "human rights," then, have to reflect more than that encoded in charters—beyond this legal discourse lies a realm of rights that is truly "socially charged" (Bakhtin, 1981: 293), a realm that is, to mix my theorists and borrow a phrase from Richard Wilson (2006; cf. Appadurai, 1986), immersed in the social life of words.

The presence of rights talk in my interlocutors' daily lives can be linked to both the political and economic conditions in Zimbabwe and South Africa and to the growing global emphasis on human rights. Wilson (2006: 77) has noted that "human rights became, in the second half of the 20th Century, a political value with global ambitions, analogous to political meta-narratives such as 'liberal democracy' or 'socialism.'" In South Africa, ideas of human and civil rights form the backbone of the Constitution: Adopted in 1996, this rights-based document is one of the most protective of the human rights of its citizens in the world (or, in neoliberal terminology, one of the world's most "progressive").

The ideas (ideals?) of human rights can usefully be examined as a set of discourses, in that the metanarrative of rights constructs particular systems of language and thought with accompanying sets of rights-based courses of action and institutions. Such systems may differ slightly in varied local contexts, as is shown ethnographically throughout this book; nonetheless, all are governed by a particular means of making sense of the world. In *The Order of Discourse* (1970), Foucault argued that all knowledge is composed of rules, systems, and procedures; together, these produce the conceptual terrains by which we are able to comprehend, and act on, the world.

Human rights can be seen to be one of the main discourses of modernity. Nyamnjoh (2012b) argues that, in the social sciences, colonial epistemology has privileged an ahistorical mode of thinking about Africa, which "sacrifices pluriversity for university and imposes a one best way of attaining a singular and universal truth" (Nyamnjoh, 2012b: 131). Under the guise of modernity, such an epistemology has "promis(ed) 'development' for individuals and groups who repent from 'retrogressive' attitudes, cultures, traditions and practices" (Nyamnjoh, 2012b: 131). Both rights discourse and ideas of development more broadly are embroiled within this historical context. It is worth considering the ways in which ideas of rights have emerged as part of the epistemological hierarchies created by modernity.

Decolonial thinking, as seen in the work of Latin American theorists such as Mignolo (2012) and Quijano (1999) and as used in Southern Africa by Ndlovu-Gatsheni (2013), is predicated on the idea that although colonialism delineates a temporal period of oppression that has come and gone, coloniality—the underlying hierarchizing logic that places peoples and knowledges into a classificatory framework such that the European is valorized—is still very much with us. Decolonial thinkers argue that modernity is predicated on coloniality and that one product of modernity has been the creation and maintenance of the kind of knowledge and ways of being in the world that are considered legitimate. Quijano thus argues that a "colonial matrix of power" (in Mignolo, 2012: ix) consisting of interrelated forms of control such as patriarchy, racism, knowledge, authority, and the economy underlies Western civilization. Although colonialism may have been and gone, the colonial matrix of power is still very much seen, lived, and felt in the present day. Mignolo draws on the colonial matrix to argue that "such a system of knowledge (the 'western code') serves not all humanity but a small portion of it that benefits from the belief that in terms of epistemology there is only one game in town" (Mignolo, 2012: xii). Coloniality is also a system of management and domination that affects the ways in which people are able to be in the world, based on the social categories to which they have been allocated by birth, geography, or other circumstance. Modernity, according to Mignolo, provides a rhetoric of salvation, whether seen through the salvation provided by Christianity, by the civilizing mission, or by, in its latest permutation, discourses of "development." Development discourse creates "the myth that there are global needs but only one (diverse) centre where knowledge is produced to solve the problems of everybody" (ibid., xvii).

Of course, critiques of development are not new. Postdevelopment theory, as seen in the work of critics of development such as James Ferguson (1990), Arturo Escobar (1995), and Majid Rahnema (1997), have long made similar claims. Escobar (1995) posits that development is driven by Western interests and Western systems of knowledge, such that development reflects Western hegemony. This results in a hierarchy of developed versus underdeveloped ("Third World") nations, and a system of categorizing the world that sees "underdeveloped" nations as needing the help of the "developed" nations to become like them. Such a hierarchized knowledge system stems from the ways in which the social world is constructed under modernity. In Mignolo's (2012) view, one theme of the colonial matrix is the narrowing down of valid possibilities, such that one way of being in the world is viewed as more valid than all others. One of the ways this can be seen to manifest is in development, which Escobar (1995) defines as a set of discourses in that it reflects knowledges, interventions, ways of viewing the world, and practices that carry the possibility of altering the social world. Although defendants of development discourse argue that the world is being changed for the better, postdevelopment critiques argue that this reflects Eurocentrism. In Mignolo's terms, such Eurocentrism is itself a product of modernity, in that modernity and coloniality are intertwined.

Development interventions are not, of course, only epistemological: On a fundamental level they constitute practical engagements with the social world. Ideals of development are also not only driven by international "aid" agencies, but they also exist at the level of neoliberal economics within and across countries.[13] Such critiques of development show the ways in which an underlying hierarchizing logic that places peoples and knowledges into a classificatory framework such that the European being valorized is still very much present in the so-called postcolonial world. Can we see such a situation occurring with regards to rights? I would argue that we can. Rather than simply being a manifestation of neocolonialism, then, neocolonialism and rights can be seen to be entwined in the same system of modernity/coloniality as is development. Like development, rights discourses create hierarchies of ways of being in the world; they thus could be read within the same Western paradigm of "salvation."

This book takes the methodological position of using "discourse" as an analytic lens. Foucault (1970, 1977, 1991) was deeply critical of modernity, arguing that modern forms of knowledge and social institutions are historically created and that the interaction of power and knowledge under modernity has developed a particular system of domination. He argued that the development of modern forms of knowledge (as analyzed through the examples of psychiatry, medicine, the penal system, and the social sciences) gave rise to forms of authority over people and their ways of being in the world. Foucault is concerned with showing "how specific ways of thinking and talking about aspects of the world are forms of knowledge and power which work like languages and which we learn in the same way as we learn ordinary languages" (Jones et al., 2011: 128). This then is discourse in the Foucauldian sense: "systems of connected ideas that give us our knowledge of the world" (ibid.). Human rights can be approached as discourse, or as a set of related discourses, in that they are one of the ways in which the authority of modernity is enacted and constructed. Discourses of rights have become invidious in the modern world, such that they are often presented as the best moral option.

Rights discourses, then, reflect both language and practices; they are a way of speaking about the world as well as a "process through which social reality comes into being" (Escobar, 1997: 85). Indeed, the idea of discourse is useful in that it breaks down the distinction between language and practice, in that language itself *is* a practice. Throughout this book, then, when referring to human rights practice I invoke the broad realm of both talk *and* other forms of behavioral action; when a distinction between talking about human rights and enacting those rights has been necessary, I refer to "rights talk" and "the performance of rights," respectively. Both talk and performance form part of the discourses of rights and are entangled within the organizing epistemologies of modernity.

Discourses such as human rights circulate globally (Inda and Rosaldo, 2008); as such they form one of the key "ideoscapes"[14] (Appadurai, 1996: 31) that characterize the modern world. Appadurai's characterization of human rights as a key "ideoscape" of globalization reflects that "rights" is one of a globally prevalent and circulating "chain of ideas, terms and images" (ibid.; cf. Robins, 2008b) that is invoked in diverse local contexts. Such circulation is not necessarily even (Tsing, 2000), but nonetheless the local contexts of varied spaces within Zimbabwe and South Africa are, like any other, globally inflected and globally informed. At times in this book it has therefore been heuristically necessary to separate the local and the global for the purposes of analysis; as such I refer to the ways in which global ideas of rights and justice play out in (and move between) local contexts. At other times it has been pertinent to complicate this distinction, examining the entanglements of the local and the global and how systems of power are implicated in the construction of both. Merry argues that the terms *local* and *global* tend to carry assumed meanings, where "local tends to stand for a lack of mobility, wealth, education, and cosmopolitanism" (Merry, 2006: 39), whereas *global* reflects the opposite. In using *local* I do not intend to bring to mind such associations; rather, I approach the term from an anthropological perspective that, unlike much of the academic consideration of globalization, is concerned not with the macro scope of such processes but rather with "how globalizing processes exist in the context of, and must come to terms with, the realities of particular societies, with their accumulated—that is to say, historical—cultures and ways of life" (Inda and Rosaldo, 2008: 7). *Local* in my usage, then, should not imply Merry's marginality but rather represents the immediate and complicated localities in which global processes happen, "the experiences of people living in specific localities when more and more of their everyday lives are contingent upon globally extensive processes" (ibid.).

It is also worth noting, as Merry (2006) does, that all global ideas are circulating locals, in that they originate in a particular locality. In the case of rights, the fact that this locality is posited as broadly "Western" has led to accusations of imperialism, particularly given the emphasis within rights discourse on their purported universality. There is a distinction to be made between the idea of rights as a related set of globalized discourses, which refers to the global circulation of rights and the processes by which rights discourses move, and the idea of rights as universal, which originates *within* rights discourse and assumes an applicability across varied contexts that has been heavily critiqued (for example, by Eriksen, 1997; Wilson, 1997; Mamdani, 2000; Englund, 2004, 2006; and Nyamnjoh, 2004).

First, however, it is helpful to historicize the legal discourse of rights. Although international human rights were first legally codified following World War II, the notion of rights as inherent and inalienable can be traced back further, to the political changes wrought during the Haitian and French Revolutions (Scully and Paton, 2005; Stearns, 2012), the slow abolition of the Atlantic slave trade and the recognition of slaves as rights-bearing persons (Scully and Paton, 2005; Martinez 2012), and to ideas of the inherent dignity of humanity as put forward in the work of Western philosophers such as Immanuel Kant (Rosen, 2012).

The international human rights architecture as it exists today in the Universal Declaration of Human Rights can be broken down into four categories, or generations, each of which reflects, in the "inalienable" rights it encodes, the historical moment from which it originated. The rights promulgated following World War II, later colloquially known as first-generation rights, were mainly concerned with political rights and the basic security of persons (Messer, 1993; Robertson, 2006). Ideas of what constitute rights are closely linked, like any ideology, to context: The violent politics of World War II led to the creation of a category of rights that allowed for basic political freedoms for all individuals. Second-generation rights, as Messer notes, carried the influence of socialism in that they are concerned with socioeconomic factors: Rights in this conceptualization include ideas around working conditions, rights to a standard of living that ensures health, rights to education, and special rights for women and children. Though these rights exist at the same level as first-generation rights on paper, they are harder to implement, and the international jurisprudence of rights law reflects a greater emphasis on the protection of first-generation rights. This is partly due to legal precedent:

It is easier to prosecute for human rights violations where prosecutions have occurred before. It is also difficult to prove responsibility for violation of these human rights. Second-generation rights, then, are not as pervasive as first generation.

Third-generation rights grew out of the postcolonial world order: African nations in particular emphasized the need for "solidarity or development rights to peace, a more equitable socioeconomic order, and a sustainable environment" (Messer, 1993: 223). Third-generation rights encompass a broad spectrum (such as the right to self-determination, the right to economic and social development, the right to environmental resources and a healthy environment, and the rights of indigenous persons) and have been characterized as aspirational "soft law" in comparison to first- and second-generation rights (Twiss, 2004), in that they are expressed mainly in documents that are only slowly gaining international recognition and endorsement. The rights in this final generation shift the emphasis away from the rights of the individual to that of the group; similarly, in Zimbabwean political rhetoric the sovereignty of the nation has been accorded greater importance than the freedoms of first-generation, individual political rights (see Chapter 1).

Human Rights in Practice

Anthropological studies that have examined human rights as practice (see, for example, Ross, 2003a; Merry, 2006; and Goodale, 2009a) use ethnographic examples to show how supposedly universal rights (where universality, as Abu-Lughod (2010) argues, presumes uniformity and neutrality across disparate contexts) become somewhat localized as they unfold and surface in varied ways in different contexts. The claims to a neutral, uniform universality that are made within the discourse can be seen to be erroneous: Merry (2006) has shown that international documents that claim universality were negotiated in particular social settings such that "the very instruments of a putatively universal international law are themselves part of a located culture, with its own transnational social spaces, rather than existing above any particular social world" (Abu-Lughod, 2010: 77). Englund (2006), in his ethnographic study of ideas of rights and freedom in Malawi, draws on Tsing's model of "friction" (2005) to argue that universals only ever emerge through "frictional encounters" and are better conceived of as "engaged universals" to highlight the fact that "universality in the abstract remains a chimera . . . universalism is situational" (Englund, 2006: 26). At times the theoretical moves made against universalism have resulted in an outright dismissal of the relevance of rights as a form of meaning making: Abu-Lughod, for example, argues that neither universality nor cultural relativism as its foil provide sufficient means of analyzing the practice of power in daily life. Rather than using a model of universal rights and/or their absence, she argues that anthropology is better served by returning to models of kinship that allow for recognition of the complexities of human life as "power-laden, productive, social and ambivalent" (Abu-Lughod, 2010: 69). Nonetheless, the model of human rights retains global relevance: as with any ideology, the "political meta-narrative" (Wilson, 2006: 77) of human rights discourse is entangled in international *and* local fields of power, and universality may be evoked as a means of justifying the sorts of interventions required by a rights-based ideology.

Rights in the Postcolony

Although rights talk and performance may be gaining ground globally, this is not to say they are evoked in the same ways in all contexts: For example, Werbner (1996) has examined the rise and localization of rights discourses in Zimbabwe in the 1990s in response to the publicization of the atrocities of *Gukurahundi*. Werbner distinguishes between two discourses of rights, the first a version of social contract theory "reflected in the rhetoric of civic culture and citizens' rights" (Werbner, 1996: 99) and the second a notion of moral partnership that is enduring and encompasses both the living and the dead (cf. Bhebhe and Ranger, 1995) and that differs greatly to rights as legally encoded. He argues that the succession of violent encounters in Zimbabwean history was seen as creating a moral debt to the living, to the dead, to God, and to the land itself,[15] which, in the 1990s, came to be spoken of through the language of human rights.[16] He argues that the legal, "universal" discourse of rights came to incorporate local cosmologies and ways of understanding the world. We can thus see two sets of knowledges about what constitutes rights coming into conversation with one another in Werbner's example. The one stems from Mignolo's modernity (2012), whereas the other stems from a different epistemological foundation. Universality, then, is not complete; nor is the organizing logic of modernity. There is always room for contestation.

What sorts of ideas lie behind the localized "Zimbabwean" alternative to rights that Werbner presents? Werbner's emphasis on the present as composed of echoes of the happenings of the past brings to mind Mbembe's (2001) postulate around the entanglements of time in the postcolony. Mbembe (2001:

16) argues that time in postcolonial Africa is not linear but "an interlocking of presents, pasts and futures that retain their depths of other presents, pasts and futures, each age bearing, altering and maintaining the previous ones." At least as regards rights and moral debt in Zimbabwe, this claim rings true in that the happenings of the present, and the ways in which rights are invoked, are seen to be entangled with the violent happenings of the past, for which a moral debt is still outstanding. Similarly, in exploring modes of temporality at play in Sierra Leone, Michael Jackson cites Oakeshott, who argues that "there are not two worlds—the world of past happenings and the world of our present knowledge of those past events—there is only one world, and it is the world of present experience" (Oakeshott, 1933, in Jackson, 2005: 355). There are different epistemological and cosmological foundations to the way the world is conceived in the postcolonies and in "the West." In postcolonial Africa, local notions of temporality differ from the linear model of time employed in human rights discourses. Differences in temporal models can have wide-reaching implications: As I argue in Chapter 2, such a disjuncture can act to limit the possibilities of localization of international human rights discourse. Although recent anthropological approaches to human rights emphasize localization, it is also important that we recognize the limits of this. In contemporary Zimbabwe, although global rights discourse is invoked as one means of addressing the entanglements of the past in the present, it is not the only form of justice at play.

A return to Werbner's first discourse of rights shows the link between human rights and modernist notions of citizenship: Human rights discourse is entwined with other endeavors of modernity. Englund (2006: 26) argues that "the idea of entitlement [to rights] presupposes membership in a political society" (cf. Geertz, 1983) and, further, that the failure of many postcolonial state apparatuses complicates the entitlements of citizenship in these contexts. In the present context of Zimbabwe, this is particularly pertinent. Cheater, writing in 1998, argued that, following the inclusiveness that occurred with the coming of majority rule at independence in 1980, the Zimbabwean state's notions of citizenship progressively narrowed, drawing on a patrilineal model of citizenship that limited both who was eligible to the entitlements of citizenship and what those entitlements were. Ten years on, Vambe (2008: 3) argued that events such as Operation *Murambatsvina*, a campaign of violent forced removals,[17] "forced the people of Zimbabwe to rethink the very notion of citizen and subject" in light of the state's disregard for the usual benefits of citizenship. I have argued elsewhere (Morreira, 2009) that some urban Zimbabweans have questioned whether they can even consider themselves citizens at all. Furthermore, although *Murambatsvina* provides an example of spectacular, episode-specific violence against citizens, the continual erosion of basic services in Zimbabwe also constitutes a shift in the basic prerogatives available to Zimbabwean people.

It is such state-based disregard for the entitlements of citizenship that lead to a surge in "rights talk" (Mamdani, 2000) among individuals and among civic organizations in Zimbabwe. On an individual level, this raises questions about the interplay between discourses of rights and the creation and maintenance of subjective political identities. For civic organizations, recourse to the international legal framework of human rights is a logical option where local moralities are being discounted. Such "lawfare" (Comaroff and Comaroff, 2007: 144) works both ways—as civic organizations use international law to protest against power, so can the state pass internal laws to enforce power and act against its citizens. In 2002, the Public Order and Security Act (POSA) was passed in Zimbabwe. The act was based on the colonial Law and Order Maintenance Act (LOMA), used by the Rhodesian government to counter African nationalist movements and later used by the Zimbabwean state to institute a state of emergency in Matabeleland in the early 1980s during *Gukurahundi* (CCJP, 1997). LOMA was repealed in 1990, only to resurface under a new name, and with extended powers, in 2002. Indeed, the state need not even introduce *new* laws to validate violence against the population—Operation *Murambatsvina*, for example, was justified by recourse to urban planning laws (Kamete, 2008). "In Zimbabwe," the Comaroffs note, "[lawfare] has mutated into a necropolitics with a rising body count" (ibid: 141, cf. Mbembe, 2003).

Comaroff and Comaroff (2007: 141) argue that "the fetishism of the law" has become a common feature of the postcolony, such that "a 'culture of legality' seems to be infusing everyday life" (ibid.: 142; also see Robins, 2008a). As Werbner's example shows, and as is argued by Robins (2008a), the language of the law is not confined to state and civic elites but is also drawn on by the marginalized. A language of human rights carries social and moral capital—or, in South African Constitutional Court Judge Albie Sachs's (2009: 57) words, "Concepts such as the rule of law, fundamental rights and the independence of the judiciary occupy distinctive, hallowed spaces from which powerfully attractive energies radiate." The realm of the legal, as the Comaroffs (2007:

141) argue, constitutes a frequent frame of reference in postcolonial Africa "even when both its spirit and its letter are violated, offended, distended, purloined."[18]

In addition to the complexities of gender, citizenship, subjectivity, sovereignty, and the realm of law, human rights discourse is, inevitability, caught up in the economics of the neoliberal world order. Human rights discourses can be further compared to development discourses, then, in that "the fact is that most NGOs and human rights projects depend on complex transnational links for their material and political survival" (Englund, 2006: 8). Englund argues, in a similar vein to anthropological critiques of development discourse (see, for example, Ferguson, 1990), that the spoken goals of rights discourses may be very different from the actual effects of such "transnational governance" (Englund, 2006: 8; cf. Foucault, 1991). Indeed, one of Englund's main arguments is that an analysis of human rights as practice in Malawi reveals how the discourse *dis*empowers, particularly with regard to struggles against poverty and structural violence. This book argues something different: Where Englund conceptualizes rights as an intrusion into the world of the poor, the Zimbabwean case shows human rights to be willingly embraced by local actors, who recognize its limitations yet still attempt to mobilize the discourse to their advantage.

For all of the seductiveness of ideas of rights, then, without empirical research it is hard to know what work rights discourse is *actually* doing. Goodale (2009a) argues that rights discourse carries with it the tensions and contradictions of Habermas's "unfinished project of modernity" (in Goodale, 2009a: 16), in that we do not yet know how to judge it, and so it can be simultaneously critiqued and embraced by ourselves and by our interlocutors. Wilson (2006: 77) has argued that there is a need within the field of human rights for an academic viewpoint that "mesh[es] an awareness of social theory with an attention to empirical specificity." Ethnography, he maintains, is particularly well suited to this purpose. Rights talk and the performance of rights are relational and situational; as such, there is value in localized studies that focus on rights implementation and resistance from the perspectives of varied social groups and actors.

Accessing Discourses of Rights

In embarking on fieldwork, my aim was to provide a contextualized ethnographic response to one fundamental query: How was the globalized ideology of human rights playing out in the contexts of urban Zimbabwe and the urban Zimbabwean diaspora in South Africa? Phillipe Bourgois has argued that "it is impossible to understand what is going on anywhere without paying attention to the power dynamics that shape inequality everywhere" (Bourgois, 2006: x–xi). These words raise an issue central to the task of devising a research methodology: the importance of finding a means to access and assess the relationship between Bourgois's "anywhere"—the small-scale, local spaces where I was able to engage in face to face research—and his "everywhere"—the larger-scale, broader processes of modernity that affected such spaces and can result in multiple alternative modernities (Gaonkar, 2001) and multiple alternative discourses of rights (cf. Goodale and Starr, 2002). Legal and popular discourses of human rights are entangled in a variety of (sometimes seemingly incommensurate) fields. However, it also seemed that the very "ideological promiscuity" (Wilson, 2006: 78) of rights talk was what made it such a pertinent and exciting field of enquiry as regards postcolonial Southern Africa and relations between the local and the global.

But the reader is entitled to ask: Why Zimbabwe? Why this topic in this place and this time? Although this book is far from autoethnographic, my own positionality has been central to the work that I have been able to do and to the topic I chose to explore. My personal and political positioning was relevant to the research I undertook from first inception through to the writing of this book. I am a white woman who has been resident in South Africa for the last decade. Although I grew up in Zimbabwe and call myself Zimbabwean, my citizenship is now South African. I have returned at least once a year to Zimbabwe, however, and have maintained my Zimbabwean residency permit. The history of my "Zimbabwean-ness"—as a member of the first postindependence urban generation of Zimbabweans, white and black, who (astonishingly) were taken by surprise at the vehemence of racial and political debates in the 1990s, as we were taught little Zimbabwean history at school and were unaware of the intricacies of the past; as a (private) high school student in Harare in the late 1990s who was an appalled witness to the multiple violences of 1999 and beyond, which led me to seek out those untold histories of colonial and postcolonial violence in Rhodesia/Zimbabwe; as a family member of a group of liberal white and black Zimbabweans who have been involved in activism against violence in the post-2000 era; as, in short, a product of the joys, tensions, despairs, and ambiguities of life in Southern Africa—is deeply interwoven into this text. Indeed, the ways in which I delineated and defined "the field" before and during research, and the questions with which I entered it, were informed by my personal, political, and academic history.

Similarly, my position in South Africa—as a member of a politicized diasporic community, as an active participant in protest against the South African state's neutral position on Mugabe's Zimbabwe and the resultant flow of Zimbabwean refugees,[19] as an individual subject to the pull and longing for home that one feels from a distance (which I tried to assuage on those yearly trips to Zimbabwe, bearing foreign currency, mealie meal, rice, DVDs, car parts, and clothing for family, friends, and "interlocutors," who were often the same people); as a bearer of South African citizenship and Zimbabwean residency, as, in short, a postcolonial African—has influenced the topic I chose, the questions I asked, and, ultimately, the research I was able to do and the stories and analysis I have written here.

Researching Rights

The emphasis in this research project on the varied manifestations of rights discourse has required a flexible methodology. I was influenced by the excellent advice provided in Mark Goodale and June Starr's edited volume *Practicing Ethnography in Law* (2002), from which I took three main points: Remain loyal to the process of seeking answers to research questions rather than loyal to any one particular method of answering them, design methods in such a way as to allow yourself to take an active role in the phenomena being studied (in other words, participate as well as observe), and, centrally, maintain awareness of the fact that investigating legal phenomena requires an awareness of the relationship between the local and the global.

Goodale (2002), in a reflexive consideration of the ethnographic research he undertook on the arrival of ideas of human rights to rural Bolivia, argues that research of this kind explores "a shifting set of normative practices and ideas that form a network that is mostly invisible" (Goodale, 2002: 64). Even before fully conceptualizing this project, it was clear to me that any consideration of rights in the Zimbabwean context could not be undertaken from any one field site or locality, precisely because any such legalities are part of much wider networks that stretch across both time and space. The presence of such networks ensured that research needed to not only incorporate multiple sites but to try to account for the spaces *between* sites. The research methods I used were designed in the hopes of exploring how human rights discourses emerged in the particular localities of Harare, Cape Town, and Musina, as well as surfacing Goodale's "invisible networks" or, in Hannerz's terms, tracing the "translocal linkages" (Hannerz, 1998: 247) at play.

With that in mind, the chapters that follow are based on ethnographic work conducted in multiple localities, working with multiple actors. Anthropological techniques such as participant observation allow for insight into the ways in which discourses form part of daily life; it is for this reason that Goodale and Starr assert that "deep and thick ethnography is one of the best routes we have in comprehending the complexity of law and legal processes" (Goodale and Starr, 2002: 8). During the course of research I have physically followed individual people and things (texts, money, goods) across geographical borders and have attempted to trace those things that were more nebulous, such as metaphors and modes of thought.

The book is based on ethnographic research within Zimbabwe, where, in addition to conducting the participant observation of daily life that forms the substance of the anthropological endeavor, I worked with two organizations. The first, the Research and Advocacy Unit (RAU), conducts research in Zimbabwe for the purposes of policy change; as such, it engages in research within the three main areas of governance, gender, and displacements and makes use of a legal framework of rights in so doing. The work done by RAU has also focused on the documentation of instances of political violence within Zimbabwe. The second organization with which I worked in Harare, the Tree of Life, is concerned more with people's subjectivities than with the legal framework of rights. This organization works with individuals who have experienced political violence, particularly torture, and utilizes a hybridized therapeutic model, based on "healing circles," that is concerned with moving beyond ideas of victimhood and rebuilding a sense of community following trauma. Although I worked closely with these two organizations, I also spent time interviewing various actors from other civil society groups and NGOs in Harare, which have opted not to be named in this text.

Rights discourses stretch across borders; as such, I also traced the movement of rights-based texts through the use of new technologies and followed the people from Zimbabwe to South Africa. I spent some time in Musina, a border town between Zimbabwe and South Africa, where I sat in on meetings held by local government and international organizations that focused on the "problem" of Zimbabwean migration and where I visited government-run Refugee Reception Offices and nongovernment-run shelters for migrants. In Cape Town I worked with a rights and advocacy organization, People

Against Suffering Oppression and Poverty (PASSOP), set up to deal with the difficulties facing migrants to South Africa, particularly those seeking refugee status. In all, I personally collected data from 102 participants across the three spaces; in addition, I draw on some data from a large-scale survey of 456 Zimbabweans living in South Africa collected by a team of researchers from PASSOP and the Solidarity Peace Trust, of which I was a member. I also enrolled in a masters course in human rights law so that I might immerse myself in the formal discourse. It was in such ways that I was able to, in Goodale's terms, "follow the legal ideas where they lead" (2002: 64).

Moving Forward

This book uses the political impasse and economic uncertainty that existed in Zimbabwe during the Global Political Agreement period (from 2008 to 2013) as a case study through which to explore how the legal framework of rights can be locally interpreted, constituted, and contested and how such interpretations travel. I explore the ways in which local moral notions are (mis) translated into discourses of rights and consider the entanglements (Mbembe, 2001; Nuttall, 2009) of legal and moral notions at play when ideas of rights are invoked. Chapter 1 provides an ethnographic examination of the public debates I encountered in 2010 around the writing of a new constitution in Zimbabwe as a means of tracing the discursive formations of "rights talk" and the difficulties of legally encoding such talk, whereas Chapter 2 explores the various modes of justice at play in contemporary Harare, where global ideas of rights are just one among a number of repertoires being mobilized to deal with political violence and the resultant so-called culture of impunity as regards political crimes. In Chapter 3 I trace the development of a set of human right reports from the early stages of research within Zimbabwe through to their global dissemination. In Chapter 4 I present a final ethnographic case study in which I examine the use of discourses of rights by Zimbabwean migrants to South Africa as they attempt to gain access to legal status, arguing that migrants employ a different concept of personhood from that used within rights discourse, which is not accepted as valid by the state. Any potential for the localization of rights discourses here is therefore seen to be constrained by unequal power relations. The concluding chapter draws together these multi-sited ethnographic explorations to argue that although rights have emerged as a dominant discourse of our time, such a discourse is neither evenly applicable across cultural contexts nor easily localized. An examination of rights talk as praxis in this context reveals the advantages and disadvantages of using a language of rights in a postcolonial context. The book develops ideas of entanglement and decoloniality and applies them to the temporal, moral, and legal dimensions of human rights discourses. Such a model allows for better insight into the complexities of the use of rights in postcolonial Africa than do ideas of localization or vernacularization.

Chapter 1

"Panel-Beating the Law"

Constitution Making in Zimbabwe

Legal Texts and Legal Talk: An Introduction

In the vignette with which I opened this book, a protester stood poised with a paintbrush over a blank expanse of white fabric and asked of his peers, "What do I write?" This is a question that is familiar to us all when faced with the naked page. His answer, found in conversation with the group, was to use the umbrella term *human rights* as shorthand for the diverse issues they wished to express at the protest. While thinking through the ways in which to structure this book, I found myself exploring the inverse of the problem—faced with a mound of data on the many ways in which ideas of "human rights," "justice," and, more broadly, "law" were being used, what should I write in order to explore what lay behind these umbrella terms? How might I begin to trace the nebulous discursive formations of "rights talk" in the Zimbabwean context, which encompassed ideas of dignity, democracy, and freedom; of personhood and moral ethics; and of proper versus improper laws and which were situationally shaped by position, politics, and power?

While first undertaking fieldwork in Cape Town, I spent most of my time in two starkly different spaces. Both were legal fields: the first a class in human rights law in the Faculty of Law at the University of Cape Town and the second a paralegal clinic run by PASSOP out of the back of a coffee shop in Mowbray (at that time, PASSOP did not have the funding for office space but had managed to strike a deal with the café owner; subsequently the organization has found donor funding and consequently become much more formal). One of the first things taught in the rights class was that human rights, as encoded in international statutes, had four basic characteristics: They were something that all people were born with (in other words, they were inherent); they applied to everyone (that is, they were universal); they were something that could not be taken away (inalienable); and they were so strongly interconnected as to be indivisible.

The contrast between this language and the realities I encountered daily in the paralegal clinic was marked.[1] As the law course progressed, it became clear that such reductionist language served as a heuristic device for the purposes of teaching and that the realities of law in action were acknowledged as far more complex: These four elements of human rights are widely understood to be political concepts in human rights and legal studies. Nonetheless, such a simplistic presentation of rights was prevalent whenever I encountered the law being taught, be it by university lecturers to masters-level students or by the staff of NGOs in Zimbabwe and South Africa to their clients. Such a reductionist language of human rights obscured rather than reflected the realities I encountered in another setting: the contextual ways in which ideas of human rights were called on, strategically mobilized, refused, and debated in the daily happenings of a paralegal clinic that catered to the legal needs of documented and undocumented immigrants. In beginning to write this book, then, I knew that I must find ways to demonstrate ethnographically the disjuncture between the performance of law as encountered in the field and the varied ways in which human rights were discursively expressed by interlocutors (in other words, to explore ethnographically the differences between the "doing" of law and the "speaking" of law), while also acknowledging the ways that various of the discursive tropes of human rights discourses (such as rights as inherent and inalienable but also some of the less openly articulated ideas, such as the entanglement of notions of dignity and freedom in human rights) *were* reflected in rights performance.[2]

One of the difficulties of ethnographically examining transnational discourses and flows is that there is not necessarily any one obvious topical (or even geographical) place to begin. This chapter considers the public debates that surrounded the writing of a new Zimbabwean constitution in 2010. I have chosen to start with the actual and attempted inscriptions of ideas of rights onto legal documents, but I may as easily have begun with Zimbabwean asylum seekers' interactions with the paralegal clinic and with the South African Department of Home Affairs or with how Zimbabwean women imaginatively engaged, through interaction with local NGOs, in ideas of national transitional justice, or, indeed, with one of many other ethnographic instances and moments. All are linked by the common thread of rights talk and the (attempted) performance of human rights law, and all exist in some relation to each other: In other words, all are part of a network of transnational discourses of human rights.

My argument here rests on the theoretical underpinnings that I laid out in the Introduction: namely, that supposedly universal notions of human rights emerge in local contexts and that rights, as Englund (2006: 26) puts it, can better be thought of as "engaged universals" as "universality in the abstract remains a chimera . . . universalism is situational." There is a need in anthropological engagement with human rights to move away from debates of relativism versus universalism and toward an examination of the ways in which human rights discourse is embedded in practice. Notions of supposedly inherent human rights "are enacted, debated, practiced, violated, envisioned and experienced" (Goodale, 2006b: 490) in global and in local contexts and exist within situationally shifting nexuses of power. Methodologically, then,

> The legal ethnographer assumes that "the field" does not denote primarily a bounded location in space . . . but rather a set of relationships which are linked by common interests. This means that the ethnographer must follow the legal ideas where they lead, and they often lead to unexpected places. (Goodale, 2002: 64)

In this chapter, I explore one direction in which the legal ideas led, showing the constellation of ideas that are embedded in rights-based texts, talk, and action. I examine the public dialogues and debates surrounding the writing of a new Zimbabwean constitution that occurred in Zimbabwe during my residence there in 2010 and that culminated in the coming into being of a constitution that an interlocuter employed by a legal NGO in Zimbabwe described as "compromised" and "unsatisfactory." Notwithstanding, this constitution was approved by a national referendum in 2013. The example demonstrates how human and civil rights are open to (political and politicized) interpretation and contestation, both during the processes of "fixing" them via legal procedures and after they have been formally encoded. The "finished" versions of legal documents such as constitutions and statutes emerge from and are enacted within fields of power. As such decisions and documents do not appear in a vacuum, "Legalities must be conceptualised as both fluid and unstable, a shifting set of normative practices and ideas that form a network that is mostly invisible" (Goodale, 2002: 64). The constitution-writing case study is able to make more tangible the partly visible regional and global networks of ideas and discourse that underpins human rights praxis.

Case Study 1: Constituting the Constitution

It is not enough that bread has returned to our shelves. Our hearts are also starving for a people-driven Constitution. We demand a living Constitution that will give us bread and roses too! Just like the thorns on a rose, love comes with pain, we must be willing to fight through the pain to get our new Constitution. Demand your Rose—stand up for love. Shine Zimbabwe Shine!

Valentine's Day Pamphlets handed out to journalists at the state-owned
newspaper The Herald by members of Women of Zimbabwe Arise (WOZA),
February 14, 2010[3]

You're of Zimbabwe
Please put in your input
Unless your hand moves
Your mouth won't eat

Towards a homely home
All shall shun dire deeds.
Our Constitution should shine like chrome,
As captivating as beads.

Stanzas 3 and 11 of a poem attributed to "The Giant," which opens the booklet
A People's Guide to Constitutional Debate, Africa Community Publishing and
Development Trust, 2009a

In mid- to late September 2008, two items dominated the South African news media. The first was the signing, in Zimbabwe, of a political agreement that sought to bring the impasse that had existed in Zimbabwean politics since the elections in March of that year to a close; the second was the fall from power of the man who brokered the deal, then-president of South Africa, Thabo Mbeki. In the very last days of his presidency in September 2008, Mbeki saw the culmination of the heavily criticized policy of "quiet diplomacy"[4] with which South Africa had approached political instability in Zimbabwe since 2000. The continual instability and increasing violence within Zimbabwean politics and the effects of the rapid economic collapse of the Zimbabwean economy on other economies in the region had caused political difficulty for Mbeki throughout his second term as president. By September 2008, however, it appeared that quiet diplomacy had at last produced a tangible result.

On September 11 Mbeki, as the SADC appointed mediator of talks between the three political parties in Zimbabwe, brought to a close a protracted process of negotiations. On September 15, to much regional and international media attention, ZANU-PF and the two Movement for Democratic Change factions (MDC-T[svangirai] and MDC-M[utambara]) signed the Global Political Agreement (GPA). Provisions within this agreement ushered in a new "inclusive government," which saw Mugabe retain the presidency and control of the National Security Council while Tsvangirai assumed the post of prime minister and control over the Council of Ministers. At almost the same moment that Mbeki's negotiations in Zimbabwe culminated in the GPA, however, his position in South Africa politics underwent a rapid shift. Five days after the signing of the GPA, on September 20, Mbeki resigned from the presidency following being recalled by the ANC's National Executive Commission for supposed political interference in the corruption trial of then deputy-president, now president, of South Africa Jacob Zuma. Mbeki retained his position as facilitator of the dialogue between the political parties in Zimbabwe, a crucial role, as, although the deal had been signed, negotiations over the implementation of the GPA were far from over.

The signing of the GPA did not bring political wrangling in Zimbabwe to a close. A photograph of Mugabe and Tsvangirai shaking hands, with a smiling Mbeki looking on, that circulated in international and local media was not the harbinger of political harmony that it appeared to be. The Zimbabweans I encountered in my daily life as anthropologist, activist, and Zimbabwean greeted the power-sharing deal with suspicion; moreover, neither political side was satisfied with the concessions that had been made. President Mugabe reportedly referred to the deal as "a humiliation" (BBC News, September 18, 2008) whereas MDC supporters I interviewed were angered by Mugabe's retention of the presidency and viewed the acceptance of the deal by Tsvangirai and Mutambara as an inappropriate legitimization of ZANU-PF's position, given the violence of the electoral process in 2008. Many Zimbabweans in Cape Town considered the power-sharing deal to be largely illusionary, with most of the "real" power still lying, for good or ill, in ZANU-PF hands. The liberal civil society organizations tended to agree with this assessment—Zimbabwean human rights lawyer Derek Matyszak, for example, wrote that "the agreement left Mugabe's powers largely unfettered and intact, though under a restructured form of government" and further that "it admits scanty hope for the return of the rule of law and democracy in Zimbabwe" (Matyszak, 2010: 15).

Nonetheless, the signing of the GPA caused a fundamental shift in the Zimbabwean political landscape and, over time, led to changes in the daily lives of Zimbabweans. The most obvious example of this was the legalization of the use of foreign currency in Zimbabwe in early 2009, which led to the discontinuation of the Zimbabwe dollar. This put an end to hyperinflation rates, which were estimated at "6.5 quindecillion novemdecillion percent a year—or 65 followed by 107 zeros" (Hanke, 2008) by December 2008, a rate that meant that prices doubled every twenty-four hours (ibid.). "Dollarisation" brought a multitude of immediately obvious daily improvements, such as the availability of food, but the changes in the political landscape of Zimbabwe were not as apparent. For our purposes here, one provision of the GPA is particularly important in this regard—Article VI, which stipulated the creation of a new Zimbabwean constitution. Before moving to an analysis of Article VI and its implementation, however, it is necessary to briefly step back in time to the late 1990s, to explore the political conditions that foreshadowed the Constitution-making debates that (re)occurred a decade later.

Constitution Making in Zimbabwe: Earlier Attempts

The Zimbabwean Constitution that existed at the time of fieldwork (prior to the signing into law of the new Constitution in 2013, the debates over the contents of which I describe in this chapter) was written and signed as part of the Lancaster House Agreement, which brought an end to the liberation war in the late 1970s. The Lancaster House Constitution, a document that was formulated with the main aim of transferring power from a colonial to a postcolonial government, had undergone nineteen amendments since its inception and was considered to have many weaknesses. Critiques take two main forms. First, it was considered to be a colonial document, drafted in London to end a war, and neither a reflection of the legal needs of independent Zimbabwe nor a reflection of the symbolic needs of the postcolonial nation. These critiques were largely shared across Zimbabwe's present political divisions. The second major critique, however, was predominantly levelled by NGOs and by ZANU-PF's political opposition. It was directed at the numerous constitutional amendments that have taken place since 1979, which had the main effect of consolidating presidential and state powers and weakening Zimbabwe's democratic architecture.

Some material examples of the changes to the law in the run-up to the constitutional processes of the 1990s can help to illustrate the ways in which the Lancaster House Constitution had seen an erosion of democratic and rights-based systems. Amendment No. 7 (Act 23 of 1987) replaced the system of ceremonial president and prime minister with an executive presidency, whereas Amendment No. 9 (Act 31 of 1989) replaced bicameral legislature with a single house of parliament, to which the executive president could appoint ministers without public consultation. Amendment No. 11 (Act 30 of 1990) instated capital punishment and in so doing reversed a constitutional court ruling; Amendment No. 13 (Act 9 of 1993) reversed a further constitutional court ruling that a delay in the enforcement of capital punishment constituted inhumane and degrading treatment; and Amendments 11 (Act 30 of 1990), 16, and 17 had the combined effect of removing the acquisition of land by the state from the jurisdiction of the courts, thus curtailing the independence of the judiciary. In terms of prevailing international notions of human rights and democracy, then, the 1990s saw a severe decline in Zimbabwe's legal architecture and a push toward a reconceptualization of land rights that placed control in the hands of the state.

Given these critiques, it is not surprising that there were multiple attempts to do away with the Lancaster House Constitution and that the constitutional debates that I witnessed in 2010 were not the first in recent Zimbabwean history. In 1997, the National Constitutional Assembly (NCA) was formed by numerous members of civil society, largely in response to the use of constitutional amendments to concentrate political power in the hands of the president. The forming of the NCA, which brought together very diverse arms of civil society, was no small endeavor. The phrase *civil society* is often used as shorthand for what can be a very diverse grouping. This is certainly true in Zimbabwe, where civil society has never been homogenous, and cooperation across various elements has often been laden with contradictions. In the 1990s, in response to changes within the politico-economic arena as brought about by structural adjustment and state responses to it, various arms of civil society proliferated in Zimbabwe. Helliker (2013) noted that this proliferation saw the rise of both internationally funded NGOs (what he refers to as liberal civil society) and of more radical forms of nongovernmental institutions such as trade unions, labor movements, and student groups. The aims of such groups were not necessarily in alignment. The 1990s were thus a moment in which human rights discourses, in the plural, bloomed within the country, with some organizations such as the Zimbabwe Human Rights Association (ZIMRIGHTS) pushing for a more "traditional" first-generation political/

democratic rights–based agenda while others such as the labor movement sought to consolidate socioeconomic rights. In the late 1990s, in response to constitutional amendments that were giving the state more and more power, the NCA was formed out of these varied groupings, with the assistance of considerable Western donor funding. The NCA was (and is) composed of a very broad array of political groups, incorporating "individual Zimbabwean citizens and civil organisations, including labour movements, student and youth groups, women's groups, churches, business groups and human rights organisations" (NCA 2007: 1). The common thread that united these diverse positions was a concern with the weakening of democratic processes in Zimbabwe and concern that the country was heading toward politicoeconomic difficulties. The endorsement of the democratic ideal by Mugabe's civil and political opposition is worth noting, given the entanglement of ideas of human rights with those of democracy and freedom, as I explore further in the following discussion. The NCA's aim was to initiate a nationwide conversation about the democratic weaknesses of the Lancaster House Amended Constitution and to advocate for constitutional reform.

By 1999, it seemed that the NCA's push for constitutional reform had been successful and that changes were in the cards—but not in the way that they had been envisioned by the NCA. In May 1999, the ZANU-PF government formed the Constitutional Commission to begin a process of drafting a new constitution (BBC News, 1999; NCA, 2009). There was thus a proliferation of human rights talk in the run-up to the making of the new constitution. The Constitutional Commission of the 1990s, like its successor in 2010, drew on the language and practices of liberal NGOs in its "outreach" process. This process, unlike the 2010 version, was extensive in practice as well as in name; by Dzinesa's (2012: 3) account,

> The commendable and extensive consultation process, guided by the much-publicised List of Constitutional Issues and Questions, offered Zimbabwean citizens an opportunity to openly discuss and debate the proposed constitution. The Commission said it organised 4,321 public meetings which were attended by a total of 556,276 individuals, and 700 special ad hoc meetings attended by a total of 150,000 people. In addition, the commission received 4,000 written submissions, and aired 31 programmes on ZBC TV as well as 143 programmes on Zimbabwe's four public radio stations: 16 programmes on Radio 1 (English); 55 programmes on Radio 2 (Shona and Ndebele); 2 pro-

grammes on Radio 3 (English); and 70 programmes on Radio 4 (minority languages such as Tonga and Venda).

The Constitutional Commission outreach program occurred during my last year of high school, a moment in which my awareness of the ways in which the political sphere could have an impact on the everyday was formed. Both civil society and the government invested large amounts of money in spreading the language of human and civil rights, using radio, print media, pamphlets, music, and "outreach programs" to inform the public as to what a new constitution should reflect. Again, the diverse views of different sectors could be seen in what sorts of rights were being pushed, with various versions of socioeconomic and political rights being put forward for consideration. At the inauguration of the Constitutional Commission, Mugabe drew on the symbolic and emotive power of the colonial critique to argue that "every sovereign people is entitled to give birth to its own constitution" (reported in BBC World News, November 19, 1999).

The constitution that the sovereign people of Zimbabwe put forward, however, was not necessarily one that found favor with the state. Dzinesa (2012) has argued that the 1990s Constitutional Commission was successful in gaining access to the views of the people and in explaining to people what their rights actually were and what they should be concerned about. The Zimbabwean people responded by expressing concern about the 1987 constitutional amendments, which extended the powers of the presidency, and by linking the constitutional amendments to the growing political and economic crisis (Dzinesa, 2012). The 1990s outreach, then, resulted in a large-scale endorsement of democratic rights.

Despite this, the Constitutional Commission's draft retained the executive presidency. It did, however, introduce a prime minister. It also included a more extensive Bill of Rights than did the Lancaster House Constitution. However, the Commission's version did not last long. A Government Gazette entitled "Draft Constitution for Zimbabwe: Corrections and Clarifications" was published toward the end of 1999, which introduced compulsory military service, prohibited same-sex marriage, and allowed for the compulsory acquisition of land without compensation from the state, with the responsibility for compensation being put on the former colonizer, Britain, rather than the present government (Dzinesa, 2012).

Taundi (2009) thus commented:

Seeing potential for populism, the government immediately hijacked the NCA idea, formed a Constitutional Commission and rolled out a massive nation-wide campaign complemented by a heavy media blitz to rally the population around *its* agenda for constitutional reform. After countrywide consultations, the Constitutional Commission produced a draft document that expanded Mugabe's executive powers and endorsed ZANU-PF's plans to seize white-owned commercial farms—issues that were never demanded by the people. (Taundi, 2009: 3)

In Dzinesa's (2012: 4) terms:

The publication of the Gazette reversed the positive steps taken during the participatory and inclusive outreach phase, and put an end to the prospect of a genuinely "people-driven" democratic constitution being produced.

I will return to a consideration of who "the people" might be said to be and what space they had for making demands, when analyzing the present-day debates in the following pages; at this point, however, the issue of importance is the struggles between the NCA and the ZANU-PF government. Although the NCA and the state were in agreement that reform was necessary, this was as far as their agreement went—as far as the actual content of reform was concerned, the state and civic society were greatly opposed. Two revisions to the constitution that were put forward by ZANU-PF were particularly important in terms of what they tell us about differing notions of "rights." First, the constitution was amended to include the compulsory acquisition of farms, which was couched in terms of a morally necessary indigenization land reform process: in other words, in terms of giving land to the people who had the right to it, rather than to white commercial farmers. The second was making an even more powerful executive presidency, which goes against conventional notions of a rights-driven democracy.

The draft constitution was presented to the nation via a national referendum in early 2000. The NCA, having been the advocate for constitutional reform, now found itself in the ironic position of advocating that people vote *against* the new constitution, with the support of the political opposition, the MDC. The NCA found itself in a media war with the state, with both political players attempting to win votes in the referendum. I still have a red "Vote No" card tucked into the corner of the noticeboard above my desk, an artifact from this media war. The NCA's "Vote No campaign" (as it has become known) and the constitutional referendum in 2000 were pivotal points in Zimbabwean politics, as the ZANU-PF government–endorsed constitution was rejected by 54.7 percent of voters (Electoral Institute for the Sustainability of Democracy in Africa, 2000). This was the first time in ZANU-PF history that the aims of the party had been thwarted by voters (Taundi, 2009). ZANU-PF would not allow this invincibility to be breached again until the power-sharing deal was struck a decade later[5]—at which point the issue of the constitution reemerged as central to the ongoing struggle between ZANU-PF and its opposition.

In spite of a vote against the new constitution, fast-track land reform went ahead, as did the entrenchment of powers of the executive presidency. The 1999 constitution-writing process, then, provided a glimpse into the ways in which ideas of human and civil rights could be touted, publicized, and popularized and also a glimpse into state disregard for notions of rights that did not fit into the state's agenda. The push to limit executive powers, extend legal protection of the right to property and the rule of law, and extend socioeconomic labor rights that were being put forward by the various arms of civil society that came together as the NCA were effectively ignored. The form of rights discourse backed by local force thus won out over the one endorsed by the outreach process and backed by foreign (and local) funders.

In the decade between that referendum and my fieldwork in 2010, the Zimbabwean political landscape was marked by violence and discord while the economy underwent a profound decline. It was in the context of this historicized politicoscape that the constitution-writing process emerged once more—and it was in the context of such power saturated and politicized fields that the rights of Zimbabweans were in the process of being constitutionally encoded during my fieldwork. The power struggles that solidified during the "Vote No campaign" have resonated throughout Zimbabwean politics since and could be seen to surface once more during the process of 2010. As in the 1990s, players in these politicized fields made strategic use of international discourses. Gluck and Tsing (2009) argue that words do work in the world, "whether organizing, mobilizing, inspiring, excluding, suppressing or covering up" (Gluck, 2009: 3) when they "become embedded in social and political practices" (ibid.).

Article VI

Under Article VI of the GPA, the inclusive government was charged with writing a new constitution. It is in the context of Article VI's assertion that "the process of making this Constitution must be "owned and driven by the people" (in a throwback to the failed outcomes of the outreach of the 1990s) that the vehement and, at times, violent debates around the writing of a new constitution began. An excerpt from Article VI immediately reveals the globally recognizable terminology of rights and democracy—with one notable exception, which is italicized in the following:

ARTICLE VI

CONSTITUTION

6. Constitution

Acknowledging that it is the fundamental right and duty of the Zimbabwean people to make a Constitution by themselves and for themselves;

Aware that the process of making this Constitution must be owned and driven by the people and must be inclusive and democratic;

Recognising that the current Constitution of Zimbabwe made at the Lancaster House Conference, London (1979) was primarily to transfer power from the colonial authority to the people of Zimbabwe;

Acknowledging the draft Constitution the Parties signed and agreed to in Kariba on the 30th of September 2007, annexed hereto as "Annexure B";

Determined to create conditions for our people to write a Constitution for themselves; and

Mindful of the need to ensure that the new Constitution deepens our democratic values and principles and the protection of the equality of all citizens, particularly the enhancement of full citizenship and equality of women.

The parties hereby agree . . .

(Excerpt from the Interparty Political Agreement ['Global Party Agreement'], 2008; italics mine)

It is clear from this excerpt that the GPA process was one that was driven by a democratizing agenda, and, indeed, this is unsurprising given the strong position of the democratic ideal within global politics and SADC's subscription to democracy as a political model. Tucked within the democratically correct language of "fundamental rights and duties"; "inclusive processes," "protection of equality," "full citizenship," and a "people-driven process," however, was a clause on the Kariba Draft Constitution. The clause made notions of democratic inclusivity suspect, as it referred to an already-written version of a new constitution (based largely on the version rejected in the referendum of 2000) that the three parties had all endorsed a year prior to the GPA, in September 2007. The writing of the Kariba Draft occurred behind closed doors; its mention in the GPA led to immediate public suspicion that the "people-driven process" of composing a new Constitution was nothing more than a semblance of a democratic consultative process and that the final version presented to "the people" would resemble the Kariba Draft, with all of its shortcomings. In 2013, after the lengthy nationwide public debates described here, this proved to be largely correct.

From the moment the constitution-making process became public knowledge in Zimbabwe, it was marked by suspicion and debate. During fieldwork in 2010, Tarisai,[6] a female rights advocacy campaigner, shrugged off my questions about the constitution-writing process with the comment, "What does it matter? They'll just give us the Kariba Draft at the end of the day, and then we'll have to campaign again to reject it." Her assertion that the Kariba Draft would be pushed through by the state was commonplace, and her lackadaisical words belie the tone in which she spoke them, which was more despairing than resigned. What's more, the Kariba Draft was endorsed by ZANU-PF *and* the two MDCs; civil society and the political opposition were no longer as closely aligned as they were during the constitution-making struggles of the late 1990s. Many rights activists, like Tarisai, felt that the MDC had sold out against their ostensibly democratic ideals. The tension between a version of the constitution that was "owned and driven by the people" and a state-driven "clandestine" version (NCA, 2009: 2) informed the public debates of 2010.

The general public was deeply invested in these debates, as evidenced in the many conversations that I had on the topic in Harare, as well as letters to newspapers, call-ins on radio stations, and debate on websites and social media. A constitution that is not yet written holds ambivalence as an imagined document—in a political power struggle such as has unfolded in Zimbabwe over the last decade, the constitution could prove enormously valuable to either side of the political divide. A version of the constitution such as the one pushed for by the NCA, liberal civil society, and rights advocacy groups would enable the legal foundations that they sought to begin to dismantle state autocratic control and put in place a thorough rights architecture; a version of the constitution that was close to the Kariba Draft would work to further entrench the powers of the state (and thereby, in the terminology of rights talk, to limit political freedom)—a state that now included ZANU-PF and the MDC, the old power and its opposition. Alex Magaisa, a Zimbabwean academic living in the diaspora, began a blog post on the politics of constitution-making in Zimbabwe with the line "the waters of Lake Kariba are both beautiful and treacherous" (Magaisa, 2009: 1). He goes on to argue:

> A Constitution should ideally outlive present-day politics; indeed, it should outlive political actors of the day. It is an enduring document between the governors and the governed—not just the present but also future generations. It is an embodiment of the nation's values, ideals and aspirations. (ibid.)

I will return to the symbolic work that the constitution is being made to do for "the nation" in the following discussion; what is of relevance here is Magaisa's awareness that the constitution was being forged within a specific set of political circumstances and his assertion that these should not play a role in the shape the constitution comes to take. However, documents of as much legal importance as constitutions are *always* created in politicised conditions, and the rights that are afforded by constitutions, for all that they come to be presented as naturalized and inevitable once they are encoded, reflect the moment in which they are made.

The struggle over constitution-making was one in which the stakes were extremely high—the law may be a social construct, but it is one with very real effects, be they limiting or liberatory. A member of Zimbabwe Lawyers for Human Rights (ZLHR) commented in an interview:

> In some ways this is the most important thing that is happening here [in Zimbabwe]. At the moment we're trying to get the law as it stands enforced, and sometimes we win and sometimes we fail. But if our constitution is rewritten so that it's harder for us to make those legal claims, then we've really lost.

The last ten years in Zimbabwe have seen, in addition to outright political and economic violence, the frequent eruption of what Comaroff and Comaroff (2007: 144) describe as "lawfare." ZLHR and others organizations have made consistent use of the courts where state actions have been illegal. Though ZLHR's legal cases have had their successes, lawfare works both ways, and, given the amendments to the present constitution in Zimbabwe, the odds are often stacked in favor of the state. In this context, then, what the new national constitution might look like matters considerably.

Article VI did not limit itself to stipulating that a new constitution must be written, as previously quoted, but also outlined the conditions under which this should occur. Although members of civil society were wary of the validity of the public consultation process, given the existence of the Kariba Draft, there was nonetheless a legal imperative on the transitional government to set up a Select Constitutional Parliamentary Committee and to begin a process of public consultation over what to include in the new constitution. This cumbersomely named committee quickly became known by the acronym COPAC, while the democratizing terminology used in the GPA was shortened in everyday speech to a "people-driven constitution," and the consultation process became known, as in the 1990s, as "outreach." In discussing the COPAC process as I encountered it in 2010, I make use of the local terms. Debates over the COPAC outreach were extensive; for reasons of expediency I have narrowed my focus here to two threads of the debate that underlie, or were interwoven into, the social construction of rights in Zimbabwe and that are themselves key tropes of global rights discourses: namely, the surfacing throughout the COPAC process of ideas of democracy and freedom.[7]

Constructions of the People's Voice and Democracy in the COPAC Process

Almost two years after the signing of the GPA, COPAC began its process of public consultation with "the people." This "outreach program" consisted of teams of COPAC members traveling around the country and holding public meetings at which Zimbabweans were expected to comment on what they thought should or should not be included in the constitution. There were a number of assumptions at play, all of which were predicated on an imagined relationship among "the people," democracy, and voice: first, that people would *want* to speak at such meetings (in other words, would have enough of an interest in the constitution-making process to want to attend); second, that people would be informed enough in the practicalities of legal documents to be *able* to speak in terms that the formal structure could "hear" at such meetings; and third, that people, given the political context of Zimbabwe and the extensive silencing of the population that has occurred historically (such as during and in the aftermath of *Gukurahundi* in the 1980s; see CCJP, 1997) as well as more recently, would be *willing* to speak freely at such meetings.

Even before these considerations of acts of speaking publicly, however, my own experiences led me to question the most basic (and, as such, initially unstated) assumption of the COPAC process: that "the people" would be *allowed* to attend the meetings at all. For example, I was advised by some members of an NGO with whom I spent time not to attend on the grounds that I was white and would attract the wrong kind of political attention. This was the experience of some others: When the outreach process eventually came to the capital city, a black attendee was assaulted by "three war veterans and some ZANU PF youth" (ZZICOMP, 2010) when he tried to defend the right to attend of a white couple who had been excluded. The process was not entirely closed to white people—personal communication with various white activists across the country showed their presence at meetings. Nonetheless, my lack of access to constitutional outreach meetings left me wondering who else was excluded and, further, what other disjunctures were occurring between the rights-based and democratic language in which the COPAC process was represented and the reality of its implementation.

The public language of the COPAC teams immediately reveals the rhetoric of democracy and public engagement: On billboards and in newspapers the COPAC logo was followed by the phrase "Ensuring a People-Driven Constitution," whereas COPAC advertisements urged Zimbabweans to "Be Heard: Take Part in the Constitution Making Process," reminded us that "It is everyone's duty to participate in the Constitution Making Process," and showed pictures of children next to the words "I am Taking Part in the Constitution Making Process—Children and youth, have your say!" Here, then, is a material manifestation of the rhetorical discourse of rights: state-sponsored advertising that presents a particular way of being in the world and aims to influence the behaviors of "the people."

This emphasis on the importance of public participation was not limited to state rhetoric: It was also a central element of rights talk as used by civil society and activist groups. A further example of the ways in which rights discourse manifested can be seen in the work of a nongovernmental group, the Africa Community Publishing and Development Trust, which published a book entitled *A People's Guide to Constitutional Debate* in 2009 (Africa Community Publishing and Development Trust 2009a). This Harare-based, externally funded organization aims to "advance human rights and good governance" through "community based, participatory publishing" (Africa Community Publishing and Development Trust, 2014). It is thus a good example of the ways in which human rights discourse works to move international ideas of human rights into local spaces. A central theme running through this text is the idea that Zimbabwean citizens should have the right, as enacted through public speech, to take part in the constitution-writing process.

But who is a citizen of Zimbabwe? This is one space in which we can see the material realities of shifting legal definition and categories as they emerged during the constitutional debates. In the language of liberal rights-based civil society, as well as the language of COPAC, the terms *citizens* and *the people* were used interchangeably. In this inclusive shorthand, "the people" were deemed to be anyone living in Zimbabwe and ex-Zimbabweans in the diaspora. However, the various versions of the constitution took different stances on who should be categorized as a citizen, with the Lancaster House Constitution and the Kariba Draft providing a more narrow definition than the NCA draft. Where the Lancaster House Constitution and Kariba Draft limited citizenship by birth to only those born in the country whose parents are also Zimbabwean citizens, the NCA draft allows children born outside the country to Zimbabwean citizens, and those born in the country regardless of parental citizenship, to have access to citizenship. Further, the Lancaster House Constitution and Kariba Draft prohibit dual citizenship, while the NCA version allows it. All three versions, however, are silent on the issue of migrant workers. Who "the people" of Zimbabwe might legally be, then, was still up for debate.

In *A People's Guide to Constitutional Debate*, who fit into the exact category of citizenship was left open ended, but the role of the citizen was nonetheless held as essential (Africa Community Publishing and Development Trust, 2009a). The authors thus asserted that "citizens are the builders of a democratic country called home" (15), argued for the necessity of "transforming the passive masses into active citizens" (25), and, beneath an illustration of five people writing in a large open book inscribed with the words "Constitution of Zimbabwe" commented that "No one should think and choose for us. As citizens we have the right to write our views for a democratic Constitution" (29). Further, the authors asserted that "A Constitution only becomes owned and legitimate (respected and accepted) in the eyes of the people if they participated in its making" (33) and that "one of the main purposes of a democratic Constitution is to protect citizens' human rights" (83).

The text also drew on a collation of Shona and Ndebele proverbs to emphasize the authors' political viewpoint within local idioms: In Ndebele, *Abaleleya bavuswa ngaba khangeleyo* ("The sleepy are awakened by the awake": 25) and *umuzi ngumuzi ngomthetho* ("A home is a home because of its laws":

30) were drawn on to emphasize the importance of public participation and the rule of law, whereas the Shona proverb *simba rehove riri mumvura* (literal translation: "The power of the fish is in the water") was evoked as a means of expressing "the trust and mutual relationship between leaders and people" (55), though the same proverb had earlier been translated as "Full participation is only realised in your country" (14). The ideals of liberal democracy were thus invoked throughout this text, which was distributed around the country by the NGO that wrote it during the COPAC outreach process. By such mechanisms do ideas of human rights materially manifest.

In both state and civil society discourse, then, the role of "the people" in writing the constitution and deciding on their rights was emphasized. This notion of public engagement is rooted in ideas of participatory democracy and reflects the human rights architecture that is often attendant to democracy as political form: freedom of speech, for example, and a free and fair electoral process. The reality of the process, of course, means that constitutions will in actuality be written by a very small elite, the few who have access to both the legal language and knowledge that a constitution requires and who have political access to the document-writing process itself. In the Zimbabwean constitutional debates, however, the attempts to encode rights unfolded within strategic use of the language of participatory democracy by the state *and* by its opponents. Given the ways in which the state has, in the last decade, instituted legal forms that expressly work to inhibit such public engagement, such as the Public Order and Security Act (POSA), it is unsurprising, however, that state rhetoric of public consultation was viewed with suspicion by the civil sectors and by Zimbabweans. Passed in 2002, this extensive piece of legislation stemmed from the Smith regime's colonial Law and Order Maintenance Act (LOMA), which was used against the nationalist parties during the struggle for independence. Among other terms, POSA prohibited public gatherings without police notification, curtailing the actions of trade unions and the political opposition. There was thus a clear contradiction between the ways in which the state used legal mechanisms, themselves based in a colonial regime, to curtail political rights while simultaneously and strategically using "rights talk" and anticolonialism for the purposes of populism.

In 2010, then, the public debates about the constitution centered on the validity of the outreach process. Could "the people" be said to be engaging in the COPAC process? For all that the state and civil society spoke in the language of rights and democracy, how effective was outreach at accessing people's views, and was the state even interested in those views? Throughout the implementation of COPAC's outreach process, this topic was hotly debated.

My experiences of the inaccessibility of the COPAC process were not unique. From the beginning, COPAC's public consultation process was marked by controversy over the degree of openness it afforded, with COPAC members insisting it was open and democratic, although their critics argued that only people who were sympathetic to ZANU-PF were allowed to speak and further that they had been told beforehand exactly what they were allowed to say. Both sides used the language of democracy and referenced "the people," and "the people's voice," and both positions were argued and reiterated in numerous forums, formal and informal—from articles, letters, and cellphone text messages published in newspapers, to call-in shows on the radio, from conversations in bars to electronic commentary via the NGO and activist community (e)mailing lists.

A sense of the extent of public concern with the process can be given by one example: The website Sokwanele, which gives as its mission statement "campaigning non-violently for freedom and democracy in Zimbabwe," devoted its home page entirely to the constitution for a period of 2011, with its other concerns (including the "ZIG Watch," which collected any and all media concerned with the Inclusive Government in its entirety) moved to tabs along the top of the page. Sokwanele amassed a hugely extensive archive of the constitutional outreach process, which they presented in the manner of a daily timeline with links to published articles from a variety of forums. This timeline was the best example I saw of presenting in a coherent manner the truly staggering numbers of articles that resulted from the outreach process— the links numbered in the thousands and serve to illustrate how much people had to say about the process.

When I asked interlocutors who argued against the validity of the outreach process why such an elaborate (and expensive) outreach process would be undertaken if there was no intention of recording the views of the people who attended, they all had a similar answer. Tarisai, for example, looked at me as though I was, at the very least, deeply naïve. "Come, Shannon," she said,

> You are Zimbabwean. You've seen the elections we have here. Why do we go through such a process all the time then, when we know it is rigged, or violent, or whatever? That's expensive too. *But you have to look like as if democracy is happening because then you can claim legitimacy.* Money on cars and salaries

and meetings is well spent if you come out of it with a constitution that is based on the people, and if *you can then talk about the rights laid down by the people themselves.* (Interview with Tarisai, 2010: emphasis mine)

In this reading of the process, performing democracy was the name of the game, and COPAC's political sentiment viewed as purely rhetorical.

The view held by Tarisai and others was not held by all other nonstate actors; firsthand evidence, as well as hearsay, from general members of the Zimbabwean public that spoke to both positions was frequently presented in various media forms. On one radio show "Norbert from Chirundu" stated that he was disallowed from speaking because he was viewed as unsympathetic to "the party" (Norbert, nobody's fool, didn't actually name *which* party, though that he meant ZANU-PF was clear enough from the political position he took); whereas "George from Kadoma" said he was moved to call in to the radio show following his experiences as it was obviously a "free and fair" consultation (thus invoking the language of the electoral process) "where every man was able to speak."

As with much of Zimbabwean politics, constitutional outreach was a male-dominated arena—whoever "the people" were, then, in much of the public discourse it appeared that they were men. Where I conducted interviews about the constitutional process, these gendered assumptions sometimes occurred hand in hand with mention of the need to better encode "women's rights"; at other times, even such ambivalence to the role of women did not arise, with interlocutors asserting that there was danger in allowing women too much power and "too many rights." Since independence, women's rights in Zimbabwe have been characterized by steady legislative erosion (Essof, 2006; Ranchod-Nilsson, 2006). Many of the activists I worked with were women who were personally aware of the gendered nature of much of Zimbabwean public participation and aware of the limits on how women could engage, as they themselves had struggled against the ostracism that accompanied involvement in political spaces. It is common in Zimbabwe to encounter derogatory terms such as "Tsvangirai's whores" being used of female politicians, political activists, and, indeed, even women who speak about political issues. Given this context, it is unsurprising that a newspaper article on an outreach meeting in rural Murehwa reported the women present to have responded to a question on whether the constitution should make 50 percent female representation in political bodies mandatory with a cry of "Aiwa hatidi!" ("No, we don't want it!") (NewsDay, 2010a). This was reported as reflecting the ignorance of the women concerned and did not consider the stigma attached to women's political involvement and the complexity of processes of speaking publicly in Zimbabwe, both of which provide better explanations for the women's expressed lack of desire to enforce female political contribution.

Although the rhetoric of participatory democracy was invoked throughout the COPAC process, then, the complexities of people's positions within society and the ways this might influence what they could or could not say, or what they did or did not want, largely went without problematization or acknowledgment. As Ross has noted of the expectations placed on public voice in the TRC (Truth and Reconciliation Commission) process in South Africa, "'Women' are considered to be the problem, rather than the institutions and processes that do not admit different experiences, that protect power from direct speech, or that do not admit the complexity of speech and silence" (Ross, 2010: 90).

Divisions over the definition of "the people" extended beyond gender: As already briefly mentioned, a vehement area of debate, on a national and transnational scale, centered around the constitutional encoding of citizenship—in other words, around who, by constitutional law, could lay claim to being Zimbabwean and to the rights attendant on that and who could not. Civil society and Zimbabweans contributing to the debate from outside the country were often in agreement in asserting that members of the diaspora should be part of the consultation process, whereas COPAC initially excluded them. Given that movement out of Zimbabwe was considered by many such people to have been politically motivated, it is unsurprising that their exclusion resulted in a public outcry. This outcry was vehement enough to result in COPAC allowing the Zimbabwe Exiles Forum to submit their own version of the constitution as part of the outreach process: In this version, dual citizenship is legalized.

Although key players were divided as to whether it reflected reality or performance, notions of participatory democracy were invoked throughout the consultation process. As Gluck, in her introduction to *Words in Motion: Toward a Global Lexicon* (Gluck and Tsing, 2009), which traces the emergence and global movement of particular terms, notes, "Important words like 'democracy' . . . and 'rights' travel the globe and appear in many local and national inflections" (Gluck, 2009: 4). Rights talk during the COPAC process also utilized another key trope of global discourses of rights, however, which, unlike democracy, did not stem from a definite type of government and political form but was much more nebulous: I refer here to notions of freedom.

Although the preceding discussion was located in the debates over the implementation of COPAC outreach, therefore, in examining recourse to ideas of freedom I am able to focus on the content of that process.

Competing Discourses of Freedom in Zimbabwe

Every sovereign people is entitled to give birth to its own Constitution.

Robert Mugabe, reported in BBC World News, November 19, 1999

We have fought for our land, we have fought for our sovereignty, small as we are we have won our independence and we are prepared to shed our blood. . . . So, Blair, keep your England, and let me keep my Zimbabwe.

Robert Mugabe, speech at the Earth Summit in Johannesburg, 2002

Let us be frank—freedom remains absent in Zimbabwe. Human rights remain violated in Zimbabwe, even under Tsvangirai. Mugabe says, "Zimbabwe for Zimbabweans" . . . but Zimbabweans are all still struggling for their political freedom.

Interview with George, fifty-three-year-old Shona man, who had considered himself a ZANU-PF supporter up until 2002

We used to call my generation, you know, those of us born after 1980, the "born-frees." But now . . . we might have been born free, but we did not stay that way for long. If anything real is to change, we need the constitution to ensure political freedom, freedom of assembly, freedom of media. And then we need to make sure that the constitution is obeyed.

Interview with Nyasha, a twenty-nine-year-old Shona woman

In postcolonial contexts, the word *freedom* is often used in relation to political independence from the colonizer and to freedom from colonial rule. This use of *freedom* has its roots in the nationalist ideologies of African independence movements and can be seen in the central political texts of that era, such as Kwame Nkrumah's *Speak of Freedom* (1961), Julius Nyerere's *Essays on Socialism* (1968), and Leopold Senghor's *On African Socialism* (1964). It is in this sense that Nyasha and her age cohort were termed the *born-frees*, and it is in this sense that President Mugabe drew on claims of autochthony to assert Zimbabwean sovereignty and independence. George's and Nyasha's quotes above are illustrative, however, of many Zimbabweans in 2010 in that, regardless of their own autochthony or Zimbabwe's sovereignty and independence, they considered freedom to be limited.

Angered by elaborate state-held Independence Day celebrations in 2011, Zimbabwean Dominic Mhiripiri wrote, in an blog entitled *Amid Lack of Freedom, Zimbabwe Reaches Independence Milestone,*

> In the aftermath of a decade-long economic crisis, gross human rights abuses, and more recently, a coalition government that is at best a cinema of childish and inconsequential drama from grown men and women—little remains for the average Zimbabweans to celebrate about independence.
>
> For the generation of those Zimbabweans who danced and sang Independence night away in 1980, the "gains" of freedom they were promised—land, access to capital, full employment, education and health—have either been confined into the circles of a tiny elite, or simply, eroded away by the economic crisis. Either way, they cannot partake of the supposed fruits of liberation. (Mhiripiri, 2011: 1)

Mhiripiri posits two distinct points in Zimbabwean history from which to consider ideas of freedom—the freedom gained in 1980, following the liberation struggle (the Second Chimurenga is most commonly translated into English in these terms—as a struggle for liberation, a struggle for freedom); and the freedoms, or lack thereof, that he observes in 2011. Mhiripiri's position is not unusual; the data I gathered during fieldwork showed a sharp division between two competing notions of freedom that were at play in Zimbabwean politics at the time. *Freedom* was considered either to refer to the political and economic freedoms associated with democracy and neoliberal capitalism or to refer to freedom from colonization (with a concomitant rhetorical return of the land to "the people") and freedom from "Western"[8] influence. Both of these options place freedom firmly in the realm of politics; beyond this, however, they tended to diverge.

This division was not unfamiliar to me, in that the competing notions of freedom drawn on by my interlocutors as they debated the constitution (in the liminal moment of a so-called transition)[9] reflect the political rift that has unfolded in Zimbabwean politics since independence. This rift led in time to the signing of the GPA and the introduction of the inclusive government and exists at present in the aftermath of the 2013 elections, which saw the closing of the "transitional" space, the dismantling of the "inclusive" government, and a return to ZANU-PF–led politics. The rift has been described by Raftopoulos (2004: 17) as the development of "a severe break . . . between the discourse and politics of the liberation struggle and that of the civic struggles for democratisation in the post-colonial period." In the post- 2000 period, the divide widened, as is reflected in the following description of the candidates in a Zimbabwean by-election: "Pfebve, 32, represents the new politics of democracy, while Manyika, 46, epitomises the old politics of the liberation struggle" (*The Daily News*, July 24, 2001; quoted in Raftopoulos, 2004: 17). "Old" and "new" politics reflect positioning rather than any one moment in time, as both political viewpoints still operated (and conflicted with each other) in "transitional" Zimbabwe as I encountered it during fieldwork. We can also see the imposition of a linear model of temporal time that does not reflect the realities of temporalities at work in postcolonial Africa (cf. Mbembe, 2001).

George's and Nyasha's comments illustrate one way of viewing freedom, one based on the ideals of a rights-based democracy. *Freedom*, used in this manner, refers to the "fundamental freedoms" that are central to the human rights–based ideal as articulated through the Universal Declaration of Human Rights (UDHR) and the International Covenant on Civil and Political Rights (ICCPR). Here, the freedom *to* act in particular ways replaces freedom *from* colonization as used in the "old politics" of the liberation struggle. In rights terminology these freedoms are freedom of association;[10] freedom of religion, belief, and opinion;[11] freedom of assembly, demonstration, and petition;[12] and freedom of expression.[13] Such political freedoms (aside from freedom of religious belief) have become progressively constrained in Zimbabwe in the last decade as the state tightened its hold on legal, media, and electoral institutions in response to political opposition, through acts such as the Public Order and Security Act (POSA), even though they were protected under the Lancaster House Constitution (albeit partially and poorly, in comparison to, for example, the South African Bill of Rights).

Throughout the constitution-making dialogue in 2010, then, human rights talk often referred to a Bill of Rights that would strengthen and protect political freedoms. An SMS sent to a local newspaper read, "COPAC must hear that we want to meet as MDC members without harassment," which can be translated into rights-based terminology as a call on the right to freedom of assembly and the right to freedom of association, whereas a guest at a meal I attended argued that "we need to be able to better protect freedom of press than we were able to do with Lancaster House" (freedom of expression), and an online comment after a news story that described one of the many arrests of WOZA members after a public protest read, "As Zimbabweans we must stand together with WOZA to protect our right to protest against an inhumane government"—or, in other words, to protect freedom of assembly.[14]

Such notions of political freedom form one of the central threads of international human rights discourses. Englund (2006), however, has argued that there is a danger where rights come to stand *only* for such freedoms. In a chapter devoted to the processes of translating rights talk into local languages and idioms, he argues that this is exactly what has occurred through the (politicized) processes of translation in Malawi and Zambia and that "activists, politicians, journalists, and others spearheading the translation have taken their particular interest in democratization as a universal concern. They have, accordingly, translated rights as freedoms, with a particular emphasis on political and civil liberties" (Englund, 2006: 48). Again, here we see an emphasis on the freedom *to* act in particular ways, rather than one on ideas of freedom *from*: colonization, as seen earlier, but also from want, as encoded in socioeconomic rights. Within rights discourse, then, particular forms of freedom have gained prominence in particular contexts, such that political rights come to take precedent over other forms.[15] The relationship between discourses of rights and discourses of democracy can be seen again here, as well as the prevailing emphasis within rights discourses on first-generation political and civil rights at the expense of socioeconomic rights, for all that such rights were presented in my law classes as "indivisible." Englund goes on to argue that, through such constrictive acts of translation, "human rights discourse . . . can be deprived of its democratizing potential and made to serve particular interests in society" (ibid.).

In the context of Zimbabwean political dialogue there lay a further impediment to the "democratizing potential" of rights discourse: that of an opposing view of freedom that draws on notions of autochthony[16] and authenticity to place the rhetoric of national liberation ahead of any (individual) rights-based considerations. The following example serves to illustrate.

At the beginning of the COPAC consultation process, long before outreach teams had come to Harare, I attended a public event where I was witness to a tense conversation between two members of the audience. The event was held in a restaurant in the city center that served food and drinks and often had live entertainment. This place was well known for its "political" nature in that, throughout the media crackdown and public silencing of the last decade, it had showcased artists and held events that spoke against state oppression.

That evening, which was not presented as political per se, a singer had seated herself at the small stage at the front of the room and, accompanied by an acoustic guitar, sung Bob Marley's well-known *Redemption Song*. This moving song includes the lyrics, "How long shall they kill our prophets while we stand aside and look?" and has as one refrain "Won't you help to sing these songs of freedom?"

I could not help but hear the song in terms of the Zimbabwean political situation, and the (politically active) people whom I was with viewed it in the same way. In such ways were artists able to speak about the state without breaking any laws. A few days prior to this occasion, human rights activist Farai Magawu had been arrested on charges of supplying false information on the happenings in the Marange Diamond fields in the Chiadzwa district in Zimbabwe; Magawu was the director of an NGO that documented conditions in the area. Magawu's arrest was, at this point in time, a widespread topic of conversation among the political activists I knew, and this, in combination with Bob Marley's lyrics, led to a conversation at our table about the state of freedom of expression in Zimbabwe. That this was not necessarily a wise topic to speak about publicly says a great deal, but the reputation of the restaurant as a safe political space (and no doubt the beer it served) loosened tongues, and the conversation became loud enough for a man at a nearby table to overhear. He swung his chair around and interrupted our conversation with the words, "Are you saying Zimbabwe is not free?" The man at our table who had been speaking replied (rather bravely, I thought), "I am saying we can't just talk about anything in this country without fear of consequences."

"But there are some things that should not be said, and if they are said then it is only right that there are consequences," replied his interlocutor, "That doesn't mean we are not free."

"Fine," replied the activist, "but there are also things that *should* be said. Look at Farai Magawu."

"Magawu? But he is a liar. Of course there must be consequences for liars. This has nothing to do with freedom. Zimbabwe was brought to freedom in 1980; we are free still. Magawu is a Western puppet spreading lies, but we know that Zimbabwe must never be a colony again."[17]

If it had not been obvious already, the reference to "Western puppets" and the oft-quoted "Zimbabwe must never be a colony again" made the man's political solidarities as a ZANU-PF supporter clear to us all. My companion placated the man and backed down from the conversation, and soon after we left. This incident served to highlight, however, a different idea of freedom that was called on in Zimbabwean politics, where freedom stood for political independence (and a concomitant possession of "the land"), and independence from outside interference, which was usually posited as "colonial" or "Western." In this vein, at a speech to ZANU-PF congress in 2003 while the Commonwealth was deliberating on whether to exclude Zimbabwe, Mugabe stated:

> If the choice was made for us, one for us to lose our sovereignty and become a member of the Commonwealth or to remain with our sovereignty and lose membership of the Commonwealth, then I would say, then let the Commonwealth go. What is it to us? Our people are overjoyed, the land is ours. We are now the rulers and owners of Zimbabwe. (Mugabe, 2003)

In this view of freedom as sovereignty, notions of human rights and fundamental freedoms are presented as Western constructs that are not relevant to Zimbabweans. Further, the very language in which such freedoms are articulated has also been turned against now former leaders of "the West":

> Let Mr. Bush read history correctly. Let him realise that both personally and in his representative capacity as the current President of the United States, he stands for this "civilisation" which occupied, which colonised, which incarcerated, which killed. He has much to atone for and very little to lecture us on the Universal Declaration of Human Rights. His hands drip with innocent blood of many nationalities. . . .
>
> Mr Bush, Mr. Blair and now Mr Brown's sense of human rights precludes our people's right to their God-given resources, which in their view must be controlled by their kith and kin. I am termed dictator because I have rejected this supremacist view and frustrated the neo-colonialists. (Both quotes from a speech given by Mugabe to the UN General Assembly on September 26, 2007)

In this version of freedom, people like Farai Magawu who speak publicly about people's suffering, and about the violence perpetrated by the state, are described as "puppets of the West" in that they are defying the political party that brought them access to their national "God-given resources" through national liberation. Such rhetoric does not reflect the realities of access to livelihoods or land in presen-day Zimbabwe, which are still deeply uneven and biased in favor of state elites (Murithi and Mawadza, 2011) but rather works to shut down alternative viewpoints on Zimbabwean politics, historically and in the present.

Curiously, given the emphasis within ZANU-PF rhetoric on such language of authenticity and anti-Western sentiment, I never came across a ZANU-PF critique of constitution-writing in itself. I say curiously as, to my mind, within the terms of Mugabe's rhetoric a constitution as a legal document should be viewed as "Western." In a speech to schoolchildren following the 2008 Independence Day celebrations, Mugabe explicitly censured such postcolonial "borrowing":

> You must also know the history of the struggle. Freedom did not come on a silver plate. Zimbabwe was once usurped by imperialists who seized it like robbers, but we got it back and we are proud to be Zimbabweans, not Rhodesians, Africans, not British. We have our own cultures. *We can borrow from other cultures, but not British.* We must remain black and be proud to be black and hence our children should inherit a culture of being proud to be African. (Mugabe, cited in Kawadza, 2008; emphasis mine)

The fact that Constitution writing, (in other words, the writing of a document immersed in the legal and moral norms of "the West") was endorsed by ZANU-PF and not disparaged serves to illustrate that Mugabe's anti-Western rhetoric is often just that: rhetoric. Where "British" or "Western" forms suit the regime (as a constitution based on the Kariba Draft would do), they are not challenged; where such forms challenge the state, such as in the articulation, by Zimbabweans, of (supposedly) fundamental freedoms, then they are vilified as colonial intrusions into sovereign Zimbabwe.

This version of freedom is informed by political context and works to justify political oppression through its rhetorical calls to sovereignty and an independent nationhood. Essentializing language such as that evoked by the man we encountered in a restaurant in Harare, and by the president of the country himself, limits an understanding of the complexities involved where human rights discourses surface in postcolonial contexts and the political forms of such contexts. In considering the tendency to autocracy, or what he terms *commandement* in postcolonial states, Mbembe (2001) attempts to account for such complexity through his assertion that:

> Postcolonial African regimes have not invented what they know of government from scratch. Their knowledge is the product of several cultures,

heritages, and traditions of which the features have become entangled over time, to the point where something has emerged that has the look of "custom" without being fully reducible to it, and partakes of "modernity" without fully being a part of it. (Mbembe, 2001: 25)

It is within contexts such as these that some of the prevalent ideas of modernity—such as rights and freedoms—are articulated in opposition to the state, and it is within such contexts that attempts are being made to reshape the Zimbabwean constitution by a plethora of players. To return then to the starting point of this chapter, in a context such as this the idea of human rights as inherent, inalienable, universal, and indivisible can be seen to obscure the deeply politicized nature of rights praxis and the situationality of calls on rights. We can also see the ways in which ideas of human rights operate as a discourse (Foucault, 1972), in that they reflect forms of legitimated knowledge in terms of how people understand the world, and they are one of the ways in which the authority of modernity (Mignolo, 2012) is enacted, constructed, and, at times, critiqued.

As far as human rights are concerned, then, the language of freedom was largely called on as a means of invoking political rights—or, in terms of generations of human rights law, those rights that fall under the banner of first-generation rights. Unlike Englund's critique of the narrow translation of rights in the Malawian and Zambian context, however, such political rights were not the only sorts of right that were called into being during constitutional dialogue. The following quotation, from a chapter on services and institutions in *A People's Guide to Constitutional Debate*, summons another sort of freedom: "Services should nurture and protect, and enable citizens to live with freedom from want." The idea of "freedom from want" is closer to the socioeconomic rights that Englund found missing in translations of rights by NGOs in Malawi and Zambia. Indeed, the Mhiripiri quotation used earlier in this section classified the "gains" of freedom that people had expected in 1980 in socioeconomic terms: "land, access to capital, full employment, education and health" (Mhiripiri, 2011: 1.) Socioeconomic rights were in no way absent from constitutional debates—the severity of economic decline in Zimbabwe has ensured that socioeconomic factors become central to most public political dialogue. In Zimbabwe, however, socioeconomic conditions were not usually spoken of in terms of freedom but in terms of another of the key tropes of international discourses of rights: dignity. I will return to this in Chapter 4, where I consider how Zimbabwean immigrants in South Africa saw (socioeconomic) dignity as integral to their understanding of human rights, and a violation of those rights.

Rights and Democratic Performance

When I returned to Cape Town from Harare in late August 2010, the COPAC process had not yet reached the capital city. I followed the media reports about Constitutional Outreach, which over time painted a more and more depressing picture, with increasing episodes of physical violence at COPAC meetings (*The Zimbabwean*, August 16, 2010), reports of the abandonment of the process in some provinces due to administrative problems and political infighting (Guma, 2010), reports of donors withdrawing funding as the process extended beyond the deadlines set out in Article VI of the GPA (NewsDay, 2010a), and reports of ZANU-PF youth militia bases being set up ahead of outreach meetings (MDC Today, August 31, 2010). In the end, COPAC found enough money to complete the process across the country. The outreach process was completed by the end of 2010, but this did not resolve debates as to the sincerity of the enterprise. In 2011, further political arguments broke out between ZANU-PF and the MDC as to the methods of data analysis that should be used to distill "the people's voice" from the data gathered at outreach meetings. By May 2011 the Crisis in Zimbabwe Coalition, a body composed of various nongovernmental organizations, reported on a methodological debate between ZANU-PF and the MDCs with the claim that "this is a directionless process meant to make the inclusive government appear busy" (Crisis in Zimbabwe Coalition, May 18, 2011: 1).

In 2011 I sent an email to a Zimbabwean legal academic asking him for his thoughts on the COPAC process. In his reply, he argued that "the voice human rights issues in this Constitution could not be as eloquent as many of us had hoped" and expressed little hope for the emergence of a rights-based constitution. In 2012, the final version of the constitution was made public; unsurprisingly, it closely resembled the Kariba Draft. In terms of human rights, Matyszak (2013: 4) noted that although the draft reflected the substance of transformative rights, when it came to the enforcement of those rights the constitution was weak. Despite its flaws, and despite the attempts of civil society to once again block its passing, this draft constitution was accepted by a national referendum in 2013. "Freedom" in the sense in which it was used by advocates of "new" politics is still largely inaccessible for ordinary Zimbabweans.

Conclusion: Outreach as Farce

This chapter has demonstrated the extent of public discussion over the new constitution and the enormous amounts of time and effort put by a "weakened" civil society into attempts to mobilize the political will to include a rights-based agenda in the constitutional dialogues. The email quoted in the previous section and the subsequent outcome of the COPAC process suggest that this time and effort had very little real effect.

I have presented this extended case study here to demonstrate three interconnected points. First, the global legal language of rights discourse that presents rights as inherent, universal, inalienable, and indivisible is one that obscures the very real effects of power and politics in rights praxis. This is something that is well known within legal studies but that nonetheless is presented as factual in popular "rights talk." Second, rights discourses are entangled within global political forms such as democracy, which use tropes such as freedom and dignity that reflect particular (historically constituted) ways of imagining politics and persons. I pursue this theme further later in the book. Finally, I have used the Zimbabwean constitutional debates to demonstrate that global ideas of rights unfold in local contexts that are highly charged. Rights discourse can thus be seen to be one means by which power is wielded within the hierarchized knowledges of modernity (Foucault, 1972; Mignolo, 2012), within which democracy is presented as the "best" political form. It is not, however, always successful. From the perspective of an analysis of the Zimbabwean situation, the outcome of the constitutional debates is telling in that it reflects the huge disparity of power between the moral versions of the political world put forward by civil society (even where divergent arms of civil society come together with a single aim) and those put forward by the postcolonial state; for such reasons it is also deeply disheartening. From the perspective of this case study as a means of understanding the supposed localization of global rights, the example shows that the politicized nature of those local contexts affects how rights discourse is used, abused, enacted, allowed, or disallowed and how it affects whether supposedly inalienable rights come to be encoded at all. In the next chapter I build on these foundations to further ethnographically explore the (limited) localization of supposedly universal ideas of rights in Zimbabwe.

Chapter 2

Justice in a Time of Impunity

Remaking Social Worlds after Political Violence

The Localization of Rights and Its Limits

Reports about avenging spirits that are terrorising a Zanu PF terror militia in Buhera have sparked a fierce debate about the existence of *ngozi* in African communities. In bars, kombis, homes and workplaces, several Zimbabweans last week reflected on the subject that has set tongues wagging in Buhera. In Harare, the rumour mill was awash with reports suggesting a prominent war veteran was among those who had been hard hit by *ngozi*. The former freedom fighter, who cannot be named for fear of criminal defamation, is said to be distributing cheap "zhing zhong" sandals to villagers in Buhera as a way of appeasing those affected by a violent campaign he led for Zanu PF during the run up to the March 2008 elections.

Excerpt from an article by Walter Marwizi, published in The Standard,
May 23, 2010

Avenging spirits, reparation for acts of political violence via cheap Chinese ("*zhing-zhong*") sandals, and fear of criminal defamation on the part of the journalist: The above excerpt from an article published in a Zimbabwean Sunday newspaper (Marwizi, 2010) captures some of the diversities and limitations of the repertoires of justice available in contemporary Zimbabwe. When this news story was brought to me by Tinashe, an interlocutor I met in Epworth, a high-density settlement on the outskirts of Harare, he did so to show me that *ngozi* were real, legitimized by their appearance in print. The article described *ngozi* as "the avenging spirits" of individuals who had died, most commonly via "the shedding of blood." "*Ngozi* have always been around," Tinashe told me, "but we did not hear of them as often as we do now." When read with a background of local knowledge, then, the article also raises the specter of the failures of the formal legal justice system and the rise of what interlocutors called, in everyday talk, "the culture of impunity" in Zimbabwe.[1] In Tinashe's view, the politics of the legal justice system in Zimbabwe went a long way toward explaining why *ngozi* were, in his words, "on the rise":

> It used to be that you could go to the police if a terrible thing happened, and maybe something happened, some arrest was made. But today that is not a possibility, not here in Epworth. Where it says there in the paper about criminal defamation, that is only because the person they're speaking of is a high-up man, a war vet. The police and the law are only for those guys now. If you have political violence against you, you can't report it. Nothing will be done, or you will be further targeted for your insolence. But at elections it isn't just property damaged and people injured: People die. And the dead must have justice, so they become *ngozi*, and they torment those who killed them. When there were police we didn't need *ngozi* so much. Now that there is impunity in Zimbabwe, we are hearing again about the existence of *ngozi*. Because there is no impunity from *ngozi*: The crime will be paid for.

In times of impunity, then, justice finds another way. On the face of it, the calls made on the ancestral world by interlocutors in Epworth contrasted strongly with other spaces in which I spent my time: In the world of Zimbabwean NGOs and rights activism, for example, the "culture of impunity" was seen as something to be challenged through legal interventions and the mechanisms of transitional justice so that the rule of law might "return" to Zimbabwe and people, including those who gave orders, would be held accountable for their crimes. Both had at root, however, a similar goal: the repair of social relationships in the wake of widespread violence. In this chapter, following a contextual introduction to the state of the legal justice system in Zimbabwe, I draw on three case studies to examine how ideas of justice and restoration, on national and on more intimate scales, were envisioned by my interlocutors in Harare. In the first, I explore the surfacing of the model of transitional justice, an increasingly globally prevalent form of postconflict resolution, in government and nongovernment interventions in Zimbabwe. In the second and third, I consider two models of social restoration as I encountered them in Epworth: the justice of the ancestral spirit world that is meted out through the actions of *ngozi* and the subsequent actions of those affected by it and the model used by the local civic organization the Tree of Life in the "healing circles" they held with Epworth inhabitants. These three case studies allow for an examination of the ways in which rights discourse presents one particular form of power and knowledge within modernity but is by no means the only alternative.

Though these three examples may seem to encompass separate spaces and separate modes of thought, all three exist within the same town and, in some cases, involved the same individuals. Although one could apply the theoretical model of legal pluralism—the existence of plural legal systems in one area (Channock, 1985; Merry, 1988) to the multiple valences at play here, I argue that the idea of entanglement (Mbembe, 2001; Nuttall, 2009) provides a more useful model. I draw on these examples to consider the stance, prevalent within anthropological literature on human rights,[2] that universal discourses of human rights become localized or "vernacularized" (Merry, 2006: 44; Shaw and Waldorf, 2010) in the day-to-day spaces in which they unfold. Sally Engle Merry's (2006) influential analytical framework for studying the use of human rights discourses in different contexts examined the ways in which local intermediaries such as NGOs and social activists convert global ideas of rights into forms that are understandable to local audiences and local ideas into forms that are legible to global rights organizations. She argues that through these acts of translation ideas of human rights become "remade in the vernacular" (Merry, 2006: 39) as they are adapted to local institutions and forms of meaning making. Merry theorizes vernacularization as occurring in one of two forms: either through replication, where the global discourse entirely sets the terms; or through hybridization, whereby local structures are merged with global ideas of rights. Shaw and Waldorf's 2010 volume draws on a similar idea of cultural translation: Entitled *Localizing Transitional Justice*, the volume traces how ordinary people respond to transitional justice mechanisms that import global ideas into local settings. In the first case study of this chapter, I track a process of supposed "localization" to argue that there are distinct limitations to the ways in which rights discourses are altered in the process. Although the models of vernacularization presented by Merry posit movement from the global to the local *and* the local to the global, I argue that although there is an insertion of global discourses into the local, we see little movement of local ideas into global discourses. This is in keeping with Shaw and Waldorf's (2010: 4) argument that, although there has been a recent emphasis within transitional justice on the need to localize justice mechanisms, "such adaptation tends to be conceptualised in ways that do not modify the

foundational assumptions of transitional justice." In other words, the hierarchies of knowledge at work give preference to particular ways of being in and
relating to the world (Mignolo, 2012).

Rights discourses are therefore flexible enough to allow for the translation
of rights norms into local cultural idioms;[3] this is one of the reasons that they
have been able to become such a prevalent global model. It does not necessarily allow, however, for the incorporation of local knowledge into the broader
global discourse. It is the very ability of rights discourses to encompass varied
ideologies and moralities and re-present them under the symbolically powerful banner of "human rights" that has made rights talk one of the most prevalent forms of resistance to political oppression in contemporary Zimbabwe
and one of the key "political metanarratives" of our time (Wilson, 2006: 77).
As regards ideas of national justice, however, there are other models at play
in Zimbabwe, some of which have been co-opted by transitional justice discourses and some of which have not. In addition to there being a limitation
to the ways in which rights discourses (encompassing both talk and performance) are localized, there are also limitations to the discourses' usefulness:
At times, other sorts of social restitution matter more.

The "Culture of Impunity" in Zimbabwe

Many, many women in my district were raped during the 2008 election violence. Some
of them are in my family. People also lost their homes, their belongings, even their
crops. But I do not see anything about it in my courtroom because the police were told
that they could not respond to political issues. Any political violence issues were off
limits to the police, so they have not reached us in the Magistrates Court. If they had
come into my court, I would not know what to do . . . because to prosecute would be
very dangerous to me.

Interview with Amelia, a magistrate in a small town in Zimbabwe

Viewed from a distance, the Zimbabwean legal system appears to protect citizens' rights and uphold the rule of law. Inherited from colonial Rhodesia,[4] it is
a system of constitutional supremacy, meaning that, at the time of fieldwork,
the Lancaster House Constitution (as described in the previous chapter) was
the supreme law and the parent act of any other legislation. On paper, the
constitution and the legal system protected rule of law principles, including
the independence of the judiciary and a nonpartisan police force. Further, in
terms of international legal obligations, Zimbabwe has ratified the African

Charter on Human and People's Rights (Banjul Charter) and the International Covenant on Civil and Political Rights (ICCPR), which obliges the state to respect due process (the legal requirement that the state respects the rights owed to persons). In reality, however, amendments to the constitution since 1980 had consolidated state powers in the hands of the president (see Chapter 1), and the legal architecture was progressively altered and disregarded, resulting in an erosion of the rule of law. Following the signing of the GPA in 2008, Human Rights Watch (2008: 1) summarized the state of the legal system in Zimbabwe as follows:

> Over the last decade, ZANU-PF has progressively and systematically compromised the independence and impartiality of Zimbabwe's judiciary and public prosecutors, and instilled one-sided partisanship into the police. Since 2000 it has purged the judiciary, packed the courts with ZANU-PF supporters and handed out "gifts" of land and goods to ensure the judges' loyalty. It has provided instructions to prosecutors to keep opposition members in jail for as long as possible. It has transformed Zimbabwe's police force into an openly partisan and unaccountable arm of ZANU-PF.

During fieldwork, the decline in the rule of law was generally described as "the culture of impunity" in Zimbabwe, terminology that is drawn from the globally circulating languages of rights and transitional justice.[5] Amelia's words at the beginning of this section provide just one example of how political impunity played out in day-to-day life; throughout my fieldwork, interlocutors brought up examples of an elitist police and legal justice system. Such partial application of the law, particularly with regard to political violence, has occurred in a context where widespread political violence has marked the (colonial and postcolonial) state—though the culture of impunity to which interlocutors referred was spoken of as a phenomenon of the last decade or so, any conversation about unresolved political crimes could bring up incidents stretching beyond living memory through to the present—from the hanging of Mbuya Nehanda in 1898,[6] through the liberation war in the 1970s and Gukurahundi in the 1980s, to the 2008 elections.

I will return to a consideration of this temporal relationship later. What is of concern here is that although unresolved violence has a long history, many of the Zimbabweans with whom I worked were most concerned about the post-2000 period—not surprising, as this most recent period has seen a marked increase in political and structural violence that has had profound effects on daily life. Interlocutors argued that one element of this was that political crimes could be carried out without fear of legal reprisal. This is supported by the wealth of reports released by academics and rights organizations in Zimbabwe (see Zimbabwe Human Rights NGO Forum, 2001; Feltoe, 2003, 2004; Kaulemu, 2010; Sachikonye, 2011.) In December 2012, Sokwanele, a rights advocacy group, released a report summarizing the findings of a four-year monitoring project that assessed the implementation of the GPA in that period (Sokwanele, 2012)—it found that breaches against Article XI of the GPA, the article concerned with the rule of law, had been the most prevalent, with a total of 4,672 breaches over four years. The authors concluded that "the rule *of* law in Zimbabwe has been replaced with rule *by* law. Instead of government power being subject to the law, Zimbabwe has become a police state in which government both invokes the law—and has created law—to justify excessive use of government force" (Sokwanele, 2012: 9).

It is thus generally accepted in the literature on Zimbabwe that the rule of law has been considerably eroded under the ZANU-PF dispensation. This literature tends to focus on the political and legal ramifications of the decline of the rule of law. However, there is more at stake. An example serves to illustrate: In 2007, interlocutors in Cape Town had explained to me that their move to South Africa had been motivated by a number of reasons. That people's motivations for migrating were political and economic[7] was not surprising to me. I was surprised, however, by the third sort of reason that people gave: that of a spiritual motivation. "I could not pray from inside Zimbabwe," one man told me, "the country is now so tainted by so many crimes and so much blood that has not been accounted for that Mwari (God) and the ancestors cannot hear you. So it is better to be here." A culture of political impunity had effects beyond the legal, then, effects so powerful so as to severely interrupt the relationships between this world and the world of (traditional and, to some extent, Christian) spirituality, at least for some interlocutors. Clearly, more than one discourse of rights and restitution is at work.

State-Based Justice and Reconciliation

When the GPA was signed in 2008, it attempted to account for the erosion of the rule of law through Article XI, in which the parties agreed that it was the duty of all politicians and political parties to respect and uphold the Constitution and to adhere to the principles of the rule of law. In addition, Article VII also provided for a mechanism "to advise on what measures might be necessary and practicable to achieving national healing, cohesion and unity." The Organ on National Healing, Reconciliation and Integration (ONHRI) resulted from this provision.

The ONHRI, with its emphasis on national healing and reconciliation, is modeled on ideas of transitional justice. The field of transitional justice is relatively new, historically speaking, in that it is less than twenty years old—but it has quickly gained international prominence such that Shaw and Waldorf (2010: 3) argue that "transitional justice has grown over the last twenty years into a normalized and globalized form of intervention following civil war and political oppression." The model is a redemptive one, predicated on an assumed relationship between the truth, narrative, and (national as well as individual) healing (see Ignatieff, 1996; Ross, 2003a) and on a linear temporality such that "the harms of the past may be repaired in order to produce a future characterized by non-recurrence of violence, the rule of law, and a culture of human rights" (Shaw and Waldorf, 2010: 4). The future is also anticipated to be democratic. The aims of transitional justice are implemented through a set of legal and restorative mechanisms, such as free and fair elections, truth commissions, prosecutions of war crimes, public memorials, and acts of reparations. Within Zimbabwe, as is probably the case throughout the Southern African region, the best-known restorative model is that of the Truth and Reconciliation Commission (TRC) used in neighboring South Africa beginning in 1996, which provided individual amnesty for political crimes on the basis of "full disclosure." Gready (2011: 1) has argued that it was the South African TRC that ushered in what he terms "the era of transitional justice."

Although the discourse is new, its global symbolic capital is such that it tends to be presented by its proponents as the "obvious" response to political conflict—in Zimbabwe, at least, the great majority of people to whom I spoke (ranging from political actors, civil servants, and members of civil society, who carry some political power, to street vendors, teachers, and the unemployed, who carry little) were clear that there was a need for a response modeled on transitional justice mechanisms. "We need a TRC here"; "we need to hear the truth like in South Africa, but we must also prosecute"; "we cannot let amnesty occur without some sort of reparation"; "there is no justice without accountability of politicians"; and "we will need special commissions for women because they have experienced violence differently" are just some of the comments I recorded in everyday interactions. In the Zimbabwean context, however, reconciliation as it is imagined through the discourses and processes of rights-based transitional justice is only one quite recent arm of a longer history of ideas of justice and reconciliation. Justice mechanisms under customary law rely heavily on the payment of reparations between the injured party and the perpetrator. Such processes are small scale, however. Reconciliation on a national scale, on the other hand, previously surfaced following the end of the liberation war or Second Chimurenga. An alternative genealogy of ideas of national reconciliation in Zimbabwe could take as its starting point President Robert Mugabe's address to the nation on the eve of Independence in 1980. Unlike transitional justice discourse, which lays an emphasis on bringing the violations of the past into the public eye, in this speech Mugabe advocated starting anew, without carrying over memories from the past:

> Independence will bestow on us a new personality, a new sovereignty, a new future and perspective, and *indeed a new history and a new past*. Tomorrow we are being born again; born again not as individuals but collectively as a people, nay, as a viable nation of Zimbabweans. Tomorrow is thus our birthday, the birth of a great Zimbabwe, and the birth of its nation.
>
> Tomorrow we shall cease to be men and women of the past and become men and women of the future. It's tomorrow then, not yesterday, which bears our destiny.
>
> As we become a new people we are called to be constructive, progressive and forever forward looking, for we cannot afford to be men of yesterday, backward-looking, retrogressive and destructive. Our new nation requires of every one of us to be a new man, with a new mind, a new heart and a new spirit.
>
> (Robert Mugabe's speech to the nation on the eve of independence,
> April 17, 1980; emphasis mine)

In this philosophy, the happenings of the past do not belong in the present or in the future; unlike in ideas of transitional justice, the past should not be brought to light but forgotten or left behind. There is a different imagining of temporality at work here than in transitional justice models, and both differ from traditional Shona and Ndebele cosmology, as explored in the following pages, where the presence of the ancestors in the daily world ensures an entanglement of what modernist narratives of time would consider to be the past in the present.[8] Similarly, the attitudes and prejudices carried by people should alter:

Our new mind must have a new vision and our new hearts a new love that spurns hate, and a new spirit that must unite and not divide. This to me is the human essence that must form the core of our political change and national independence.

Henceforth, you and I must strive to adapt ourselves, intellectually and spiritually to the reality of our political change and relate to each other as brothers bound one to another by a bond of national comradeship.[9]

If yesterday I fought as an enemy, today you have become a friend and ally with the same national interest, loyalty, rights and duties as myself. If yesterday you hated me, today you cannot avoid the love that binds you to me and me to you.

Though Mugabe lays an emphasis on a national unity, comradeship, and love, this is not seen as being brought about through a process of surfacing the past and coming to terms with it, as in the case of transitional justice. Rather, one "strives to adapt" within the present. "Forgiveness" goes hand in hand with forgetting, rather than with remembering, in this viewpoint:

Is it not folly, therefore, that in these circumstances anybody should seek to revive the wounds and grievances of the past? The wrongs of the past must now stand forgiven and forgotten.

It is worth noting that "the nation" figures here as the medium through which such forgiveness and forgetting can occur. In neighboring South Africa during the TRC, "the nation" was perceived as being unable to come into being without truth and reconciliation; here, "the nation" is already imagined as present and as constituting the grounds for commonality.

The insistence of interlocutors in Harare[10] that a process of national justice, based on international models, should take place should be viewed in light of this earlier branch in Zimbabwe's postconflict reconciliation lineage. In the ensuing years, Mugabe's insistence on forgetting the past did not, in reality, unfold as neatly as in his independence speech. Rather, the politics of remembrance and forgetting have been deeply politicized and strategic. By 2000, for example, ZANU-PF revived and publicized the atrocities of the Rhodesian past for political means, to justify the illegal occupation of white-owned commercial farmland, while simultaneously refusing to acknowledge the atrocities committed by the (state-sponsored) Fifth Brigade in Matabeleland and the Midlands in the 1980s. Forgetting was not as clean cut as it was presented to be.[11]

Unlike Mugabe's earlier model, then, the ONHRI took as its main stance the viewpoints of transitional justice discourses as previously outlined. This was indubitably influenced by the fact that the GPA was signed under international pressure and orchestrated by Thabo Mbeki, the ex-president of the country that carried out the TRC. Given this, one might think that such an organ[12] would be expected to incorporate the legal and spiritual as previously referred to. Indeed, transitional justice discourses, with their emphasis on forgiveness, truth, and healing (Ignatieff, 1996), tend to draw on the law and on spirituality. In Southern Africa, Archbishop Desmond Tutu has been particularly influential in this regard. While I was resident in Zimbabwe in 2010, however, very few interlocutors had even heard of the Organ of National Healing and Reconciliation; those who had were people who worked in the field of rights and transitional justice, and they tended to consider it largely ineffectual and irrelevant. As with the constitution-writing process, it was within the mandate of the ONHRI to begin a process of public consultation to establish the "necessary measures for national healing" as outlined in the GPA; unlike the constitution-writing process, however, this did not lead to a widespread campaign. In keeping with this, research conducted by the Zimbabwe Human Rights NGO Forum in 2011 showed 74 percent of the 3,491 respondents from across the country never to have heard of the ONHRI; of the 26 percent who had heard of it, only 34 percent rated it as performing well (Zimbabwe Human Rights NGO Forum, 2011). A study conducted on the ONHRI's lack of success to date (Mbire, 2011) concluded that it has been limited by a number of factors. First, there was no clear legal mandate within the GPA as to how the ONHRI was to be constituted or what its precise functions were. Second (as with the rest of the outcomes of the GPA), the ONHRI is composed of members of all three major political parties in Zimbabwe, which ensured that the process was deeply politicized and led to infighting and polarization. Finally, the political will (and attendant economic impetus) behind the ONHRI was limited: From 2008 onward, the Inclusive Government was faced with enormous socioeconomic and political challenges, and as such the more immediately pragmatic issues (such as rebuilding industry and the health care sector) were given priority, whereas processes of "national healing" fell by the wayside. Although Zimbabwe had been perceived as "in transition" since the signing of the GPA, it was unclear during fieldwork what the country was transitioning from or what it was transitioning to (Murithi and Mawadza, 2011; Morreira, 2012b); subsequent events have shown that the "transition" was in fact just a brief anomaly within a continuation of ZANU-PF rule. The particular set of historical circumstances at play in Zimbabwe, which has maintained at the very least a façade of democracy since independence, ensures that the country fits uneasily within the conventional transitional justice paradigm that imagines transition to a democratic state, given that technically—in law if not fact—Zimbabwe has been a democratic state from 1980.[13] State-based interventions have done little so far to challenge the erosion of the rule of law and the rise of impunity for political crimes and to put into practice any actions toward the goals of "national healing, cohesion and unity."

NGOs and the Transitional Justice Paradigm

In the absence of state-based processes of justice and reparation, it is unsurprising that local NGOs made attempts to fill the gap. As with state-based responses, this also occurred in the context of the effects of Mugabe's assertion in 1980 that remembering can be "retrogressive and destructive." In Zimbabwean politics since 1980 the tendency has been for violence to be disregarded. Yet, "There is a line between forgetting, and silencing," the director of a local NGO told me. "And what has occurred in Zimbabwe is silencing." The most obvious and terrible example of this is Gukurahundi in the 1980s, where thousands of Ndebele citizens were massacred as "dissidents" by the state-sponsored Fifth Brigade, a special wing of the military that reported directly to the president. The full extent of the violence was unveiled only in the late 1990s through the work of an NGO, the Catholic Commission for Justice and Peace, which published its findings in a report entitled *Breaking the Silence* (CCJP, 1997). In contrast to Mugabe's 1980 avocation of forgetting, then, NGOs and civil society (such as the CCJP, Zimbabwe Lawyers for Human Rights, the Solidarity Peace Trust, the Zimbabwe Human Rights NGO Forum—the list goes on) have emphasized the necessity for truth telling and (legal) accountability. In this section, I explore the work that was done by one such NGO to imagine a process of national justice, unpacking how global ideas of transitional justice materialized throughout the process.

Case Study: The Transitional Justice Model

Each Monday morning for eight weeks, I drove across central Harare, through chaotic traffic that stopped and started as motorists negotiated their way through multilaned intersections with nonoperational traffic lights. At each street corner, and at times in the center of the road, men stood selling airtime vouchers and newspapers. My destination was removed from the turmoil of central town, tucked down a quiet side street scattered with speed bumps to slow down passing traffic. I was headed to a state-sponsored "Woman's Centre," which was acting as the venue for a series of eight focus groups being run by a local[14] rights advocacy NGO, the Research and Advocacy Unit (RAU), that were aimed at deepening an understanding of the relationship between women and politics. Though the questions asked during the daylong focus group were extensive, for my purposes here those that focused on processes of "transition" and "reconciliation" are most important. In focus group after focus group, the NGO raised questions around processes of justice and accountability, and the female respondents spoke in great detail about the ways in which they imagined a postconflict Zimbabwe. Though Zimbabwe was still embroiled in political and economic crisis at the time, NGOs and ordinary citizens were looking to the future and using the globalized norms of transitional justice to think through how a national process of "reconciliation" might begin.

That the NGO was drawing on a model of transitional justice was immediately apparent from the questions asked of the groups. On the focus group interview schedule that facilitators worked from, sections were devoted to "Special Commissions and Processes" ("Do you know what a truth commission is?"; "What kind of commission would you like to see in Zimbabwe?"; "How should commissions be formed?"); "truth telling" ("Is there a need to tell the truth about violence in Zimbabwe?"; "Which time periods should we cover?"; "What are the major obstacles to truth-telling?"); "accountability" ('What does accountability mean to you?"; "Should a person found to have been involved in political violence be removed from their political position?"; "Should perpetrators of violence be able to hold public office?": "Should there be a process to identify and remove violators of human rights from public service?"; "Should perpetrators be pardoned?"); and "compensation" ("Should people be compensated for their losses?"; "Who should compensate them?"). Such questions led to broad and diverse debate in the focus groups; in this case study I wish to narrow the discussion down to three threads through which to consider the interplay of the local and the global in imaginaries of justice: ideas of truth telling, ideas of temporality, and ideas of legal accountability. Though I have separated them here for purposes of analysis, these three threads are of course entwined, as the preceding questions show.

When I first started attending the focus group sessions, I went armed with a scattering of chiShona from my school days in Zimbabwe, and a Shona-to-English dictionary that I had borrowed from a friend. Focus groups were usually bilingual, with English and chiShona being spoken interchangeably, and I found myself able to follow the majority of the conversations. However, on that first day there was one word that kept coming up again and again that I did not know and couldn't find in my dictionary because the relevant page was missing—the dictionary I had was old and well thumbed. That word was *chokwadi*—truth, as I learned when I asked the woman I sat next to during the morning tea break. As can be seen from the preceding questions, issues of truth telling were considered central by the NGO. This can be read in relation to the silencings within Zimbabwe but is also a key component of rights discourses.

In answer to the first question asked of truth telling ("Do we need to tell the truth in Zimbabwe?"), respondents invariably answered yes. What does it mean "to tell the truth," however? In chiShona, *chokwadi* translates as both *truth* and as *certainty*; therefore a question which asks, in chiShona, if there is a need for truth about violence in Zimbabwe is also asking if there is a need for certainty around the events of the past. On the one hand, this maps well onto transitional justice discourses that, being rooted in the law, are concerned with establishing a certain, authoritative version of events. On the other hand, though, it raises a weakness within transitional justice. Ignatieff (1996) argues:

> One should distinguish between factual truth and moral truth, between narratives that tell what happened and narratives that attempt to explain why things happened and who is responsible. Truth commissions were more successful at promoting the first than the second.

For people with whom I worked, and Shona-speaking Zimbabweans more generally, *chokwadi*'s linking of truth and certainty raised the expectation of establishing a moral truth, a certainty about the happenings of the past that is more than factual. As Englund (2006) notes, issues of translation are at the heart of much of the contextual application of human rights discourse; in the Zimbabwean context as in others, then, the "truth" that is assumed in transitional justice discourse could differ from the truth that is assumed by people gaining access to and using that discourse.

Furthermore, processes of truth making, as with all knowledge (Foucault, 1972), are imbued with power. Focus groups tackled such issues: In what sort of a forum might the creation of truth be possible, and how do we ensure that truth is truthful? Whose truth is it, anyway—particularly in a context where ZANU-PF strategies of maintaining power have written what Muponde describes as "a virulent, narrowed down version of Zimbabwean history, oversimplified and made rigid" (Muponde, 2004: 276)? Focus group debates covered such material (albeit not in such academic terms), and it was in response to these uncertainties that focus group facilitators guided participants toward the models of transitional justice. "Did they know what a Truth Commission was?" facilitators asked. How about a Truth and Reconciliation Commission? Or a Truth, Justice, and Reconciliation Commission? Focus group participants frequently did know of truth commissions broadly, if not down to the differences between the three models. The South African Truth and Reconciliation Commission, after all, happened just across the border and had been widely broadcast in media Zimbabweans used. When facilitators explained the subtle differences between the three models—with the first constituting a forum for establishing narratives about instances of violence, the second providing amnesty in return for a truthful telling, and the third asking for both truth and reparative punishment of some kind, be it through a jail sentence, reparations, or community service—the majority of participants opted for the need for a Truth, Justice, and Reconciliation Commission.

Within this model, the creation of truth was held as central to processes of national transition. The emphasis on a Truth, *Justice*, and Reconciliation Commission raises a further thread that is central to the transitional justice model as it was being applied in Zimbabwe: that of accountability. "Look across the border [to South Africa]," one participant said. "There, there is so much crime and violence and fighting, against their own people and in xenophobia. That is because after apartheid there was no justice. It is not possible to forgive and move on unless there is justice, unless people are seen to have paid for what they did to others. Truth, *justice*, and reconciliation. That is what we want." The women emphasized truth telling and legal accountability, rejecting the TRC with its amnesty provisions.

This raises two points. First, as in the South African case, it highlights the trend within transitional justice to link truth telling to ideas of forgiveness and, through this, to healing and reconciliation on a national scale. But, as

Ignatieff asks, "Can a nation or contending parts of it be reconciled to their past, as individuals can, by replacing myth with fact and lies with truth?" (Ignatieff, 1996: 3). In the model of transitional justice generated during focus groups, it could not. Second, then, it brings us to the idea of legal accountability as central to an imagined process of national "transition": a further material manifestation of the discourses of rights that present particular forms of dealing with conflict as preferable to other forms. Furthermore, legal accountability was overtly linked to ideas of reconciliation: In one woman's words, "There's no peace in Zimbabwe because perpetrators are not being convicted, and so there's no reconciliation. How can we have peace and national unity without having convictions?" Thus, although the model propagated in workshops questioned ideas of national unity on the basis of truth telling, it did not reject the possibilities of national unity per se. Rather, the legal mechanisms of transitional justice were seen as a means of bringing this about. As in Mugabe's speech, this is another instance where the nation is figured as already present and in need of "repair": Unlike in the South African case where the TRC was used as an imaginative means of building a new nation.

The final thread of rights and transitional justice discourses that I wish to emphasize here is the model of time that is at play in the tropes explored thus far. In the focus groups, as in conventional ideas of transitional justice, the facilitators drew on a linear model of time where, although the violence of the past is seen to inform the present, this is viewed as an anomaly that can be "fixed" by a process of national healing and/or justice. For example, questions asked in focus groups such as, "How must we deal with the events of the past in order to move forward?" assume the intrusions of the past into the present are interfering with an imagined future. One aim of reconciliation, then, is to prevent the interference of such a past in the present. Although there was debate in focus groups as to where "the past" should begin and end in processes of national justice (did one include the liberation war? Gukurahundi? Or did one focus on the events of the "post-2000" period—and even then, all of it, or only the most recent elections?), the emphasis was clearly on a linear model of time.

Mbembe (2001), however, argues that time in postcolonial Africa is not experienced as linear but is better conceived of as entangled, "an interlocking of presents, pasts and futures that retain their depths of other presents, pasts and futures, each age bearing, altering and maintaining the previous ones" (Mbembe, 2001: 16; cf. Cole, 2001). Mbembe's model of time is partially similar to that of transitional justice discourse, in that it emphasizes the over-laps between past and present; it differs, however, in that the relationship between the past and the present is not theorized as linear but as multiple and simultaneous. Furthermore, *dis*continuities and reversals are given more emphasis than in transitional justice discourse, which is predicated on the as-sumed continuation of the harms of the past into the present. In this reading of time, the past, the future, and the present operate simultaneously, and it is not seen as "out of place" for the "past" to exist in the "present," or, rather, temporality is not necessarily or inevitably differentiated in everyday life.

This view of time is echoed in Shona cosmology, where the social world is composed of individuals both living and dead and ancestors play a cen-tral role in the maintenance of familial and social relationships (Gelfand, 1970; Bourdillon, 1987). In such a worldview it is perfectly normal for one to maintain a relationship with people who, in a chronological model of time, should be firmly situated in the past. Although it was clear from conversa-tions conducted in different settings that many of the participants, and some of the facilitators, viewed ancestors as relevant, such a model was not applied to discussions of transitional justice in Zimbabwe. Within the construction of valid knowledge within that context (Mignolo, 2012), such a view of time and personhood was considered to carry no relevance, though almost everyone in the room considered it to be relevant in other contexts. In such ways do we see both the power of rights discourses in constructing ways of being in, know-ing about, and relating to the world, and the limitations to their power in that they do not always matter.

This case study can be read as an example of the social life of rights in action. It shows that although there has been a recent emphasis within tran-sitional justice on the need to localize justice mechanisms, the comparative global symbolic (and attendant economic) capital of rights talk ensures that Zimbabwean NGOs, like the state, largely operate within the constraints of the global norm. Any localisation or vernacularization that occurs, then, occurs in a top-down direction and within the terms of the dominant dis-course. This can be advantageous: Rights models are globally powerful and as such give NGOs leverage that they would not otherwise have. Furthermore, such interventions as the RAU focus groups allow for individuals to exercise agency in engaging with political and legal ideas. Unlike in Merry's (2006) model, however, the case study shows no opportunity for local ideas to influ-ence broader global discourses of rights. Furthermore, there is a danger in limiting justice to particular repertoires, particularly given that the state is still not actually implementing any process of nationwide (transitional) justice. Let us turn to two further case studies to explore other ways in which social restitution and justice is being imagined and (unlike transitional justice) actually enacted in contemporary Zimbabwe.

Responses to Political Violence in Epworth

Welcome to my community. I think it is one of the most violated-against communities. There have been all sorts of evils. People have disappeared. There are stories that they have been thrown into the dam up there, alive, weighed with stones so they drown. Did you see the dam? I should have shown you when we were driving in. We have had rape here, beatings, people's houses being burnt. There are many disabled people here now. All the violence is started by politicians. They come here and make the violence happen. But the people remain.

Tinashe's description of Epworth

The Tree of Life

The first time I met Robert and Elias was at the annual meeting of the Tree of Life, an organization founded to assist victims of torture in rebuilding their lives and their communities after violence. The meeting was held in a spacious garden in suburban Harare. Members had come from across the country; seated in a large circle under a jacaranda tree, they spoke one by one, passing a stone between them to signify whose moment it was to speak as they shared information about what had been happening in their areas. Most of the people present had been tortured at some point in their lives; this was a hard reality to come to terms with in the sunshine of a suburban garden on a Harare winter morning. Of the fifty or so people present, ten were the Tree of Life "guardians," individuals who assist with the running of the organization, whereas the rest were people who had been to a Tree of Life workshop in the past and who had now become facilitators of workshops in their own towns and villages. The news they shared was often grim—it was two years after the violence of the 2008 elections, but most speakers still referred to it. The general mood was not somber, however, and many speakers shared good news: Local successes as chiefs or headmen had agreed to attend workshops, or the youth militia[15] in an area were persuaded that workshops could continue, or the crops had been good that year and it seemed that food security was assured for a time.

One of the organization's founders introduced me to Robert after the circle was over. Robert and I stood on the yellowing lawn (winter is the dry season in Harare) and had a cup of tea together, speaking about Zimbabwe, my research, and the Tree of Life. When I told him that I had recently been observing cases at the Magistrate's Court in Harare, he shook his head. "Justice is hard to find in Zimbabwe—if you want to see it, come to our neighborhood or to a workshop, not to the court. This organization brings peace to people," he told me. "You must come to Epworth and talk with the people there about what we are doing." He called over his friend Elias, and together they invited me to come and visit them in Epworth to spend some time talking about the Tree of Life and seeing how things were done in Epworth. A week or so later I picked up Elias from Parirenyatwa Hospital in central Harare, where he was attending a course, and we drove together to his home.

Originally a Methodist Mission, Epworth experienced an influx of migrants in the 1970s and was transferred to the Ministry of Local Government in 1983. Today, Epworth is a high-density suburb composed of a mixture of formal housing and informal *magada* (shacks), with a little over around 100,000 (mostly poor) inhabitants (Zimbabwe Central Statistic Office, 2004; McGreal, 2008). It is a place of scarce resources, with ensuing tensions and rivalries among inhabitants who arrived as part of different waves of migration. The urban poor in Epworth, like their counterparts across the country, have been vulnerable to interference and violence at the hands of the postcolonial state.[16] In the 1980s the various urban "clean-up" campaigns that were initiated in response to the perceived unruliness of urban informality (Kamete, 2008) affected Epworth; in 1991, people were again displaced as the Harare City Council prepared for a visit by Britain's Queen Elizabeth II (Musiyiwa, 2008).

In both the 2000 and the 2005 elections, the majority of voters in Epworth voted in favor of the MDC (Musiyiwa, 2008), as it became apparent countrywide that ZANU–PF had lost its hold on urban areas to the MDC and was supported by a largely rural constituency. ZANU-PF has sought to reassert and consolidate its control by increasingly coercive means. In 2005, in Epworth as elsewhere, Operation Murambatsvina resulted in widespread displacement and the loss of homes and livelihoods (Musiyiwa, 2008; Vambe, 2008; Morreira, 2010a), which were locally perceived as a punishment for voting for the MDC. Three years later, in the 2008 elections, Tsvangirai and the MDC again won by a large majority in Epworth. This was followed by a severe backlash of violence in the area that saw three deaths, more than 200 abductions, and many cases of torture and destruction of property (McGreal, 2008). The political violence occurred against the backdrop of the already existing divisions over land ownership and belonging. Thus, when I asked Amelia (the wife of Tinashe, the interlocuter with whose views on *ngozi* I opened this chapter) to tell me about politics in Epworth, she answered with a litany of violence, counting on her fingers as she spoke: "In Epworth we've had police, bulldozers, green bombers, killing, abduction, *falanga*,[17] rape. Not just from the outside, people who know each other, too." The inhabitants of Epworth, then, are no strangers to political violence, to the extent that a question about politics elicits a reply about the harms it inflicts.

As Elias and I drove down the Chiremba Road toward the suburb in 2010, the multiple forms of violence of the last five years were not far from my mind. When we encountered a police roadblock I wondered if I would be allowed to continue, but we were waved through with a smile by the ZRP official. Urban spaces can be traversed differently at different points in time: In an election year, I would not have gained access so easily, as urban spaces would have been more closely controlled by the state.[18] Epworth's setting is beautiful: It is situated in a place of rounded balancing granite rocks, with large weathered boulders scattered along the Chiremba Road and throughout the suburb. The rocks are colored by lichen; in recent years, some have been covered in the conflicting painted slogans of politics: "ZANU-PF *mbava*" (ZANU-PF thieves); "MDC 2005"; "the fist" (a reference to Mugabe's telling 2008 election slogan, "Vote for the Fist"). The area's beauty is literally inscribed with political conflict. The rocks of Epworth act as more than political billboards, however. Epworth is unique among the suburbs of Harare in that it is the home to a number of rock formations with deep religious significance. Domboramwari ("The Rock of God") is the largest physical feature in the area and has been considered sacred since precolonial times, whereas Domboremaziso ("The Rock of Eyes," so named because it is shaped like a head with many eyes that weep when rain falls) and the surrounding caves are significant spaces of prayer. The rocks have most significance within traditional cosmology, but spaces around them are also vied for by the *vapostori* (an Apostolic sect whose church meetings are always held outdoors), and Christian churches have been built around significant rock formations. Following Murambatsvina, people whose houses had been destroyed congregated at Domboremwari to pray about what they should do next (Musiyiwa, 2008).

It is, furthermore, a place of poverty, with the balancing rocks acting as backdrop to deeply rutted roads (which became less and less formal as Elias directed me along them toward his home) and tightly packed houses and *magada*. Children said hello as we went slowly past; one shouted out, "Murungu!" ("White person!"), and I laughed. Elias pretended not to have heard. People went about their lives in the winter dry season as we drove—washing clothes, watching over cooking fires, tending dusty vegetable gardens, and walking between places. After negotiating our way past a man on a bicycle carrying a pallet packed with loaves of bread, we turned down a final dirt track and entered Elias's yard. Here, his friend Robert was waiting to greet me and take me inside. Seated on comfortable armchairs, surrounded by family photographs, we began to talk about the Tree of Life.

The Tree of Life was started by a small group of Zimbabweans in South Africa in 2003, with the first workshops held with victims of political violence and torture who had migrated across the border to South Africa. The initial model was adapted from a preexisting "empowerment workshop" that "was developed from traditional ways of dealing with difficult issues in communities, notably amongst the Native Americans, and shares common features with many similar circle processes" (Reeler et al., 2009: 182).[19] The Tree of Life model subsequently traveled back to Zimbabwe in 2004 as its proponents felt it safe enough to return home as political violence and police intimidation subsided. Although the organization has grown in the subsequent years, it remains small, with a core of "guardians" who founded the organization, or who have subsequently been asked by the organization to be involved, and a series of facilitators, all of whom have survived some form of organized violence.

Elias and Robert had both been participants in workshops and had subsequently become facilitators. This is a key element of the model, which aims at the "empowerment" of individuals who have had their autonomy and control, including over their own bodies, wrested from them during experiences of politically motivated torture, violence, and rape, or who have been responsible for acts of violence toward others. The organization works with people who have experienced political violence or torture from different standpoints, be it as victim ("although we do not like to use the word *victim*," Robert told me) or perpetrator.[20] Facilitators find participants locally, working carefully and slowly to connect and build trust with others in their areas who have been affected by violence. Though participants usually come from the same area, the model values residential workshops, where the participants are able to live together for three days, removed from the spaces in which they experienced violence.

Robert attended his first workshop in 2009. Initially, the attraction of the workshop was that he would receive food for the three days that he was there. "At first I did not want to go—I was sick of these organizations coming in and out, saying they will change things in Epworth, and they don't." He was encouraged to attend by his mother and other older women who had been to a workshop, and he was persuaded to go only on hearing that he would be given food: "That was when there was no food in Harare, and everyone was very hungry. I'm glad now I was hungry, because I went to that first workshop and saw that it was very different from any other NGOs." Initially, he was struck by the fact that the workshop was held out of town "where I was able to be in nature, in a very quiet place with a lot of trees. I felt at home." Like the workshops that Robert now facilitates himself, the workshop consisted of a series of "circles" held over the three days. Each circle is modeled on the Shona *dare*, a (traditionally male) space of consultation and conflict resolution "where everyone sits face to face and equal, and we are all able to speak." In Tree of Life, the patriarchal element is removed, and the equality is extended to women. Thus, though predicated on (in the words of a Tree of Life guardian) "traditional modes of addressing conflict," a key aim of the workshops is to alter some of the "traditional" power relationships within communities, and the circle is one way of doing this. Participants are guided by facilitators to set their own rules at the beginning of the first circle and are encouraged to use a talking piece—a stone—that is passed around the circle so that each participant has equal chance to speak should he or she wish to.

The process uses the tree as metaphor for human lives and human relationships. Early circles, where participants get to know one another, center on discussion of the tree's roots, where participants place themselves in the world in terms of their kinship, describing their ancestral and totemic[21] histories to other participants. This can be a powerful way of building *communitas* as, in Elias's words, "We can see that even though we think we are from different places, underneath we have much in common. So that's how we weave relationships. You realize that this person you thought was just your neighbor is actually your mother, is actually the same totem as you." In a Zimbabwe that has increasingly questioned the "authenticity" and right to belong of various categories of the population, a discussion of roots can also have powerful individual effects: In Robert's case, "My mother is Mozambican, and my father Malawian. But when we were in the circle I began to feel at home again, that I am a citizen again. I found out that Zimbabwe is built up of a lot of people whose ancestors are not from here." One need not have a totem to feel this sense of *communitas*—in a circle I attended, I was able, as a white Zimbabwean, to find historical connections with the other (Shona and Ndebele) participants and experienced firsthand the relief of having a group acknowledge that my Zimbabwean-ness was of as much relevance as anyone else's. Further, one need not be Zimbabwean—a conversation with a foreign visitor showed that he too had been placed in a web of connected social relationships via diasporic connections. In Epworth, where political violence has followed the fracture lines caused by tensions over who has rightful access to the land, the building of a shared sense of kinship can have powerful effects on local relationships.

As the workshop progresses, the circles move on from ancestral roots to the trunk of people's lives. Circles devoted to the trunk discuss participants' childhoods, as a further means of sharing stories and building trust. Following this is the most difficult part of the process: the trauma circle, where participants relate their life histories, with an emphasis on experiences of harm. Elias explained that participants begin by going

> . . . to sit under a tree and write, draw, and narrate their stories alone. Then they bring them and come and narrate their histories to you. We must be sure that what people say won't be heard in the community. Because if it's heard in the community, there won't be any healing. It would be another trauma. As a facilitator, and as a participant, you must listen attentively, be there. Let people cry to let out the bitterness within themselves. These stories of trauma have to be done in one sitting, even if it takes up to midnight for everyone to tell his or her story. We all need to be able to speak. Afterwards, people often like to pray.

Participants begin this process alone and end it as part of a group. Emphasis is placed on the value of narrative as a means of addressing trauma and on attentive listening. Although forgiveness is an aim that facilitators are striving for, Robert emphasized that "we never mention the word. People must come to it on their own or not come to it at all. You cannot push someone to forgive."

He continued,

In the next circle, the next day, we ask everyone to tell us what they think of by the word *power*. Then we make a list and get them to split it into the negatives and positives of power. The shapes of triangle and circle show the different kinds of power. This always comes from the people themselves, that these are the shapes that work well for power. The circle shows power to be shared within the group or community. But people also see that within the power circle there needs to be a triangle. For example, if you are a parent and your child doesn't want to go to school, you need to have the power to make him. So, sometimes you need a triangle. So, even though we share equal ideas, there have to be people who collect those ideas and implement them. This is what we want people to understand about power when they leave. We all have power; we all have a say, but we are also all part of communities, and we must work with each other, sometimes in circles, sometimes in triangles, but always together.

The model is clearly predicated on building social relationships as a means of overcoming violence and violation.

In the final circle of the workshop, participants explore and discuss the last aspect of their trees: the fruits and leaves. These refer to the gifts they have in life and what abilities they have to offer the world and others. In Elias's words, "People often mention the gifts in their hands and brain. A gift is what you need within you to produce things. People make drawings of their fruits and leaves, so the drawings resemble people's lives, their abilities. Sometimes the drawings are very strange! But when people explain them you understand." The workshops close with participants going and finding a tree that is representative of a new life. He continued,

People bring a leaf or bark from the tree and start a narration about their experience. Then, you find something to do with the pieces of tree that have witnessed. We decide as a group to bury them, or burn them, or put them in a river. People usually decide to bury them—it is best to make them compost like this. We bury them together as a group in silence. After the workshop, we encourage people to go home and to put into practice what they have learned and to share it. We want change to happen from the very bottom, in people's homes. That's what I mean when I say *empowerment*.

The model reflects the structure of ritual as uncovered in classic anthropological analyses of rites of passage and other ritual processes (van Gennep,

1960; Turner, 1969), with participants removed from their usual social context to a liminal space where the ordinary is temporarily suspended. Following rituals of reincorporation, participants leave the workshops having undergone a social transition: In this case, to an "empowered" state. This model was clearly effective for participants in terms of their subjective understandings of violence.[22] However, Robert noted:

> What we are doing here is not justice, and for some people that makes it hard to forgive. The people in circles are also saying that if we are to forgive these people, they need to pass through the legal system and be punished.[23] But the legal system is malfunctioning. There is no transitional justice. So, for now, we must try to get people to forgive themselves before they try to forgive someone else. To stop blaming themselves for the things that happened. So, while we wait for those systems to be put into place, we are doing something here. On a grassroots level, we are building community systems, building the roads, building together. We are showing people how to practice democracy in your own homes, and it will spill from there to the neighbors. And one day there will be legal systems in place again, and justice on that level will operate too.

Robert's differentiation between the work being done by the Tree of Life and the work of justice is key to an understanding of the model and its efficacy. The Tree of Life is concerned with making and remaking social relationships and with doing away with ideas of victimhood to remake individual lives, not with justice. It differs from discourses of transitional justice, then, in two important ways. First, it steps away from the binary construction of victim and perpetrator that has characterized much of international transitional justice precedent thus far. Clarke (2007) has argued that the discursive and legal creation of victimhood reduces people to a state of "bare life" (Agamben, 1995) rather than acknowledging their roles as political actors. The Tree of Life process, which placed people within a web of social relationships and emphasized the power they held as individuals and communities, shifts people from bare life. Second, it places emphasis on the immediate (psychosocial) needs of the people it works with rather than on legal matters, although, as Robert points out, this does not preclude a desire for prosecutions. Weinstein and his coauthors (2010: 47) have argued that a weakness of transitional justice has been its tendency to "lose sight of its goals in favour of developing and maintaining an international system of criminal law over and above what might be the needs and the desires of the victims of abuse." It is worth noting, however, that in this example, as in the RAU focus groups, legal justice was also considered a priority.

The Tree of Life model draws widely on a variety of repertoires of social and individual healing. The language used by these two practitioners of the Tree of Life model moved between local idioms of conflict resolution (such as the role of the *dare*); metaphors of nature that drew on a mixture of local cosmology (such as the role of totems) and the new ideas of the Tree of Life model (with trees bearing witness to trauma and the symbolic burning or burial of leaves); psychological ideas of healing;[24] *and* a globally inflected language of violation, democracy, and transitional justice.

There is a pluralism of ways of making meaning at work in the organization's model and in the ways it is taken on and adapted by its facilitators and by participants. Let us pause a moment here to consider some of the theoretical lenses that could be brought to bear on such multiplicity. Ideas of *legal pluralism* (Merry, 1988) are clearly inadequate as a means of analysis here: for one thing, the majority of the ideas at play are clearly not legal. Bhabha's (1994) concept of hybridity (which is drawn on by Merry, 2006, in her analysis of vernacularization) could also be brought to bear on the preceding case study in that it emphasizes the outcomes of interplay between the local and the global but does not seem adequate either. The metaphor of hybridity implies a purity of "local" and "outside" contexts that is not convincing in that "local"/"global" or "insider"/"outsider" spaces are always hybrid; there is no one earlier point in time at which a "pure" version existed, though the metaphor requires one. Hybridity thus draws on the very essentialist categories it seeks to subvert (Englund, 2004); further, there is no room in this conceptualization for the work that is done by structures of power in creating the hybrid local. A third option in the genealogy of multiplicity I am presenting here is the idea of polyphony (Bahktin, 1984; Clifford, 1988). This seems more useful, in that multiple voices or points of view are woven into the Tree of Life model itself and into the ways it is used. Furthermore, Bahktin's polyphony, as developed in *Problems of Dostoevsky's Poetics*, does not aim to describe a unified singularity: Unlike Bhabha's new hybrid whole, polyphony allows for conflict, ambiguity, and unevenness. This seems a better way of unpacking the emergence of various modes of thought, from human rights to totems, in the Tree of Life model. Indeed, as with the idea of entanglement as discussed in the following paragraphs, polyphony seems a useful model for examining the surfacing of global discourses of human rights in local contexts more generally.

Polyphony is not the only useful theoretical lens we can apply: The concept of entanglement, as used by Achille Mbembe (2001) and Sarah Nuttall (2009), is also helpful here as a means of analyzing the pluralities of meaning making at play in the case study. Mbembe uses entanglement as a means of theorizing the state of the African postcolony, which he characterizes as composed of "multiple *durées* made up of discontinuities, reversals, inertias and swings that overlay one another, interpenetrate one another, and envelop one another: an entanglement" (Mbembe, 2001: 14). I have already considered Mbembe's model elsewhere in light of the ideas of temporality as they exist in rights discourses and in postcolonial settings; here I wish to highlight the ideas of *discontinuity, overlay, interpenetration,* and *envelopment* as a means of viewing the relationships among the multiple cosmological, psychological, and legal threads that the preceding case study raises. Nuttall's (2009) use of entanglement differs from Mbembe's: Situated in postapartheid South Africa, Nuttall's analysis centers on the definition of entanglement as an uneasy intimacy ("even if it was resisted, or ignored, or uninvited" [2009: 1]), which we can use to analyze the intersections of sites such as identity, space, and history in understanding race in South Africa.[25] The Tree of Life provides a case study of the complex entanglements at play in small-scale "local" settings. Further, in keeping with Goodale's (2006b) critique, such an analysis of the Tree of Life model can be seen to complicate the simplistic distinctions made between local, national, regional, and global levels, as, although it could be defined as a distinctly local phenomenon, it is inflected with circulating national, regional, and global ideas, and, although distinctly local, it bears remarkable resemblance to focus group interventions elsewhere on the Continent (see Curling 2005; Kayser 2005; Forcier 2010). Further, notions of discontinuity, overlay, interpenetration, and envelopment can be expanded beyond the Tree of Life case study to be seen in the surfacing of rights discourses in everyday life more generally: As is explored in subsequent chapters, however, such entanglements are not always as benevolent as they are in the Tree of Life. I will return to such theoretical considerations in later chapters.

The Tree of Life incorporated multiple modes of meaning making. The diversity of ways of making sense of political violence that emerged during the time I spent with Robert and Elias was not yet exhausted, however. At the very end of our first long conversation, Elias turned to me and said, "And of course, while we wait for the legal system to come back to Zimbabwe, we are not seeing justice coming from the top. Justice *must* come from the top, or else it is pointless. But that is not how *ngozi* work: They come for the one who did the crime, or for his family, but not the one who caused the crime." Here, another model of justice was at play. Before returning to ideas of transitional justice, let us turn to a consideration of the role played by ancestral spirits.

The Justice Meted Out by Ngozi

Although it was Elias who first mentioned the existence of *ngozi* in Epworth to me, I came to understand the role of these ancestral spirits better through conversations held with another Epworth resident, Tinashe, who brought me the newspaper article about *ngozi* in Buhera with which I opened this chapter. I was introduced to Tinashe as someone who had firsthand experience of *ngozi*; the story he told me serves as a case study of justice as it played out beyond the legal realm.

In the Shona worldview, as is the case across Southern Africa, the social world is composed of both living persons and the ancestors. Ancestral spirits encompass both clan spirits (*Mhondoro*), originating from the founders of clans or chiefdoms (and thus of political significance), and family spirits (*Vadzimu;* sing., *Mudzimu*): an individual's deceased parents and grandparents (and thus of more immediate kinship significance) (Gelfand, 1970). Gelfand has argued that a key role of the ancestors lies in their creation of the ethical person—one who has the quality of *Unhu*, which can loosely be translated as *decency* or *goodness*. *Vadzimu* play the greatest role in this (as indeed they did in life). The *Mhondoro* continue to care for the territories they once ruled and the people within them, and in return those same people maintain the *Mhondoro* through remembrance and ritual. The *vadzimu* keep their descendents on the straight and narrow, as to go against moral norms would constitute an affront to the *vadzimu*, and social relations between people and their *vadzimu* are also maintained through a lifelong cycle of rituals, which are closely linked to the land that is inhabited by the living and the dead.

Such then are the (ideal) relationships between the inhabitants of the social world—but there are also categories of spirit that result from a serious ethical transgression against that social world. *Ngozi* is the overarching term for spirits who return after death to haunt those who committed a serious violation against them. According to Tirivangani (in Marwizi, 2010), archetypical *ngozi* result from a sanguine crime, where blood has been shed (such as murder), but *ngozi* can also result from a breach of marriage that results in suicide, from crimes by children against their parents, and from an incomplete marital or financial transaction where one side fails to fulfil obligations. In such cases, *ngozi* can return after death to harass the person, and/or the families of the person, who wronged them, causing serious misfortunes or madness and mental torment (Mupinda, 1997). Unlike in law, where the emphasis is placed on the individual (be it as "victim" or "perpetrator"), the fact that *ngozi* may affect the direct perpetrator of a crime *or that person's family* shows the social unit to be located here at the level of the kinship group. Retribution can thus be visited on a child for harms inflicted on others by his parents: *Ngozi* do not provide a benign form of justice. To appease *ngozi*, reparations, mediated by diviners, must be made to the family of the deceased or wronged person(s).

Tinashe's family had been affected by political violence in 2008. His younger brother was involved in campaigning for the MDC in the run-up to the 2008 elections; when the area voted in favor of the MDC, his brother Patrick was abducted from his home in the ensuing backlash. For three days they did not know his brother's whereabouts; on the fourth day his badly beaten body was discovered abandoned near a dam in the area (the same dam mentioned in the quotation with which I opened the description of Epworth). The police removed Patrick's body to the local mortuary. Tinashe is convinced he knows the identity of his brother's killers: "I could tell them exactly which man came and took my brother from the house; it was _____ , and he was accompanied by that woman who is involved in politics here." Tinashe imparted this information to the police, but nothing ever came of it; as far as he is aware, no investigation was ever carried out. Initially, the family did not wish to inter Patrick's body until some acknowledgment of responsibility for his death had been made by the people who had abducted him or until it was clear the police were investigating the family's accusations. However, neither occurred, and the local mortuary insisted on the family removing Patrick's remains. The family conducted a Christian burial but were also intending, after the requisite amount of time had passed, to conduct the traditional ceremony of *kurova guva*, which aims to guide the deceased back to his family's land in order that he may take his place among the *vadzimu*.

Some seven months later, before *kurova guva* was due to take place, the man who Tinashe was sure had abducted Patrick from the family home began experiencing problems, as did his family members. First, his car broke down. Then, his wife's rape (canola) crop failed even though the neighboring crops were fine and there was water available. Next, his older brother lost his job. At this point, people in the neighbourhood began to talk about *ngozi*. In Tinashe's words, "It's possible for the spirit to bother the living," as Patrick's *kurova guva* ceremony had not yet been performed. When, a few weeks later, another man who was known to have been involved in the political violence was killed in a minibus taxi accident, "Then we knew that there was a restless spirit." It was "well known" within the area that the man had been involved in political violence that had seen more than one death; as such, local consensus decided that *ngozi* were definitely at work. Given that more than one person had died during political violence, moreover, it was impossible to know whose spirit was aggrieved. "So, the only thing for this man to do was to come to the families of all of us and pay compensation. But he refused." The man maintained that *ngozi* were superstition, not reality. By 2010, Tinashe's family had performed *kurova guva* but were unsure whether the spirit had been settled or not. Tinashe emphasized, furthermore, that "we are still waiting for him to make amends." Tinashe said that he was "comforted" by the knowledge that the man had been harassed by *ngozi* and thus not been entirely immune to ramifications, "but obviously it would be better if he would admit his responsibility so we can do the right rituals, and so that we can send him to prison." Again, as in the previous case studies, a diversity of justice repertoires are at play—and, again, questions of legal impunity are raised.

In such cases, then, particularly as regards blood crimes, legal justice alone is considered necessary but inadequate: Although a jail sentence should be part of the response to murder, this alone cannot repair the harm that has been done. In Tinashe's words, "Even if they had gone to prison, they need to make amends before the *ngozi* will stop tormenting them." In the newspaper article with which I opened this chapter, Augustine Tirivangana (who was approached as a local expert as he had written a PhD thesis on the *ngozi* theme in Zimbabwean literature) argued that "the idea of *ngozi* is not to punish but to build bridges. The key value of Africans is peace. If someone pays for the *ngozi*, they would have restored the peace in the community."

A key element in the model of justice at work here is the way in which harm is perceived. Whereas in rights discourse violations are linked to individuals, in this model harm has been inflicted on the family group. In Tirivangana's terms[26] (2010: 1), life is "the fundamental intangible asset" that is a gift from Mwari (god) and belongs to the family group, not just to an individual. Therefore, "a deprivation of material or immaterial possessions of any member of the group is a deprivation to all the members. This is the context in which *ngozi* should be understood" (Tirivangana, 2010: 1). As in the Tree of Life example, then, social restitution here is viewed in terms of a repair of damaged relationships, not only between people but also between people and the spirits (themselves considered alive and able to exert influence on the mundane world) who have the power to animate relationships.

Of particular relevance, however, is that Tirivangana uses a language of rights in his explanation of *ngozi*: "The spirit of the departed *has the right* to approach the offending family for compensation" (emphasis mine). Other experts approached in the media debate that followed the article about *ngozi* in Buhera also framed it in legal terms, with University of Zimbabwe lecturer Vimbai Chivura defining *ngozi* as "a crime that demands restitution" (Marwizi, 2010), and local historian Pathisa Nyathi (drawing parallels between *ngozi* and the Ndebele *uzimu*) stating that "in Matabeleland, death will result around the family, until the *perpetrator* realises that he or she has to pay for the crime" (ibid.; emphasis mine). *Rights, crime, restitution,* and *perpetrators*: These terms, drawn from globalized legal discourses, thus surfaced in a debate around spirit possession. Here, legal terminology is applied to a kind of justice that has its roots in an entirely different metaphysics and cosmology.

The entanglement of legal and spiritual ideas of justice has been carried further, however. In 2010, a second case of *ngozi* made it to the newspapers ("High Drama as *Ngozi* Fears Grip Gokwe"; Sifile, 2010). Here, a family in Gokwe refused to bury the body of their son who was killed in 2009, allegedly after being removed by the sons of two prominent ZANU-PF members, who (again allegedly) took him away in a ZANU-PF–branded vehicle. The family of the deceased would not perform traditional rites of burial until the families of the accused killers admitted to the crime (Sifile, 2010). According to the article, the father of the murdered boy demanded an apology and an explanation and that the families of the accused murderers seek forgiveness. Until then, his deceased son would continue to help "sort them out" through his actions as an *ngozi*. Although he originally refused to admit any responsibility, after the *ngozi* had been active for some time the father of one of the accused paid thirty-five head of cattle and US$15,000 in compensation (Dube, 2011). This was in addition to the case (most unusually) actually being brought to court, where the four accused were found guilty of murder in 2011.

The media upheld the "Gokwe saga" as a "test case" (Sifile, 2010) for the ONHRI, which I earlier argued was modeled on transitional justice mechanisms. As was noted earlier, there has been a move in transitional justice over the last decade to "localise justice mechanisms" (Shaw and Waldorf, 2010: 4); in keeping with this it was reported in the media that "the Organ said the process of healing would be done according to everyone's customs and beliefs" (Sifile, 2010). *Ngozi*, however, have one very serious flaw as a means of implementing some of the wider aims of transitional justice: They influence only the direct perpetrator of a crime or his or her family, not the persons or political parties who may have instigated such crimes.

Nonetheless, in 2011, following the legal *and* compensatory outcome, a newspaper report framed the case as "a template to address the problematic issue of political violence and impunity" (Dube, 2011). The fact that compensation was paid is central here; throughout the focus groups run by the NGO discussed in the previous pages, issues of reparation through compensation were raised time and again. "Justice" here can be seen to be multilayered, drawing on a diversity of repertoires: legal (court cases and transitional justice mechanisms), spiritual (the angered *ngozi* is appeased and is able to take his place as a *madzimu*), and customary (through compensation). As a template, then, the case in Gokwe is called on as it encompasses a wide range of entangled justicial discourses. Using *ngozi* as a template, however, means that the "culture of impunity" with which I opened this chapter is not really resolved: In Phatisa Nyathi's words, "The sender is very safe and the one who spilt the blood suffers" (quoted in Dube, 2011). (Given that the family members of "the one who spilt blood" may suffer too, "the one" here is composite and collective.) In the justice meted out by *ngozi*, the powerful elite who instigated crimes and gave the orders remain untouched. In a context such as this, then, the template seems inadequate, and NGOs call for nationwide legal commissions, as outlined in the preceding case study, resume importance.

Conclusion: Entanglements of Justice

Can "justice" ever be complete? There is, of course, no "perfect" justice: The three case studies discussed in this chapter all deal with justice in intersecting but different ways, none of which is absolute. It is thus unsurprising that people draw on as wide an array of repertoires as are available: Legal pluralism through customary, national, and international law; cosmological justice through the work of the spirits; and traditional compensatory mechanisms are all invoked. We see multiple forms of knowledge at play, within which rights discourses are only one strand. Three in-depth case studies may seem too much for a single chapter, but all were at play in Zimbabwe, and it was not possible to speak about justice without incorporating all three intertwined examples. Such a rich repertoire of practices and meanings cannot easily be separated into binaries of "tradition" versus "modernity," or "Western" versus "African"—and neither should they be. Rather, they show the ways in which modernity is composed of all these things. An examination of rights as praxis in this context shows the futility of such binaries and highlights the importance of a historicized understanding of local contexts to processes of post-conflict justice.

As Wilson (2006: 78) notes, rights discourses "do not provide the basis for a fully worked out moral or political philosophy. This must be formulated elsewhere and then brought to discussions of rights." Thus, local forms of cosmology and meaning making are brought into conversation with the more globally powerful discourse of rights. Though global ideas of rights can be brought to local cosmologies and ideologies and situationally incorporated, however, there is little movement in the other direction. These processes are imbued with power; as Cowan (2006) has argued human rights discourses can simultaneously be enabling and constraining. The earlier ethnographic analysis of ideas of justice in action reveals the dangers as well as the possibilities offered where ideas of justice are embedded in local and global systems of meaning.

Chapter 3

Producing Knowledge about Human Rights in Harare

Global Connections and Disconnections

In the introduction to *The Anthropology of Globalization* (2002), Inda and Rosaldo note that the world today is characterized by "complex mobilities" such that we can view globalization as "an intensification of global interconnectedness" (2002: 2). They caution, however, that the processes of interconnection are not necessarily smooth: Even in a world of increasing mobility and flow of information, people, and things, some things move with more ease than others, and "Not every person and every place participates equally in the circuits of interconnection that traverse the globe" (ibid: 4). Human rights discourses follow (and constitute some of) these global circuits and could be said to form one of the key ideologies of our time: As such, Appadurai (1996) conceptualizes rights as one of the key ideoscapes of a globalized world, whereas Goodale (2009a: 16) frames globalized discourses of rights, along with those of development, as one of the central "dilemmas of modernity."[1] I have explored some of the complexities using the concept of entanglement. Now I examine the fractures of global circuits through an ethnographic exploration of the construction of human rights reports in Harare and their mobilities as they leave Zimbabwe, tracing two rights-based texts from their origins in Zimbabwe through to their national and international dissemination. One aspect of the political and economic situation in Zimbabwe has been increased movement out of the country. Although a wealth of literature (including some of my own earlier work) has focused on the movement of people across the country's borders (Bloch, 2008; Betts and Kaytaz, 2009; FMSP, 2009b, 2010; Morreira, 2009, 2015b; Elphick and Amit, 2012), little consideration has been given to the increased global flow of information about the country, from within and beyond its borders, that has emanated from a combination of crisis and the advent of new technologies. This then is another material manifestation of rights discourses—particularized constructions about people, place, and happenings that follow a genre and contribute to global hierarchies of knowledge. Rights discourses have a great impact at the discursive level—as such, it is worth considering the conditions under which rights-based texts such as reports are created, what they include and what they don't, and the ways in which the finished product moves. As the two reports on which I focus in this chapter are concerned with violations against women's rights in Zimbabwe, I begin with a brief contextualization of the ways in which discourses of gendered rights have historically manifested in that country since the colonial period.

Women and Rights in Zimbabwe: The Legal History

The Zimbabwe in which I grew up, and to which I returned to conduct fieldwork as an adult, is deeply patriarchal. Ranchod-Nilsson (2006: 49) has outlined what she refers to as "the swinging pendulum" of progress with regards to gender equality in Zimbabwe. During colonialism, African women had few rights even in comparison with African men (Schmidt, 1992), and even poorer protection in comparison with the rights of Europeans. At independence in 1980 Zimbabwe maintained a dual system of customary and common law inherited from the colonial government. The implementation of the Legal Age of Majority Act (1982) gave majority status to women of age eighteen and above regardless of race (Stewart 1990), increasing women's legal equality. (Previously women had been considered perpetual minors.) Similarly, in 1991 Zimbabwe signed the International Covenant on Economic, Social and Cultural Rights (ICESCR), the International Covenant on Civil and Political Rights (ICCPR) and the Convention on the Elimination of All Forms of Discrimination Against Women (CEDAW) without reservations, thus agreeing to provisions that specified that women and men were equal before the law (Sisterhood Is Global Institute, 1999). Nonetheless, the retention of customary law has at times worked against gender equality: Women married under (more patriarchal) customary law, for example, had fewer rights within marriage than did women married under common law. Even where the law does protect women, it is often not implemented due to lack of knowledge and/or lack of political will (Essof, 2005).

Thus, a rights framework may not even be the most useful or relevant approach to the needs of Zimbabwean women. Nonetheless, women's groups within Zimbabwe continue to use local law and international rights ideas and instruments (as seen in the work done by WOZA and WCoZ[2]), emphasizing that in Zimbabwe at present the rights of women stand on shaky ground (McFadden, 2000; Ranchod-Nilsson, 2006; Tamale, 2008). Essof (2005) argues that, despite the "terrain of women's mobilising in Zimbabwe [being] both rich and deep," (2005: 29) such movements face an "increasingly hostile political environment" (2005: 40). Rights discourses have provided a useful tool that carries a global validity as a means of promoting the needs of women in the face of such an environment. Nonetheless, the textual record of rights reports emerging from Zimbabwe reflects a bias in favor of discussions of violations against political rights that do not take gender differentiations into account; the particular example of research, resulting in two rights reports, that I draw on in this chapter was done in response to this trend and deliberately aimed to access women's experiences. As such, it allows for an examination both of agency within the constraints of the dominant rights discourses, in that the NGOs are able to write to fill gaps, and an examination of the ways in which women's experiences are nonetheless structurally constrained within the terms of rights discourses and thus turned into data that is then used in a rights report.

Kinds of Mobility

By way of ethnographic introduction, consider the following three vignettes:

Snapshot One: It is a muggy Wednesday morning in January 2011, and I am traveling in the backseat of a white 4 by 4 vehicle, my body covered in a filmy layer of sweat and dust. My companions are three staff members of the International Organisation for Migration (IOM), two of whom are permanently based in the Musina office, on the border between Zimbabwe and South Africa, and the third of whom is visiting from Johannesburg. We turn off a tarred road onto a dirt track that initially runs alongside a secondhand car dealership and scrap yard but that then turns away from the outskirts of town into the surrounding bush, heading north toward the Limpopo River, the border between Zimbabwe and South Africa. The road straightens to run parallel to the river, and we see what it is we have come here to see today: a seemingly unending stretch of a double-layered fence (locally known as "the fence") that runs as far as I can see in either direction, blocking off no-man's-land from

South Africa. Beyond it lies the Limpopo, the geographical and political border with Zimbabwe. This fence seems strange to me in its very physicality, bringing home that the edges of the modern nation-state are not only metaphorical: Here lies an actual fence, which cuts one country off from another. IOM travels along here often to monitor[3] this barrier; other patrols are conducted by border officials, by the police, and occasionally by members of the army. We do not have to travel for long along the road before we come across a physical reminder of the permeability of borders: A hole has been raggedly cut into the wire of the fence furthest from us, then there is a path through the dusty space between the two fences, ending in a corresponding hole in the fence closest to us. Lying next to this hole is an abandoned woman's shoe. I stare at the fence. I stare at the holes. I stare at the shoe. This is how my Zimbabwean country(wo)men cross into South Africa, which is also my country. I belong in both worlds, legally, whereas they do not. I stare at the fence. Gloria Anzaldúa's words on the Mexico–United States border enter my mind, unbidden: "The border is an open wound, *una herida abierta*" (Anzaldúa, 2007: 25).

Snapshot Two: I am at a *braai* in Cape Town in 2005, and the man seated across from me has been telling a story about how he had worked with a rights advocacy NGO in Harare a few years previously. It is a gray day; all the people present are Zimbabweans, all wearing warm clothes, all still unused to Cape Town's winters, even though some of us have been here for five years. The man pulls his sleeves down over his hands as he tells his story, as he describes being given a pen in the first days of flash drives: "a pen that wasn't really a pen, a pen that made me feel like a spy"; a pen that doubled as a miniature portable hard drive. Leaving Zimbabwe to come to South Africa to attend university, he had carried the pen on his person, carried it from the offices where he worked into his car, along the winding roads past Masvingo and to Beitbridge, and then across the border (did he use it to fill in the forms? I did not ask), carried his pen filled with data, with information on violence and violation, with names, dates, and places. When he arrived in Johannesburg he dropped off his pen at the offices of a South African rights organization, having served as an information mule, carrying data from one country to another. We listen to the story and shake our heads at the necessity of physically smuggling out information from our homeland to this, our new country.

Snapshot Three: It is five years later, late in 2010. I am in Harare, and the electricity has just gone off again. I hear a frustrated muttering from the workstation next to me; the final version of a report is being written and is shortly due to be sent out on numerous electronic mailing lists. The office in which I am spending the afternoon is only temporarily impeded, however: The administrator rises from her desk and goes outside to start the generator. The rest of us take advantage of the break in power supply to go and stand in the sunshine outside for a few minutes. We talk about the report; it has been a few weeks in the writing and is based on research a few months in the making. "It will be done by tomorrow," Tarisai[4] says confidently. "And then we can send it out to everyone. Then we can let everyone know even more about the goings on in the 2008 elections, about the ways it affected women. Women are always left out of these stories." The generator roars into life, and we turn to go back inside. I think to myself, there's no more need for smuggling flash drives across the border. No need for words to crawl through holes in the fence as do people. Now we just send a report out via email. Now information about human rights in Zimbabwe is always on the move; now there are reports upon reports upon reports out there. A mushrooming of rights reports in Zimbabwe, circulating around the world. Where do they go to? What do they do?

What can these snapshots tell us about rights and mobility? The first tells us that people are on the move, and that governmental and nongovernmental institutions are responding to that movement. Border officials and NGOs monitored the fence; in Musina itself (the closest South African town to the Zimbabwe border) many international and local NGOs have sprung up as a result of, or shifted their mandates in light of, the increased movement of Zimbabweans across the border. At a meeting of the Migrants Health Forum that I attended in Musina in 2011, for example, local government representatives attended from the South African Departments of Labour; Safety, Security and Liason; Home Affairs; and Health and Service Delivery, while representatives from international NGOs such as Médicins Sans Frontières (MSF, or Doctors Without Borders), Save the Children, the UN High Commission for Refugees (UNHCR), and the US Agency for International Development (USAID) were present, as well as from a local NGO, the Musina Legal Advice Office. The meeting was attended by thirty-four people and took place in the Civic Centre's biggest conference room: Migration from Zimbabwe could perhaps be said to drive a rights and aid industry in Musina.

The first snapshot shows us both the permeability and the impermeability of borders: They are crossed, but not without effort. Within the ways in which nation-states have been constructed during modernity/coloniality (Mignolo,

2012), movement is considered problematic, and attempts are made to prevent it—the legal border post entails a lengthy bureaucratic process that is not open to everyone (given the difficulty and expense of gaining access to, first, passports in Zimbabwe [Musarandega, 2009] and, second, a visa to enter South Africa), and "the fence" is patrolled. Crossing the borderlands is also dangerous, as they are spaces of violence and of violation (Morreira, 2015b). The physicality of the border stands in stark contrast to the electronic documents, which bypass such physical barriers with greater ease. The pen stands as reminder that it was not always possible for documents to be moved without greater effort. Increases in technology, and the advent of improved Internet connectivity in Zimbabwe, however, have subsequently facilitated the movement of words and numbers into and out of the country. Although I have been unable to find statistical data on the number of rights reports to be disseminated from Zimbabwe in any given year, it would appear that over the last decade such reports have proliferated, as a result both of the increasing dominance of the rights paradigm globally and of the deteriorating socioeconomic and political conditions in Zimbabwe. A Google search for "Zimbabwe Human Rights Reports" today results in about 20 million hits; although these are of course not all actual reports, this number gives an idea of the prevalence of the terminology. A scan of the first few pages of hits shows that documents about human rights in Zimbabwe originate from international organizations such as Amnesty International or Human Rights Watch and from local organizations such as the Zimbabwe Human Rights NGO Forum (a coalition of nineteen local rights organizations), ZIMRIGHTS, and Zimbabwe Lawyers for Human Rights (which are often funded by international organizations). A quantitative survey of my email inbox over the last twelve months shows an average of two new comprehensive reports a month and ten media articles about human rights in Zimbabwe per month. Further, although I subscribe to a few mailing lists, I know that I do not receive all the rights reports to emerge from Zimbabwe or about Zimbabwe by any stretch. The language of rights is thus speaking very loudly to, and from, Zimbabwe.

What these snapshots tell us then is that both documents and people are moving in and out of Zimbabwe and, further, that the movement of texts is not as controlled as that of people: Rights reports do not need wire cutters or passports to traverse between two countries and to move even further beyond (although they are required to fit into a particular format to be circulated and read). In considering the movement of discourses of rights between Zimbabwe and South Africa, then, a dichotomy emerges: Although ideas of rights can circulate relatively easily between the two countries, crossing back and forth across the border in the form of electronic documents between institutions and between individuals, it is harder for people to move and to enact their rights during that movement. It is therefore necessary that, in addition to the existing literature on the movement of people, anthropological engagements with movement and migration situate ethnographic analyses in the construction and mobility of texts and technologies—what sorts of texts travel, and where do they go to? It is such an analysis I present here.

Mobile Texts: The Construction and Movement of Human Rights Reports

Although texts may move with greater ease than people, the contents of such texts are created within the terms of rights discourses, and they therefore circulate a particular form of representation. Foucault (1991: 194) argues:

> We must cease once and for all to describe the effects of power in [only] negative terms: it "excludes," it "represses," it "censors," it "abstracts," it "masks," it "conceals." In fact, power produces; it produces reality; it produces domains of knowledge and rituals of truth.

One of the ways in which power produces reality is through discursive practices, characterized by the "delimitation of a field of objects, the definition of a legitimate perspective for the agent of knowledge, and the fixing of norms for the elaboration of concepts and theories" (Foucault, 1977: 199). Rights reports constitute one kind of discursive practice and are one way in which knowledge is produced as legitimate. Constructed within the terms of the discourse, which "governs the way that a topic can be meaningfully talked about and reasoned about" (Hall, 2001b [1997]: 72), rights reports constitute a particular domain of knowledge, a way of knowing the political, economic, and social situation in Zimbabwe that follows certain structures and rules and that may differ to other ways of knowing. As I've already demonstrated, the term *human rights* can encompass a variety of positions, so an examination of the similarities in structure of rights reports is not to deny the multiple positions organizations and authors could take within the bounds of the discourse (cf. Wilson and Brown, 2009).

The discursive framework of rights documents is, as I have shown in Chapter 1, driven by an emphasis on the individualized political rights of persons. Reports are predicated on the collection of data, usually about situations where rights are being denied or violated. The feminist historian Joan Scott (1991) has considered the process by which people's "experiences" become "data," arguing that locating the object of study in events and social reality obscures the broader discursive systems at work that shape how that reality is perceived and constructed. Within rights discourse, "experiences" are accessed in very particular ways: Unlike the feminist historiography that Scott discusses, which encourages gaining access to women's "experiences" as broadly as possible, rights reports are mainly concerned with those elements of social life that fall within a legal category of violation (as I will discuss in the following paragraphs), such that the discursive practices are even more constraining than they are in the texts Scott critiques.

Rights reports about women constitute a subsection of the discursive framework of rights and one in which women are considered a particularly vulnerable population. A U.S.–based NGO concerned with women's rights globally, Stop Violence Against Women (STOPVAW) offers the following description of the role of documentation, which I present here as an example of the globalized discourse:

> Investigation and documentation of women's human rights violations[5] (sometimes referred to as "fact-finding") is one of the most commonly used and important advocacy tools in the promotion of human rights. In order to be effective, it is vital that the information gathered in the documenting process be accurate, valid and as timely as possible. The documentation of human rights abuses serves many functions, from putting pressure on government institutions to improve their response to violations of women's rights, to bringing public awareness to serious human rights violations, which have typically remained hidden, to forming the basis of a needs-assessment for future work. (STOPVAW, 2003)

This quotation brings together some of the key elements of those rights reports that are intended not only for use in a court of law but also for circulation among governments, other organizations, and the general public. First, the translation of investigation and documentation into "fact finding" reveals a particular conceptual understanding of research as revealing a knowable truth, in that one is establishing accurate and valid knowledge. This leads to an emphasis on the collation of statistical or numeric data (Dudai, 2009), which I will discuss in more detail later. Second, the STOPVAW quotation shows knowledge to focus on rights violations and abuses, not rights adherence: The emphasis is on gathering and presenting knowledge of harm, spoken of as *violation* and *abuse*, terms that carry connotations of violence and that reflect specifically structured legal categories. Violations are legally encoded classifications—such as violations against bodily integrity or the infliction of gender-based violence or violations against the right to equality before the law (Robertson, 2006), and documentation is therefore geared toward gaining access to information about such preestablished categories. Finally, the quotation reveals the intended social life of such reports, which start off in the field through investigation and end in broad circulation to international organizations, government institutions, and the public in order to surface violations "which have typically remained hidden." Rights reports, then, are presented in a particular way and with particular aims in mind (Wilson, 1997).

Data and Temporality

The knowledge presented in rights reports is often established through a particular form of data collection known as "monitoring." The UN Office for the High Commissioner for Human Rights defines "monitoring" as:

> A broad term describing the *active collection, verification and immediate use of* information to address human rights problems. Human rights monitoring includes gathering information about incidents, observing events (elections, trials, demonstrations, etc.), visiting sites such as places of detention and refugee camps, discussions with Government authorities to obtain information and to pursue remedies and other immediate follow-up. (UN OHCHR, 2001: 9; emphasis in the original)

In the same report, *fact finding* is defined as:

> . . . a process of drawing conclusions of fact from monitoring activities. Hence, "fact-finding" is necessarily a narrower term than "monitoring." Fact-finding entails a great deal of *information gathering* in order to *establish and verify* the facts surrounding an alleged *human rights violation*. Moreover, fact-finding means *pursuing reliability* through the use of generally accepted procedures and by establishing a reputation for fairness and impartiality. (UN OHCHR, 2001: 9; emphasis in the original)

The emphasis here is on factual knowledge that is perceived as impartial, verifiable, and reliable. Often, this knowledge is numeric: The information gathered during monitoring is collated into a statistical format. Dudai (2009), in his analysis of the construction of rights reports, has argued that statistics are considered the best way to collect and disseminate objective and neutral information. Neutrality is highly regarded. Rights methodology, then, as with much of Western thought, is based on an ideology in which the numeric is central: As an IOM staff member explained to me in an interview, if statistics cannot be provided, then organizations find themselves unable to be heard. This is particularly the case as concerns reports intended for strictly legal audiences (Dudai, 2009) but also occurs in those reports intended for broader circulation.

The sorts of large numbers gathered in big surveys provide information that is considered to be more accurate and valid than smaller scale, or less quantitative, research. Hastrup (1993) argues that such "hard facts" often constitute the discursive basis of engagements with human hardship and suffering: Presenting numeric data provides "objective" facts about human experiences that otherwise seem too subjective for serious study. Hastrup has elsewhere argued (Hastrup, 2001) that the removal of subjectivity is a key component of legal language, such that "its appeal to reason is based on a view of the disengaged mind and of instrumental modes of thought" (Hastrup, 2001: 25). Of course, as Dudai (2009) argues, the removal of subjective language from rights reports does not remove subjectivity; furthermore, the presentation of rights reports as neutral obscures the fact that they too are specific kinds of narrative constructions. The numeric, however, is accorded emphasis within rights discourse. Emphasis on numbers and statistics is not confined to rights reports: As Guyer et al. (2010: 36) note, "Anthropologists are seeing numbers as insurgently prominent in people's descriptions, imaginations and efforts to influence their social worlds in the 21st century." Guyer and her coauthors refer to the "number regimes" (ibid.: 37) by which social worlds come to be ordered: As Nelson (2010) shows in the same volume, rights discourse constitutes one of many such regimes. For example, the process of tallying the effects of the civil war in Guatemala was accorded central importance at the end of the war as a means of identifying rights violations for the purposes of reparation and legal accountability, despite what Nelson (2010: 88) refers to as "the slipperiness of counting." Although Nelson shows that the process of identifying the numbers of rights violations that occurred during the war was complex and far from neutral (and possibly far from accurate), the numbers to come out of the Commission for Historical Clarification came to take on the status of facts "cited in almost every analysis of Guatemala" (ibid.: 88). Furthermore, these numerically established "facts" resulted in the Guatemalan state being found guilty of genocide under international law. Within rights discourses, then, numbers carry weight and can have real consequences.

One day Tarisai said of a piece of research the rights advocacy organization she worked for had just completed, "It was good to get those numbers, to do that survey. We must base it in facts, so that we can get the information out there. We need to know on a broad scale what is happening to women across Zimbabwe; if we have that data then we have something very solid to say." Numbers here were read as more factual than words or subjective experiences: In Tarisai's terms, they were more "solid" than other sorts of data. In Tarisai's estimation, numbers were doing a particular kind of work—they provided what I refer to as a "broadness" and "scale," which the rights organization could then use to confidently disseminate information. As is seen in Nelson (2010) and Guyer and her coauthors (2010), analyses of the roles of the numeric, then, quantification is viewed as essential to the process of producing fact and producing knowledge. The numeric produces a particular way of comprehending the world, which, while it may render subjectivities invisible, as Hastrup (1993, 2003) argues, simultaneously renders certain kinds of facts visible (Nelson, 2010).

Tarisai's comments on broadness and scale were not the end of our conversation, however. She followed her endorsement of numbers by saying, "But those stats were not enough. We need to know why those numbers are happening, why there's so much violence against women, and how they are dealing with it. We need to know what is *actually happening*, you know?" (emphasis mine). Numbers, then are not all that matter: For all that they present a particular kind of truth and one that carries weight and the authority of supposed validity, they do not necessarily tell us everything that is "actually happening." Similarly, when I carried out interviews for a well-known global rights organization in 2007, the brief I was given in conversation with a consultant (who had flown to South Africa for one week to conduct research on Zimbabwean migrants) first required that I "get the demographic stuff, as we need that to make our argument." "The demographic stuff" constituted data on people's age, gender, educational level, immigration status, and employment in South Africa, and, an important point, numeric data on whether political violence had been experienced, and if so what sort, when, and on how many occasions, and whether medical treatment had been necessary and had been received. Here we see the gathering of information that can be statistically collated in terms of already preconceived categories of violation. The verbal brief I was given also required, however, that I "get some stories, because we need those stories to make our argument convincing, and to carry our numbers across." In the views of both a consultant from a well-funded and internationally powerful organization and Tarisai, numbers had primacy, but elements of narrative and personalized stories were also needed to give the numbers a different sort of valence.

It is worth pausing here to consider these different typologies of fact making and value. The inclusion of personalized narratives in rights reports draws in a value that is very different to the capital accorded to neutrality within the discourse. The difference seems to be one of scale and intensity.[6] Numbers are essential for producing convincing legal arguments, but emotion also has a valence and weight. Audiences have a quick response to the numeric; there is also clearly a place for emotion in rights work, however. Though the *scale* of harm matters in rights reporting, the previous examples suggest that the *intensity* of that harm can only be "fully" told through the inclusion of more personalized narratives. The emotional charge of those narratives carries a force or value in itself that causes a response in the audience. Wilson and Brown (2009: 1) argue that "the mobilization of empathy" through narratives of suffering is a central element in why some humanitarian crises are ignored whereas others incite national or international emergency responses. Wilson and Brown argue that, unlike human rights law, which is based in (supposedly neutral) legal categories, humanitarianism's wider agenda allows for the inclusion of a different more moral and emotive tone to the work it does. The instructions given to me by the consultant and Tarisai's emphasis on stories suggest that where rights documents are prepared for global circulation among other organizations, governments, or individuals and not only for presentation in court, such an emotive register is also apparent and important. However, as Dudai (2009: 225) notes, the inclusion of first-person narratives in human rights reports occurs "to support the organization's factual and legal claims, not the other way around." The terms of inclusion are thus driven by rights organizations' legal interpretations. Scott (1991: 776) argues that "evidence only counts as evidence and is only recognized as such in relation to a potential narrative." In the case of rights reports, this potential narrative is determined by legal categories and arguments.

A second structural pressure that influences the textual construction of reports is that of temporality: The documentation work done by rights organizations must be produced as quickly as possible for knowledge to be considered relevant within the rights field. The UN OHCR Training Manual on Human Rights Monitoring previously quoted emphasizes the "immediate use" (UNOCHCR, 2001: 9) of information gathered; whereas the earlier STOPVAW quotation emphasizes that rights reports be "as timely as possible." Where organizations are involved in monitoring the rights situations within a particular place, reports may be expected to be sent from the field office to the main branch as often as once a week detailing the violations that have been monitored in the time that has elapsed since the last report. This emphasis on timeliness reflects an attention to detail that is located in the legal discourse's thorough documentation of the facts, but it also reflects the moral urgency that can at times be seen to lie behind rights work. Chido, a rights advocacy worker I interviewed in Harare, argued:

> We need to be gathering information all the time, and then we need to write it up and circulate it quickly, because these are big issues we're dealing with. If the youth militia is raping women, that information must be collated and shared as quickly as possible. We need to get it out there; we have a responsibility to do so.

The pressure to get information "out there" was one I commonly encountered among rights practitioners in Zimbabwe. This was driven in part by the constraints at work within the country, where internal legal systems were often inadequate as a means of securing rights or securing convictions for violations against rights (see Chapter 2). In such a context, a global audience was seen as a more effective means of campaigning for rights than a local one. In getting the information "out there," Zimbabwean rights organizations attempted to mobilize international support from what Slaughter (2007: 116) refers to as an "imagined community of readers and rights holders." Whether these attempts are effective or not is a different issue; suffice to say at this point that reports are composed with particular imagined audiences in mind and are driven by a sense of moral urgency and responsibility.

Urgency, however, has drawbacks: Such intense time constraints limit what sort of information one can gather. The pressures of time constraints in combination with the need to fit into a legal framework work against analytic categories arising from the field itself, ensuring instead that the terms of the legal discourse dictate what is seen or not seen, counted or not counted, during rights monitoring. Human rights discourse is a legal one; in order that reports might be relevant, they need to prove that they are presenting data worthy of attention and advocacy. As such, the data that are focused on within the structured short-term temporality of the discourse tend to be those that carry legal precedent. The data collected thus generally center on first-generation political rights and incidents of political violence at the expense of second-generation rights and structural violence (see Introduction). This external bias, in combination with the emphasis on presenting numerical data, effectively excludes some kinds of analysis.

The rights practitioners I interviewed in Zimbabwe knew the limitations of this and found it frustrating. One commented:

> Sometimes it seems we have all this information that is being wasted, that we don't have time to go back to. You gather information, analyse it, and write it up, and then it's done—but you know there is so much more you could have done with it. You also know that that is people's lives that you have sent off so quickly into the world, and then you don't think about it again. It has been done. And that makes us all uncomfortable, so sometimes you're able to do a longer-term project, and then you feel that you are producing something a little less short-lived, a little more detailed.

The discomfort described here links to the emotional valences I have already described: Rights work is emotionally difficult for fieldworkers, who speak to the human beings behind the numbers and who have a sense of the personalized stories that lie behind the data. Although time pressures and extant legal categories work against the inclusion of detail, practitioners felt a need to include more of that emotive detail where they could and, at times, were able to do so, as I describe in the following case study.

Case Study: The Social Life of Reports on Zimbabwean Women

An example serves to illustrate the points presented in the previous section. The pair of reports which I am using here were produced by the NGO with which I spent most time in Zimbabwe—the Research and Advocacy Unit (RAU)—in conjunction with IDASA (the Institute for Democracy in Africa), ICTJ (the International Center for Transitional Justice), and WCoZ (the Women's Coalition of Zimbabwe). Already we can see transnational ties and linkages: RAU is based in Harare and is staffed by Zimbabweans, WCoZ is a national umbrella body of Zimbabwean women's organizations, IDASA is a South African organization, and the ICTJ is an international organization with its head office in New York. All four organizations have connections with the world of human rights advocacy: RAU and WCoZ are both members of the Zimbabwe Human Rights NGO Forum, and WCoZ states on its website that "its central role is to provide a focal point for activism on women and girl's rights" (WCoZ, 2012); IDASA's mandated commitment to "building sustainable democracies" entails a support of the rights agenda (IDASA, 2012), and the ICTJ describes itself as "dedicated to pursuing accountability for mass atrocity and human rights abuse" (ICTJ, 2012).

The two reports analyzed here are entitled, "Women, Politics and the Zimbabwe Crisis" (RAU et al., 2010c) and "'When the Going Gets Tough, the Man Gets Going!': Zimbabwean Women's Views on Politics, Governance, Political Violence, and Transitional Justice" (RAU et al., 2010b). I present them together as the reports were released within a few months of one another and are based on two related sets of research: first, a large-scale survey that set out to gain access to women's views on politics in Zimbabwe and, second, a follow-up set of focus groups carried out to gather qualitative data to speak to the quantitative findings of the survey, which resulted in the second report. Both reports were written by RAU staff,[7] although the research process that led to the final report was funded by the other organizations.

The RAU women's reports began their social life in a quantitative study. The survey incorporated 2,158 respondents and was carried out across the country, in urban and rural areas. The questionnaire comprised over 100 questions and was administered by women trained by the rights organizations running the survey, who were identified by member organizations of WCoZ from across the country. Each interviewer administered fifty questionnaires in their local area with the cases selected from every tenth household. The questionnaire followed conventional format, with a mixture of yes/no and multiple choice questions designed at eliciting quantitative data about the relationship between women and politics in Zimbabwe. Questions ranged from the demographic (age, education level, home language) through the informative (such as what years women had voted in an election or whether they had ever been involved in political violence), through to those designed to elicit opinions (for example: "Sometimes it is acceptable for violence to be used in politics: Strongly Agree; Agree; Neither Agree nor Disagree; Disagree;

Strongly Disagree"). The scale of the study, both in terms of the number of respondents and the breadth of the questions, ensured it elicited a great deal of previously unknown information on the relationship between women and politics in Zimbabwe at the time. It thus provided a very valuable data source for advocacy.

The study was followed up some months later by a set of qualitative focus groups, which I attended as described in Chapter 2. Each focus group, although aiming to solicit women's opinions, nonetheless followed a strict schedule based on the statistical findings of the survey. Sections of the day-long groups were allocated to a discussion of the findings with regard to the numbers of women affected by political violence, for example, or the numbers of women who had voted in different presidential and parliamentary elections. Unsurprisingly, qualitative responses were sought within the terms of rights discourse itself; given the time constraints of focused research, there was little room for conversations to extend beyond it. Even where conversations did extend, transcriptions were taken by RAU staff with a particularized rights agenda in mind, and some information was excluded from the final versions of data gathered at each session. The notes I had from focus groups thus sometimes differed in emphasis from those of the organization. Nonetheless, the work carried out by RAU was unusual in that focus groups were so extensive and carried out over such a long period, with an aim not of getting quotable quotes to scatter through a report but rather of eliciting a much deeper understanding of the political situation as it affected women in Zimbabwe.

The elicitation of quantitative data and of complementary qualitative data that nonetheless fits within categories to emerge from the quantitative is at the heart of an ideology of "fact finding," and such an ideology was reflected in the reports themselves. In both reports, these quantitative facts formed the core of the documents, with the statistical findings being presented to show that women experienced violence and violation as a result of the political situation in Zimbabwe—and that their experiences have differed to that of men. For example, 52 percent of the women interviewed stated they had been victims of political violence, 2 percent reported being raped, 3 percent reported that a family member had been raped, and 16 percent reported that someone in the community had been raped (RAU et al., 2010c: 3). In both reports, furthermore, physical violations against women took center stage, as these statistics show. In the first report in particular, *Women, Politics and the Zimbabwean Crisis* (RAU et al., 2010c), which was based on the survey, violence was central. In this report, six tables of data concerned with demographics (geographical distribution, age, marital status, education, religion, and ethnic affiliation) were presented, followed by a further fifteen tables of data concerned with four broad categories of elections, violations, peace, and the transitional government. All four categories devoted some space to statistical consideration of violence. Of the fifteen tables presented across the categories, five were concerned entirely with data on incidents of political violence, including politically motivated rape, and another three addressed violence in some way (such as a single column within a table on the Inclusive Government's ability to deliver being devoted to personal security). More than half of the fifteen data tables concerned physical violations against women.

The core of the first report lay in numeric data, providing the necessary scale; the second, although still based on the numbers presented in the first, drew in more qualitative commentary and in so doing produced intensity. Instead of being structured around tables of numeric data, the report was based on quotations that spoke to that data. For example, in response to 52 percent of women in the survey stating they had been victims of violence, focus group attendees were asked both for their opinions on this statistic and for their own definitions of violence. The quotes reproduced in the report invoke both a depth of understanding that is missing from the bare numbers, and an emotional valence. For example:

> Everything was centred on women. Say if my husband was involved in politics even if I wasn't I was affected in a certain way because if they came and didn't find my husband I ended up being raped. And if my son or my daughter, my mother or even my grandmother was involved I ended up being victimised. So the whole politics was centred on women. (Quoted in RAU et al., 2010b: 11)

And

> Assault is physical when a woman is hit with a closed fist and raped whereas torture can also be emotional abuse, where women are made to live under fear of the perpetrators. For example they are told to avail themselves or something will be done to them. Torture is also a planned attack on the emotions of women. (ibid.)

Aside from providing emotionally haunting images of closed fists and political rape, the quotations also illustrate one of the dangers of relying on the collation of data in terms of predefined categories: What respondents understand the categories to mean may not be the same as legal definitions. "Torture" in the second quotation refers to emotional abuse and fear; this is a different definition than that used in the UN Convention against Torture.[8]

The emotivity invoked in the report was not limited to the narratives of respondents: The report also drew in the subjective emotional response of Munashe Mkaronda, a young woman who, although not a staff member of the organization, attended some of the focus groups and transcribed conversations. The report opens with a poem she wrote about the relationship among men, women, and politics in Zimbabwe after listening to women speak at focus groups. The title of the report, *When the Going Gets Tough, the Man Gets Going*, is drawn from her poem:

> . . . Because of you . . .
>
> Many of us have lost our pride and dignity because of you
>
> Many of us have lost all we had because of you
>
> Families have been destroyed because of you
>
> Hearts have been broken because of you
>
> Lives have ended because of you
>
> Yet you still continue to say that you're needed
>
> Needed for what?
>
> More destruction?
>
> More heartbreak?
>
> You're the one who says your job is to take care of women
>
> Yet you're the first one to run when problems surface
>
> When the going gets tough the man gets going!
>
> Because of you, my child has no future
>
> Because of you, my sister has AIDS
>
> Because of you, my mother is scarred for life,
>
> And because of you
>
> I cannot bear to look at my own reflection in the mirror
>
> (Munashe Mkaronda, cited in RAU et al., 2010b: 2)

This text is a far cry from the bare numbers presented in data tables. It illustrates a different means of presenting information about rights violations.

The social life of rights reports begins with knowledge being ordered in such structured ways. Koptyoff (1986) argues that commodities are not only materially produced as things but are "culturally marked" as being a certain kind of thing; the process of structuring rights report outlined earlier is another form of cultural production, where reports are marked in recognizable ways such that they are, in Foucauldian terms, recognized as emanating from a "legitimate perspective" (Foucault, 1977: 199) within the discourse. Koptyoff (1986: 64) further argued that things can be followed via their "cultural biographies." The idea of a cultural biography is centered on the chain of events that a material object follows during its social lifetime, from production through to its eventual end. Cultural biographies begin when objects are produced, before they circulate, and it is this process that I have traced so far. Once produced and legitimized, however, Zimbabwean rights reports are distributed: As Chido noted earlier, the information has to "get out there." It is to this aspect of the texts' social lives that I now turn.

Circuits of Distribution

> Much of the work here is about information: We share the stories of what is happening here [in Zimbabwe], the evidence of violations this week, the outcomes of court cases that week, with our colleagues at home and in other parts of the world. We get information on violators out, and we store it outside of Zimbabwe. And we look to other parts of the world for inspiration, for jurisprudence, for ideas. There is communication back and forth, back and forth. Like everyone else, much of our day is spent on email. (Interview with a Zimbabwean human rights lawyer)

Reports can be considered through a similar lens as was applied to commodities in Appadurai's *The Social Life of Things*, in that the conduits of exchange and circulation are based in the political realm:

> Focusing on the forms or functions of exchange makes it possible to argue that what creates the link between exchange and value is politics, construed broadly. This argument . . . justifies the conceit that commodities, like persons, have social lives. (Appadurai 1986: 3)

As Wilson and Brown (2009) note, information is presented in reports as a means of transforming knowledge about a particular situation into humanitarian or political action. Access to the value of reports is gained through movement; to be effective in bringing about political action, reports must circulate among other rights institutions, state-based institutions (both locally and nationally), academics, legal practitioners, and the general public. Although nation-states may ratify international rights treaties, there is often a gap between policy and practice. Hafner-Burton and Tsutsui (2005) argue that, in the face of this gap, civil society organizations play an important role in pushing for the realization of rights. Their quantitative study, which utilized time-series analyses of human rights practices from 1976 to 1999 and is based on data drawn from around the globe, examined whether state linkages to NGOs affected human rights behavior. Hafner-Burton and Tsutsui found that although the ratification of treaties did not automatically translate into government adherence to human rights norms,

> . . . linkage to global civil society improves human rights practices. Even though treaties often do not directly contribute to improvement in practice, the norms codified in these treaties are spread through NGOs that strategically leverage the human rights legal regime to pressure governments to change their human rights behavior. (Hafner-Burton and Tsutsui, 2005: 1399)

This is the kind of result that rights organizations hope for in producing knowledge about the situation of rights adherence or violation "on the ground." Once reports are written, the finished products need to circulate for them to spread information and potentially bring about change; in the Zimbabwean case, interlocutors continually stressed the necessity of reports moving both internally and across national borders. The following quotation from a rights NGO practitioner in Zimbabwe illustrates:

> We have to get this both to the government, and outside the country. Internally, it's important that the state cannot say they don't know what is happening at somewhere like a youth militia camp, for example. We make sure they know; we make sure everyone knows that this camp is being run by the police or the army or whatever. Because there must be accountability. We know this country . . . we have a history here of politicians pretending that they knew nothing, that they didn't give the orders, that this or that atrocity had nothing to do with state structures.
>
> So that's one thing. But the state is not enough. They're not making any changes any time soon; the violence is continuing. So we need pressure to come from outside also: from SADC countries and from further afield. So reports are sent to other governments and to the people who are involved in mediating Zimbabwe's political crisis and to international organisations. And slowly, slowly, the pressure builds. It's like the end of apartheid: For that to happen, people had to fight the system from inside the country. But there also

had to be international pressure. It's not enough to have one or the other. You need both.

As the second vignette with which I opened this chapter showed, the movement of data and written reports out of Zimbabwe used to be difficult, involving the covert physical movement of actual documents or electronic storage devices out of the country, such that in 2002 a friend smuggled electronic documents out of the country in a flash drive disguised as a pen. My interlocutors indicated that, at that point in time, providing information generated by local NGOs to the state could have resulted in their (illegal) detention. In the buildup to the 2005 and 2008 elections, the Zimbabwean state went so far as to ban NGOs from operating (Ndlovu, 2012). Although this was justified as a means of preventing Western infiltration, the action was widely understood by rights activists to be an attempt to maintain control of the country and silence opposition to state policy and violence. Political conditions under the GPA, however, worked to ensure that organizations were able to overtly publish their findings inside and out of the country when I conducted fieldwork in 2010, and even to present their findings to government officials when relevant.

Nonetheless, sharing reports around the country still carried some challenges. At the focus groups, for example, the women who attended were given copies of *Women, Politics and the Zimbabwean Crisis*, which most took back with them to their areas of origin (both rural and urban). The organizers of the focus groups, however, were legitimately concerned that carrying such reports might be dangerous to the women. By carrying information about state violence, there was a possibility they could be targeted by state or nonstate actors (the police or "party supporters," for example) in their hometowns or as they traveled. Each separate focus group discussed the likelihood of this, and at all of those where I was present, most women decided nonetheless that taking copies was worth it. Women emphasized that information such as this was important to take back to their communities: In the words of one focus group participant, "People have not seen numbers like this before. They do not know that this is happening everywhere; it would be good for them to see it on paper like this."[9] Furthermore, their decisions were based on a nuanced analysis of political conditions as they stood at that point in time: One woman commented, "This would not be a good thing to carry in an election year, but for now I think it is safe; politics is not so bad at the moment."

Here, then, is one example of the unevenness of circuits and flow that exist even in an increasingly globalized world: Sharing reports and findings with the general Zimbabwean public within the country's borders can be complicated, whereas the advent of new technologies has worked to ensure that sharing it with international and national organizations and individuals with Internet access has become much simpler than previously. Rights organizations in Zimbabwe today circulate their work electronically, and reports can immediately become available in numerous different spaces. The RAU reports on women became mobile as soon as they were complete, initially circulated among RAU's contacts via email. This mailing list goes out to over 400 addresses: The majority are those of local organizations (both governmental and nongovernmental), but reports are also sent to, in the words of a RAU staff member, "international governments, international organisations, regional organisations, and a large number of individuals." RAU reports are also increasingly picked up by the local media, with Zimbabwean newspapers *The Independent* and *The Zimbabwean* reporting on RAU's findings. In addition to circulation via mailing lists, reports are available on the organization's website for downloading. The organization's data on the number of "hits" (that is, the number of times material was viewed) in 2012 showed that, over a period of six months, more than two years after it was released, the first statistics-based report was viewed 1,753 times, whereas the second statistical and qualitative report was viewed 3,916 times. Despite the apparent value of numbers, it is the qualitative material that is most frequently viewed. Data also showed that each month the number of hits rises: This may be due to the fact that RAU's website is fairly new and is becoming increasingly well-known as a source of information on the Zimbabwean politico-legal situation. It is interesting that the organization has also started writing about rights using a different type of textual format, blogs.[10] RAU's blogs are written by staff members and provide more personal reflections on various issues concerning Zimbabwean politics and governance, allowing rights advocacy workers to move further beyond the conventional bounds of the discourse if they wish.

Along "the Curious Grapevine"

In such ways is knowledge constructed and organized and moved, with the aim of bringing about political change, rights adherence, and accountability. Words and numbers about the Zimbabwean situation are mobile. Goodale (2009b: 91) has noted that "what was important about the rise of transnational rights networks was the fact that they interconnected both above and below the radar of a (formal) international human rights system"; in other words, that the social life of rights exists beyond international courts and treaties in other less formally legal spaces, such as those provided by rights monitoring and advocacy organizations. Liberal civil society (Helliker, 2013), in all its complexity, plays a large role in the institutional structuring of rights discourses. Goodale draws on Eleanor Roosevelt, an early proponent of rights, who envisioned "a curious grapevine" of rights that would allow for information to "seep in even when governments are not so anxious for it" (Roosevelt, quoted in Goodale, 2009b: 93). Rights talk and texts—products of the dominant discourses of modernity—traverse this "curious grapevine," allowing for the movement and development of rights discourses around the globe. Such movement is one of the products of globalization, as is the increasing movement of people around the world. In the following chapter, I further follow the social life of rights, considering the ways in which rights are mobilized, debated, enacted, and denied once Zimbabweans themselves have crossed the border and are living in South Africa.

Chapter 4

Personhood and Rights among Zimbabwean Migrants in South Africa

Postcolonial Legalities in a Time of Migration

In this chapter I consider the use of law and ideas of human and civil rights by Zimbabweans living in, yet still seeking secure legal residence in,[1] neighboring South Africa. Over the last fifteen years, migration out of Zimbabwe has become increasingly common, such that one interlocutor commented that "Bob Marley's 'Exodus' should be our national anthem," whereas another identified *transnationalism* as a central element of "being Zimbabwean" ("To be a Zimbabwean is to live in another country from your sister or your brother or your father or your mother"). Official statistics are hard to come by due to the extent of illegal movement; even so, Zimbabwe has shifted from its historic position of having a migration profile mixed between origin and destination to being primarily one of origin (ZIMSTAT and IOM, 2010); it is a place from which, statistically speaking, people leave rather than one to which they go. Statistics collected by Zimbabwean immigration and border control indicate that South Africa is the primary destination country for legal migrants, followed by Botswana, though migration further afield to the United Kingdom, America, and even Australia is also common for those with greater resources (ZIMSTAT and IOM, 2010). Many more migrants leave the country without documentation, however. In 2010, the Forced Migration Studies Program estimated that there were between 1 and 1.5 million Zimbabweans in South Africa (FMSP, 2010), the majority without legal status. It is in the context of these migrants that notions of illegality become central.

Ideas of law and legality have become increasing prevalent within the postcolonial state: Comaroff and Comaroff (2007: 142) argue that "a 'culture' of legality" has become a common feature of the postcolony, whereas Robins (2008b: 185) has argued that *rights* has become a "notable keyword in South African political discourse" across social classes. On one level this is unsurprising, given that notions of legality lie at the heart of the modern state, where relationships between people and the state are mediated through laws and through the civil rights and responsibilities attendant on such laws. Law, however, is not the only form of meaning making that people draw on: It is worth examining, then, under what circumstances "the law," or language that invokes legal relationships such as rights, becomes the relevant medium for negotiating one's position, attempting to resolve difference, addressing perceived wrongs, or seeking security of place. It is also worth examining the limitations of a public discourse that emphasizes rights over other forms of political meaning making: as Robins, drawing on ANC MP Ben Turok, notes, "the limited, legalistic formulation" (Turok, 2005, quoted in Robins, 2008b: 185) of civil rights discourse may be "incompatible with radical politics and the structural transformation of highly unequal societies" (Robins, 2008b: 185; cf. Ross, 2003c).

The legal mediation of relationships between people and the state is further complicated when considering immigration: Where "outsiders" to a country attempt to lay claim to it, they need to do so by following the correct avenues created by the state, so they ultimately might fit into a recognized legal and/ or bureaucratic category (cf. Scott, 1998; Merry and Goodale, 2007), or they need to accept a status of illegality. In this chapter I am concerned with Zimbabwean migrants who were not able to obtain a South African work permit before arrival; specifically, those who applied for asylum-seeking papers with the ultimate view to achieving refugee status. Comaroff and Comaroff (2004: 200) have conceptualized law as it unfolds in postcolonial Southern Africa as "a dialectic-in-motion, a historical process that pivots on the horns of a contradiction," where the contradiction reflects the tensions between ideas of equal citizenship and ideas of legal respect for difference. In the case of immigration law and noncitizens' relationships with the South African state, the contradictions at work are more complex, as I demonstrate through an ethnographic consideration of the contextual use of rights discourses as used by migrants. Although the site of study has shifted to South Africa, my focus is still on the ways in which Zimbabweans are using discourses of rights.

The Legal Framework

Apart from a brief window afforded by the Zimbabwean Dispensation Project[2] in 2010, for most Zimbabwean migrants the only available avenue to legality within South Africa has been via a process of accessing asylum-seeking papers, which in turn give migrants the possibility of gaining refugee status. Other alternatives were rarely open to Zimbabweans; work permits were very difficult to get and relied on the Zimbabwean applicant having a passport and a job lined up in South Africa before arrival. The great majority of Zimbabwean migrants to enter the country since 2000 have done so without a work permit (Bloch, 2008; FMSP, 2010; Elphick and Amit, 2012). During fieldwork it became apparent, however, that even though Zimbabwean migrants tended to enter the country illegally, they did not intend to remain illegal; rather, they made use of asylum-seeking legislation in an attempt to gain access to a refugee permit. Gaining legal status had not been easy for the majority of applicants. When I first began research into Zimbabwean migration in 2007, the Refugee Reception Centres across South Africa were unable to keep up with the number of applicants (FMSP, 2009a), to the extent that in Cape Town potential applicants slept outside the offices for weeks at a time while queuing for an appointment (Morreira, 2009; 2010b). Once in the building, the chances of success were still very slim; for example, the statistics available from 2009 show that in that year Home Affairs received 223,324 new applications for refugee status. Of these, 4,567 were approved, 46,055 were rejected, and 172,702 were added to the backlog of unprocessed cases (FMSP, 2009b).

The possibilities open to people living in contemporary Zimbabwe are constrained by a combination of both socioeconomic *and* political conditions. This means that in the case of migration out of Zimbabwe, the varied conditions that led to what Betts and Kaytaz (2009: 1) refer to as "the Zimbabwean exodus" have sat uneasily with the limited legal categories that are available to undocumented migrants on arrival. Essentially, these categories are either that of the asylum seeker aiming to achieve refugee status who, due to the international and national conventions endorsed by South Africa, has a right to reside in South Africa or that of the economic migrant who has no such claim and should thus (apart from during a period from 2009 to 2011 when a moratorium on deportation of Zimbabweans was in place) be deported back to his or her country of origin. Such categorization rests on whether migrants are considered by the South African state to have been forcibly displaced or voluntarily mobile (Morreira, 2010b; Elphick and Amit, 2012). The effects of falling between legal categories can be extensive; as Elphick and Amit (2012: 7) note:

> While a number of Zimbabweans are fleeing the effects of the economic crisis—including economic deprivation and food scarcity—these effects cannot easily be divorced from the underlying political causes, making it hard to distinctly categorise them as either economic migrants or as asylum seekers. South Africa, however, categorises most migrants who do not fall unequivocally into the category of refugees as economic migrants. Since legal avenues of migration for economic migrants—particularly those who are relatively unskilled—are highly restricted, many Zimbabwean migrants are left with no means to regularise their status in South Africa.

In South Africa, refugee status is closely based on international refugee instruments and norms; indeed, the South African Refugee Act reproduces exactly the definition of refugee as found in the UN Convention on Refugee Rights (Khan, Chennells, and Heaney, 2009). In the terms of the Refugees Act, a person is eligible for refugee status if that person:

> 3. (a) Owing to a well-founded fear of being persecuted by reason of his or her race, tribe, religion, nationality, political opinion or membership of a particular social group, is outside the country of his or her nationality and is unable or unwilling to avail himself or herself of the protection of that country, or, not having a nationality and being outside the country of his or her former habitual residence is unable or, owing to such fear, unwilling to return to it; or
>
> (b) Owing to external aggression, occupation, foreign domination or events seriously disturbing or disrupting public order in either a part or the whole of his or her country of origin or nationality, is compelled to leave his or her place of habitual residence in order to seek refuge elsewhere. (South African Refugees Act of 1998)

To apply for refugee status people must follow a convoluted series of bureaucratized legal procedures. Initially, the applicant reports to a Home Affairs Refugee Reception Office[3] as soon as possible on arrival in the country, where he or she fills in an Eligibility Determination Form with the assistance of a Refugee Reception Officer. After capturing such information as deemed necessary (name, age, fingerprints, dependents, reasons for applying for asylum, and photocopies of any documents that might act as supporting evidence for a claim, such as medical records or political party membership cards), the applicant is issued with an Asylum Seeker Permit, often referred to as a "Section 22" after the section of the Refugee Act that determines such documentation. All applicants receive Asylum Seeker Permits, which are temporary; if the permit expires before the date on which the applicant has been granted a status determination interview (the next stage of the process), another visit to the Refugee Reception Office is needed to extend the permit. At the status determination interview, also called the second interview, the burden of proof rests with applicants, who must convince the Refugee Status Determination Officer (RSDO) that they fulfill the criteria of the Refugee Act, again supplying as much supporting evidence as possible. Following this interview, one of five outcomes is possible: The claim can be approved and Refugee Status granted; the claim can be rejected as manifestly unfounded, fraudulent, or abusive; or the claim can be rejected as unfounded. A rejection does not necessarily mean the end of the road for applicants, as there is a process of appeal. However, if any appeal is rejected, applicants need to approach a lawyer to take the matter to the High Court or leave the country.

This convoluted process of applying for asylum is predicated on an examination of individuals' migration histories and the motivations behind their movement, which need to be political rather than economic. Refugee status also relies on the applicant not returning to his or her country of origin due to a "well-founded fear of persecution." Although Zimbabwe has experienced periods of intense political violence, persecution on political grounds became more common over the last decade[4] (though, as Sachikonye [2011] shows, it also existed prior to this in independent Zimbabwe and colonial Rhodesia). Zimbabwean migrants often move for a combination of reasons and often wish to return home for short intervals.[5] Their reasons for movement are thus not always overtly political; indeed, the research I have carried out since 2007 indicates that the extreme decline in the Zimbabwean economy was always a relevant factor in interlocutors' migration histories, though overtly political violence might also have been present. This emphasis on socioeconomic factors for migration means that Zimbabwean applicants usually do not fulfill the criteria necessary for refugee status.

Nonetheless, as I will discuss in the following, interlocutors vehemently asserted that socioeconomic factors for movement constituted a violation of their basic rights and were grounds for seeking asylum, regardless of the fact that this was not in accordance with the Refugee Act. The Refugee Act, as based on international UN instruments, uses a narrow definition of rights and violation: Internationally, human rights charters recognize both political and socioeconomic rights. Though the different generations of rights (as described in Chapter 1) are recognized as equally important in comprehensive rights documents such as the Universal Declaration of Human Rights; the International Covenant on Civil and Political Rights (ICCPR); the International Covenant on Economic, Social and Cultural Rights (ICESCR); and the South African Constitution, this is not carried through to the more specific Refugee Act. This is partly because it is more difficult to prove direct responsibility for a violation of socioeconomic rights, and there is not the same legal precedent as there is for political violation, but also because many countries such as South Africa are not necessarily able to secure the socioeconomic rights of their citizens. Most states do not accept socioeconomic reasons as valid for refugee status.

Academic and policy debates in the field of rights law have emphasized the necessity of a holistic approach to rights, which does away with different "generations" and recognizes that all rights are intertwined and dependent on one another (Deng, 2005; Haas, 2008). In other words, the enjoyment of one right will often depend on the enjoyment of others; for example, a woman is much more likely to be able to fulfill her (political) rights to freedom of expression if she has been able to access a (socioeconomic) right to basic education. At the level of asylum seeking, however, a violation against economic rights and a violation against civil or political rights still carry different legal entitlements. The binaries at work in South African and international refugee law do not adequately map onto the complex realities of migration histories. In terms of these binaries, a person is considered either displaced or mobile, having moved because of either a political violation or an economic motivation, with the end result that he or she is considered to be either a refugee or an economic migrant. The binary structure this establishes is depicted as follows:

Political Violation	vs.	Economic Motivation
Forcibly Displaced	vs.	Voluntarily Mobile
Refugee	vs.	Economic Migrant

The inadequacy of these binaries is becoming increasingly recognized in Southern Africa and beyond, particularly as concerns the case of Zimbabweans. Zimbabwean migrants sit uncomfortably at the interstices of legal categories. As Zimbabwean migration increased from 2008 following the violent elections of that year and the continued and rapid decline of the economy, Zimbabweans' precarious position became increasingly obvious. A report by the UNHCR released in 2009 conceded that:

> The case (of Zimbabwean migration) poses a particular challenge for the international refugee protection regime because the majority of people leaving fall neither within the legal definition of a "refugee" nor are they voluntary, economic migrants. Rather, they fall within a broader category of "survival migration," fleeing an existential threat to which they have no domestic remedy. The reasons for their flight have mainly been a combination of state collapse, livelihood failure, and environmental disaster. (Betts and Kaytaz, 2009: 1)

The category of "survival migration" is a new one to rights discourse: This emergent term has been developed most prominently in the work of Alexander Betts (Betts and Kaytaz, 2009; Betts, 2010). Betts, a former UN High Commissioner for Refugees employee now situated at the University of Oxford, argues that the narrow focus within refugee rights discourse on providing protection to persons who have suffered from individualized political persecution or violence is no longer adequate. Betts (2010: 361) argues that in recent years "a range of new drivers of external displacement—particularly related to the interaction of environmental change, livelihood collapse, and state fragility—have emerged that fall outside the framework of the (modern refugee) regime." Betts's use of the word *regime* to describe the refugee rights framework is worth noting here, as it highlights the intertwined institutional, legal, and discursive elements of the discourse,[6] which, in combination, create and constitute a particular domain of knowledge (Foucault, 1970). Drawing on case studies of the state responses to the migration patterns of persons from the DRC to Angola and Tanzania, from Somalia to Yemen and Kenya, and from Zimbabwe to South Africa and Botswana, Betts argues that state responses to these unusual (from the perspective of the refugee rights regime) cases have largely been ad hoc. One such example is seen in the temporary Zimbabwean Dispensation Project, which briefly created a new category as a means of regularizing the many Zimbabwean migrants who did not fall into categories recognizable by the state. Ad hoc state responses are due to the fact that at the level of national and international refugee institutions, the narrow framework relying on particular sorts of violation is still used. Instead, Betts argues that there is a need for "regime stretching" (Betts, 2010: 361), which allows for the inclusion of new categories such as that of survival migration within refugee law. In other words, the formal discourse needs to expand.

The surfacing of such a debate within refugee rights discourse reflects the inadequacy of current categories and is exciting in that it shows the potential for the emergence of new possibilities within rights law. However, within international and national refugee law as it stands, category shifts and "regime stretching" (ibid.) have not occurred. In Southern Africa, academic commentators have noted that the law as it stands in the countries that neighbor Zimbabwe is not adequate to "irregular" (FMSP, 2009b: 42) Zimbabwean migration. The Zimbabweans I encountered during fieldwork thus had to negotiate this interstitial position between legal categories. As such, Zimbabwean migrants traverse a difficult line that can easily result in their remaining undocumented and without rights or protection in South Africa.

In *Seeing Like a State* (1998), James Scott argues that the modern state operates on ideals of centralized authority; one result of this is that the state seeks to render the complexity of society "legible," which requires disregarding the particular and the contextually dependent for that which fits into recognized bureaucratic categories (Scott, 1998: 26).[7] The following case study serve to illustrate the disjuncture between Zimbabwean migrants' particularized histories and their motivation for movement, and that which was legible to the South African state.

"I Had Nothing to Show Them but My Story"

I first met Chenai, a twenty-six-year-old Shona woman from a small town in central Zimbabwe, in Cape Town in early 2010, at the paralegal clinic where I was working at the time. This small, badly funded clinic provided free legal advice to refugees and asylum seekers. Chenai came to see us because she had received a letter telling her that her application for asylum had been rejected as unfounded, and she had thirty days to appeal or to leave the country. We met because she had tried to find a way to fit her migration history, which had elements of both political and economic motivations for crossing the border, into the bureaucratic framework of asylum seeking—and failed. Her story of migration and displacement is a good place to begin a conversation about how individual experiences become ordered within various domains of knowledge, and the ways in which rights discourse was drawn on by migrants in their attempts to gain refugee status. In January 2008, Chenai gave birth to her first child, a daughter whom she named Rumbidzai. She was newly married and living with her in-laws in a town in central Zimbabwe while her husband David looked for work in Harare, a five-hour bus ride away. Economically, things were extremely difficult, and the family often went hungry. In Chenai's words,

> At that point there was little food; we were eating *sadza*[8] once a day when things were good and making relish from the rape we grew or sometimes from wild food we gathered. We never had meat; we often didn't have *sadza* either. It was a very hungry time.

In addition to hunger, the family was caught in the growing tensions of the preelection period. In mid-March, Chenai was walking home from a nearby house where she had gone to fetch water—municipal water had not been available for weeks, and so the neighborhood relied on the one property that had a borehole. As she was carrying a heavy load, she had left her baby at home with her mother-in-law. On her way home, Chenai encountered a group of young men who were chanting election songs. They forced her to walk with them to a rally that was being held a few kilometers away. Chenai asked them if she could go home to drop off the water first, but:

> They made me pour it out on the road. I wanted to go back to get my child, so then I said that is why I really want to go back. They said I was lying so I wouldn't go to the rally—so they did not let me go home.

Chenai was held at the rally for close to six hours, having to sing and dance in praise of ZANU-PF in order not to draw attention to herself. "But you know," she said to me,

> I did not care at all about politics. I just wanted to get home to my baby, who I knew was very hungry and who needed me to feed her. There was nothing there (at home) to give her instead of my milk; I knew there wasn't even water because I had taken the container with me when I left.

Chenai leaked breast milk onto her shirt at the rally and was deeply embarrassed. Her breasts, engorged to feed a child, were also extremely painful. An older woman lent her a jersey to cover herself but could do nothing to help with the pain. Eventually, the rally was over, and Chenai could go home to a hysterically hungry Rumbidzai. Chenai remained in Zimbabwe over the election period and for the rest of the year, but when her husband suggested they try to move to South Africa she agreed, "because the politics in Zimbabwe nearly killed my child of hunger and kept me from going to her when I needed to." David left first, and Chenai followed a few months later. Her movement across the border was motivated by politics and by a failing economy, reasons that she and her husband thought might grant them asylum in South Africa. Unlike many women, Chenai crossed the border without incident.

In 2007, when I first started working with newly arrived Zimbabwean migrants in South Africa, most of my interlocutors expected that on telling their stories to representatives of the South African state, they would be granted refugee status (Morreira, 2010b). In the words of one informant, Simba, "We thought they would see that if we stayed at home we would be suffering too much, that we might even die." In most cases, "suffering" was shorthand for socioeconomic, not political, conditions; nonetheless, interlocutors conceptualized such suffering as, again in Simba's words, "going against my human rights." By the time of Chenai's arrival in South Africa in late 2008, however, it was obvious to Zimbabweans that getting refugee status was not so easy. Zimbabwean migrants' perceptions of socioeconomic "suffering" or "violations" as a means of securing legal access to South Africa were shown on many occasions to be incorrect.

Data collated from across my research with Zimbabweans in South Africa (including that gathered from a large-scale survey carried out with PASSOP and the Solidarity Peace Trust in 2010) show that, out of 522 migrants, 511 had attempted to begin the process of seeking asylum. Of those, only sixty-six (13 percent) had gotten as far in the process of seeking asylum as to have gone for a refugee status determination interview. Of those sixty-six, twenty-eight (42 percent) had been granted refugee status, and thirty-eight (58 percent) were denied it. Of the total number of migrants who attempted to begin the asylum-seeking process, therefore, only twenty-eight (5 percent) had been granted refugee status at the time of fieldwork. It is worth emphasizing that because these data were gathered in South Africa, they do not reflect the numbers of refugee applications that failed and resulted in migrants being deported or returning to Zimbabwe but only those who risked illegality and stayed. It is clearly not easy for Zimbabweans in South Africa to use a language of rights to achieve refugee status.

Framing Harm: Speaking to the State

Given the difficulties of refugee applications, as illustrated in the numeric data in the previous section, the migrants I interviewed had quickly learned that it was not enough to expect that officials would "see" the dangers of remaining in Zimbabwe through the sorts of empathetic solidarities that statements such as Simba's in the previous section hinge on. The ways in which the state rendered people's experiences "legible" (Scott, 1998) was different to their own interpretations of such experiences, which needed to be ordered in such a way that narratives reflected the categories that the law accepted as legitimate.

During fieldwork, I spent time at Refugee Reception Centres, where Zimbabwean migrants attempted to formalize their status. Here, the queues were long, and rumors about what was the best thing to say to officials reverberated along them. Interlocutors emphasized in interviews that they learned what to say from others while waiting for an appointment to fill in an application form and from conversations with other migrants in their home areas before visiting Home Affairs. One interlocutor told me that he

> . . . learned that it's better not to talk about the economy; you should provide proof of politics. But if you don't have that, you can try to say you were starving and going to die of hunger if you returned. But then someone else would say, no, it's better to say you are ill and there was no medicine.

In another woman's words,

> They told me that I mustn't say I am looking for work even though I was, even though I needed that work to keep my family going. I must say something about politics, and then I must provide evidence. I had been beaten once, so I told that story. But I had no evidence; what evidence is there? There was no point in going to a clinic after the beating, so I did not go. I had nothing to show them but my story.

Another informant told me that he had learned in the queue that applications were being granted on the grounds that homosexuality was illegal in Zimbabwe, "so I swallowed my pride and told them, I am a gay man, and they will put me in prison for that if I return." He was not in fact homosexual; in the country to find work to send money home to his common-law wife and two children, he asserted that "I felt okay about lying, because my reason for being there was an honest one; it was just one they would not accept. But I had to be allowed to stay somehow."

To return to my original case study: Chenai had drawn on both political and socioeconomic factors—her fear and suffering during the election rally and the fact that the family were unable to survive economically and had existed in conditions of continual hunger—in the hope that this would satisfy the stringent application criteria. Chenai's story exemplifies how political and socioeconomic factors are entangled—it was, after all, a socioeconomic issue, the absence of water, that put her in the path of political danger. Chenai's claim was rejected as unfounded, however, on the grounds that her life was not deemed to be endangered were she to return to Zimbabwe.

Her husband, David, who had applied for asylum before Chenai's arrival in South Africa, had also had his application rejected as unfounded. In his interview with a Refugee Reception Officer, he had emphasized that he was unable to earn enough money to feed and clothe himself, his wife, and his child and that he could not afford basic medications if one of the family were to get ill:

> I said to him, even if I was to find five jobs, with inflation as it is I would still be a starving billionaire. But how can I find even one job with unemployment above 80 percent? But to him that wasn't enough violation of my rights. I got a letter saying my application was unfounded.

Despite David's emphasis that being able to maintain his family consti-tuted, in his opinion, a basic right, both Chenai and her husband were deemed economic migrants, not refugees. In a legal setting, this type of naming is extremely powerful. As I have argued elsewhere (Morreira, 2010b, 2011), asy-lum seekers' livelihoods rest on whether they are categorized by the state as "displaced" or as economically "mobile," as refugees or illegal immigrants.

The emphasis on socioeconomic factors in Chenai and David's narratives was not unusual in the migration histories I collected from informants. In-deed, quantitative data from the in-depth interviews conducted with thirty-five migrants in Cape Town showed socioeconomic factors to be central in male and female migrants' reasons for movement *and* in their understandings of what constituted their human rights. During interviews, I asked people to describe what they understood their human rights to be and then to rate those rights in order of importance, giving the options of rating the right as a "very important" one, "somewhat important," or "not important." The categories that consistently emerged in interviews, in order of importance, were access to work (this was the only category considered by *everyone* in the sample to be a "very important right"), freedom from political violence or torture (90 per-cent of the sample saw it as "very important"), the ability to fulfill family ob-ligations and rituals ("very important" to 80 percent of the sample), freedom from intimidation or arrest (also "very important" to 80 percent of the sample), the right to vote without intimidation ("very important" to 78 percent), access to health care ("very important" to 68 percent), access to education ("very important" to 65 percent), access to documentation ("very important" to 47 percent), and access to water ("very important" to 45 percent).

These results were surprising to me, in that they do not reflect the definitions of rights as given within the international framework, and neither do they reflect the importance accorded within this framework to different rights. Access to work, which is not a human right per se in conventional discourse, was considered by *all* respondents, male and female, to be a "very important" right. This idea of rights was recently endorsed by Zimbabwean Deputy Prime Minister, Hon. Thokozani Khupe, who, when addressing the audience at the International Human Rights Day Commemorations organized by the Zimbabwe Human Rights Association (ZIMRIGHTS) in Harare in December 2012, asserted:

> Decent employment is a human right. Everyone has a right to have a job and a decent salary. Once the right to employment is realized, it also ensures that other rights such as entitlement to food, shelter, health and clean water can also be easily enjoyed. (Reported by Crisis in Zimbabwe Coalition, December 10, 2012)

In terms of the Refugee Act, however, this socioeconomic idea of rights is not legally relevant. Freedom from political violence, which followed closely behind access to work in interlocutors' ratings, *is* in keeping with the definitions of rights that underlie the Refugee Act. This was followed by the ability to fulfill family obligations, by which informants meant that they should be able to feed, clothe, shelter, and care for their families, as well as maintain important relationships with kin (living and dead) via necessary rituals, such as the payment of *ilobolo* (bridewealth) or the correct burial procedures. Again, this category is not one that exists within conventional rights law but was one that was central to interlocutors understanding of human rights.

The case studies already presented demonstrate that interlocutors translated experiences of "suffering" into a language of human rights violations, that the things that they considered a violation did not map easily onto the South African state's definition of a violation of human rights, and finally that in an official state setting, rights talk alone did not carry enough weight to secure refugee status. Narratives of rights have to fit within the "correct" categories of violation and within a strictly policed domain of knowledge, and they need to provide evidence that the state recognizes as valid. We can thus see discourse at work—systems of ideas that give us valid ways of knowing and acting on the world. Though socioeconomic rights such as the right to health and education are protected by human rights charters and recognized in international law, a violation of these rights is not viewed in the same light as political violations, and such violations do not form grounds for refugee status. Ideas such as familial obligations are not recognized in *any* rights charters. Scott (1998) argues that the state is able to relate to citizens only within the bounds of the categories it has created and that bureaucrats are not legitimately able to recognize anything outside of these closely specified boundaries due to the constraints of what is officially legible. As Kihato (2004: 280) phrases it, "Anything not in the required format cannot be understood by the state." The state and asylum seekers both drew on a language of rights; where they referred to violation, however, they meant very different things.

Anna Tsing (2005: xi) argues that the creation of such "zones of awkward engagement" is one of the effects of a globalized world, where power-laden interactions across difference involve multiple translations such that "words (may) mean something different across a divide, even where people agree to speak." She refers to such episodes as instances of "cultural friction" (ibid.); such misunderstandings occur within existing systems of power, and, as such, they carry the potential to limit possibilities as well as provide a means of resistance. Sarah Nuttall's (2009) understanding of entanglement as an instance of uneasy intimacy is also useful here: Though different legal and moral systems were entangled where violations were called on, this entanglement was an uncomfortable one. In what follows I consider *why* such friction and mistranslation occurred where Zimbabwean migrants spoke of socioeconomic difficulties in Zimbabwe in the language of human rights. I argue that there is more to how claims are made by Zimbabwean asylum seekers than is raised by the conventional dichotomy between socioeconomic versus political rights. We can better understand the tensions Zimbabweans seeking asylum in South Africa place on conventional rights law if we locate our analysis outside rights discourse and examine Southern African conceptualizations of personhood. It is here that we can begin to understand the uneasy relationships between Zimbabweans and the South African state, in that ideas about personhood allow us to understand the gap between a localized version of rights discourse that is based on ideas of what constitutes a person and proper relations between persons as understood by Zimbabwean migrants and the official version held by the South African state, which essentially replicates international refugee rights norms and categories. Examining ideas of Southern African sociality reveals particular ideas about the social construction of moral persons (cf. Englund and Nyamnjoh, 2004) that underpin migrants' ideas of rights and violation. Ironically, given their illegibility to RSDOs, these ideas are very close to the notions of *ubuntu* that have gained symbolic capital in South Africa since democracy and that have begun to be reflected in South African jurisprudence (Sachs, 2009; Cornell and Muvangua, 2012) but are not applied in immigration law. It is to this that I now turn.

Immigrants' Knowledge of Harm: What Constitutes the Rights of a Person?

One day in 2008, George, a Zimbabwean newly arrived in South Africa, said to me, "If I am here to prevent my family from starving, how am I different from someone here running away from imprisonment or torture by ZANU-PF? I am also running away from ZANU. I am also fulfilling my rights if I am trying to keep my family." When I used this quotation in previous work (Morreira, 2009: 110), I left out the final sentence of it, as it seemed extraneous. It was only later, after many more conversations with Zimbabweans about ideas of human rights, that I came to fully understand what he was telling me and the importance of the sentence I had discarded from my finished product. "I am also fulfilling my rights if I am trying to keep my family" points to a central way in which Zimbabweans translated local cultural norms of sociality into the internationally recognized language of human rights: that of the importance of family relations to what it means to be human, to be a social person, in both Shona and Ndebele contexts.

Consider the following set of responses to an interview question in which I asked interlocutors to explain to me what they understood their human rights to be:

"I have the right to keep myself and my family safe and well."

"My human rights are the things that I have because I am a human . . . like, I should have the right to a home, to a husband who is able to care for me and my children, to be able to go to church and to pray."

"I think human rights are many things: to be healthy or to go to a clinic if you are sick and there is medicine there. You must send your children to school, that is their right, so that they can get an education and then they can care for you when you are older. You must be able to get work, to get food. You must be able to care for your family."

"Human rights mean that you are able to live your life with dignity. What do I mean by *dignity*? It is to be able to work hard for fair wages, to look after your family, big and small. Rights are also about being able to vote for whom you want to; to talk about what you want to. But for me the most important is to be able to live your life decently and properly."

Sociality was central to Zimbabweans' understandings of rights. Their responses show how people broadened definitions of human rights beyond political rights, to incorporate what they considered the key elements of living a "proper" or "dignified" life, including the maintenance of family relations across the generations. The responses point to local ideas of personhood.

The anthropological concept of personhood refers to the ways in which social persons are created in different societal contexts. Conklin and Morgan (1996) argue that "Euro-American" personhood is based on the social construction of individualism and that:

Western ideologies of personhood prize egocentrism, self-containment, self-reliance, and social autonomy. This individualistic emphasis is evident in key values such as privacy, personal freedom, independence, and economic self-interest. (Conklin and Morgan, 1996: 664)

Human rights as presented in law rest on an idea of an autonomous individual (Messer, 1993). Individualism, however, is not only means by which social groups have made sense of what it means to be a person. Indeed, Comaroff and Comaroff (2001: 267; emphasis in the original), argue that "'the *autonomous* person,' that familiar trope of European bourgeois modernity, is a Eurocentric idea." The literature on personhood among the Shona emphasizes social relationships. Mawere (2010: 270), for example, argues that personhood "is defined by reference to other members of the same community, both the living and the living dead," while Chimuka (2001: 31) argues that "since life is a shared enterprise . . . one's humanity is affirmed as one affirms the humanity of others." In the Shona context, as is the case throughout Southern Africa, one is not a person without the intricate connections one holds to other people: To be human is to maintain relationships through, for example, caring for family members or paying bridewealth (Bourdillon, 1987; Mutambirwa, 1989; Engelke, 1999). This view of personhood is not limited to Zimbabwe. Indeed, there is a tendency in philosophical texts to generalize across Africa; hence Mbiti (1969: 145) argues that the dictum, "I am because we are and since we are therefore I am" sums up "African personhood" whereas Mawere (2010: 270) refers to "personhood in the African context"—yet the maintenance of relationships is not something international law would claim as a basic right[9] (cf. Nyamnjoh, 2004). These sorts of relationships, however, *were* taken by my interlocutors as an inherent right of the person and to be prevented from fulfilling them by political *or* economic reasons were translated into the weighty realm of legalese as an infringement of human rights. Interlocutors also justified the fact that they wished to be able to go home occasionally on these grounds, contrary to the expectations of refugee law that a refugee does not return to his or her country of origin: Being able to go home and then return to South Africa was integral to maintaining familial ties and, as such, was also viewed as a basic right.

Although social persons are constructed differently in different contexts, then, human rights discourses contain at heart the idea that such rights apply to all "humans," universally. What happens, however, where people encounter rights discourse and use its language, but with a different idea of what it means to be a human? Might "human rights" be assumed to refer to something different in such a case—might we in fact encounter an instance of Tsing's (2005: xi) friction, "where words mean something different across a divide," even where the words being used are exactly the same? Englund (2006) highlights the dangers of translation at work in the fields of human rights: In Malawi, he argues, rights have been translated into local languages with an emphasis on freedoms that has the end result of limiting the liberatory potential of such ideas, such that rights discourse constrains the poor rather than offering a means of resistance to structural violence. My argument here, however, concerns a mistranslation across ways of being in the world rather than a mistranslation across languages. To my interlocutors, personhood was relational, and to be human was to be enmeshed in a web of social relationships. A violation against human rights, then, was anything that damaged or limited their ability to properly partake in those social relationships, such as an economic crisis so severe that ordinary sociality could not be maintained.

Further Friction: Unhu, Ubuntu, and Dignity

To delve more deeply into the worldview underlying such (mis)translations, it is necessary to explore the Shona concept of *Unhu/Hunhu*, which was variously translated to me as decency, dignity, good manners, and character. A perusal of Shona philosophy shows that ideas of personhood are closely entwined with the construction of an ethical being (Gelfand, 1970; Chimuka, 2001; Mawere, 2010). The ethical Shona person is constructed in relation to the social world, which is composed of both living persons and ancestors (as is the case across Southern Africa). As explored in Chapter 3, for example, one of the roles of the *vadzimu* is to ensure that their descendants behave in a moral manner, as to oppose the moral order constitutes an affront against the *vadzimu*, which carries dangers for individuals and communities. Gelfand (1970) and Chimuka (2001) argue that the ethical person is one who embodies what they transcribe as *unhu* (Gelfand) and *hunhu* (Chimuka). Chimuka translates *hunhu* variously as humanity (2001: 27), as commendable character (ibid.: 26), and, drawing on Ramose (1999), as "the ontological, epistemological and moral fountain of African philosophy" (Chimuka, 2001: 29). Gelfand's translations are perhaps less encompassing but nonetheless also varied: He describes *unhu* as a quality, such that "a good man (is) one whom the Shona say has *unhu*—a man of good behavior, respectful to others, pleasant and honest" (Gelfand, 1970: 1). The *Standard Shona Dictionary* interestingly defines *unhu* as "Good manners; Culture." The Shona word for person is *munhu* (plural: *vanhu*): A cultured/socialized person, then, is not just a biological being but one who has learnt the values of *unhu*.

It is important to note that *hunhu*, when used in everyday speech, does not directly refer to rights; rather, it is much broader than this and, when used with like terms such as *tsika*, can refer to good manners and deference to age and authority. Some interlocutors argued that *hunhu/tsika* was racialized, such that they were particular to black Zimbabweans as white Zimbabweans did not fulfill the necessary way of being in the world to be so categorized. It is this idea of humanity that interlocutors drew on when they insisted that deteriorating socioeconomic conditions in Zimbabwe, which interrupted relationships, were a violation of *human* rights. This version of humanity, however—which deliberately creates hierarchies of respect and excludes particular kinds of person—is clearly contradictory to the explicit aims of human rights discourses, which set out all persons as equally valid. Nonetheless, *hunhu* has been used to talk about rights. Although Shona also has another term for rights—*kodzero*—this is usually specific to kinship relations and exchanges in situations such as bridewealth, for example (Gelfand, 1970). Interestingly, interlocutors in South Africa expanded the term *hunhu* to include human rights (which is not to say it is not still used in other, potentially incompatible, contexts) but did not draw on *kodzero*, as they considered the definition of this to be too limiting for the purposes of seeking asylum. I thus confine my discussion here to what this usage of *hunhu* reflects about competing discourses of personhood and rights.

Conceptually, *unhu* is very similar to the South African moral concept of *Ubuntu*, which has recently (re)surfaced in the South African popular imagination and in some legal jurisprudence. Indeed, Samkange and Samkange's 1980 treatise *Hunhuism or Ubuntuism: A Zimbabwe Indigenous Political Philosophy* holds the two concepts as identical. Similarly, Chimuka (2001) cites Ramose's (1999) arguments around *ubuntu* to argue that "*Ubuntu (Hunhu)* philosophy [constitutes] the basis of ontology and epistemology for the Bantu-speaking people, of which the Shona is part" (Chimuka, 2001: 29). Some Shona philosophers at least, then, hold *unhuism* and *ubuntu* as mutually translatable. That the ideas are closely interlinked seems undeniable: Consider the definition of *ubuntu* as invoked by Justice Yvonne Mokgoro in a case where the South African Constitutional Court declared capital punishment to be in conflict with the Bill of Rights:

> Generally, *ubuntu* translates as "humaneness." In its most fundamental sense, it translates as personhood and "morality." Metaphorically, it expresses itself in *umuntu ngumuntu ngabantu*, describing the significance of group solidarity, compassion, respect, human dignity, conformity to basic norms and collective unity, in its fundamental sense it denotes humanity and morality. Its spirit emphasizes a respect for human dignity, marking a shift from confrontation to conciliation. (Mokgoro, cited in Sachs, 2009: 106).

The similar idea of personhood at work in ideas of *ubuntu* and *unhu* raises interesting implications, given the failure of refugee law to recognize the ideas of personhood at play in migrants' calls on human rights, despite the use of *ubuntu* in some South African jurisprudence.[10] *Ubuntu* has most frequently surfaced at the level of constitutional law, making its first appearance in a case considered under the interim constitution, the Makwanyane case, where the Interim Constitutional Court drew on ideas of *ubuntu* in finding capital punishment to be unconstitutional (cited in Sachs, 2009). *Ubuntu* has subsequently been called on in constitutional cases concerning restorative justice, amnesty, reconciliation, customary law, and the right to culture (Cornell and Mavangua, 2012); most pertinently for our purposes here, however, it has been prominent in cases concerning socioeconomic rights (ibid.). What we see here, then, is a localization of law at the *constitutional* level, which is not applied at the level of the Refugee Act, where international norms still hold sway and where particular categories, based in a Euromodern understanding of the autonomous person, are all that is legible to the state. The relationship between the local and the global here, then, is one that is imbued with power; South African law carries an entanglement of philosophical and legal traditions that surface differently at different points in the country's legal architecture.

Though there are multiple systems of meaning making at work in the translations given in the preceding paragraphs, there is one English word that arises in all of them: *dignity*. The idea of dignity forms one of the epistemological foundations of South African constitutional law and is also a key trope of rights discourse. Furthermore, an examination of the meanings already allocated to *unhu* and *ubuntu* show that both draw on this same word in their translations into English. Engelke (1999: 301), for example, directly translates one into the other, stating that "the Shona word for 'human dignity' or 'humanity' in the most general sense is *unhu*," whereas the quotation from Justice Mokgoro previously cited notes of *ubuntu* that "its spirit emphasizes a respect for human dignity" (in Sachs, 2009: 106). Dignity is also central to human rights: indeed, it is the first article in the UNDHR:

> All human beings are born free and equal in dignity and rights. They are endowed with reason and conscience and should act towards one another in a spirit of brotherhood. (UNHDR, Article 1)

Francis Deng (2005), in a discussion of human rights in the African context, uses the idea of dignity as a means of justifying the claims to universality made in international rights discourses, arguing that "the more profound roots of the claim to universality lie in the fact that human rights reflect the universal quest for human dignity" (Deng, 2005: 499). That human beings have dignity, then, seems to be one point on which multiple discourses and modes of thought converge: What is meant, however, by dignity when it is invoked? A justification of the universality of rights through the calls to dignity such as are made by Deng would imply that the concept carries the same meaning in different geographical, temporal, and philosophical locations. Could this possibly be the case? Does *dignity* mean the same thing in rights charters as it does in South African constitutional decisions or in migrants' perceptions of *unhu*, or South African perceptions of *Ubuntu*? I would argue that this is not the case: The occurrence of ideas of dignity in these varied modes of thought and meaning making does not reflect a convergence of meaning but rather reflects that the term is broad enough to encompass multiple interpretations and valences and is also open to instances of friction.

Let us begin with the European history of the term. It is with the writings of Kant that dignity as used in law today comes to the forefront (Rosen, 2012). The particular version of dignity that emerges in rights law today is based on a Kantian conceptualization: a secular, egalitarian view of dignity as something intrinsic, incomparable, and unconditional that is limited to humans as "only human beings (so far as we know) are capable of acting morally and feeling the force of morality's claims" (ibid.: 23–24). Dignity in this conceptualization is a moral concept and is linked to the autonomous, individual person who is capable of making moral decisions: As such, it is an inherent characteristic of all people. In contrast to earlier European definitions of dignity as the province only of the upper classes (Rosen, 2012), Kantian dignity is inclusive. It is this idea of dignity that becomes codified in rights law. Dignity here, then, is located firmly in the realm of the individual and is concerned with that individual's ability to make moral decisions.

Ideas of *Ubuntu* and *unhu*, however, for all that they also invoke dignity, are essentially social and relational: Where dignity surfaces in such definitions it is not confined to an individual agent. Engelke (1999: 301) defines *unhu* as *both* human dignity and humanity, whereas the definitions of dignity given by interlocutors in the preceding pages also show dignity to be relational; as previously quoted, "Human rights mean that you are able to live your life with dignity. What do I mean by dignity? It is to be able to work hard for fair wages, *to look after your family, big and small*" (emphasis mine). In these conceptualizations, furthermore, dignity is closely aligned to socioeconomic conditions within which social relations are played out. Emmanuel, an Ndebele immigrant in Cape Town, commented:

> One of the things that this situation in Zimbabwe has done is to take away people's dignity . . . we cannot live with dignity when there is no food for our families, no schooling, no health care. At one point no one even had money

for coffins, so even if you died you did it without dignity. Imagine that! Not being able to bury your brother or your uncle properly! That is not right, not right at all.

Theresa, a Zimbabwean studying law at UCT, had this to say:

> At the end of the day, what is *ubuntu*? It is about living with dignity, treating others with dignity. Zimbabweans have a similar concept to *ubuntu*—*uhunhu*—but at home it's certainly not law. It's part of daily life. I would like to see it in the constitution at home, though. That would be something.

There are clearly competing kinds of knowledge at work here. Where dignity invokes morality in these conceptualizations, it is a socioeconomic morality: Dignity involves being able to work for fair wages, for example. In South Africa, dignity is also often located in the socioeconomic realm. Consider the following excerpts from a talk given by the South African founder of Abahlahi baseMjondolo (the Shack Dwellers' Movement) Lindela Figlan, at the Anarchist Bookfair in London. The transcript of this talk was sent to me by a staff member of PASSOP after I had asked him to think about and share with me what dignity meant to him. The talk beautifully expresses the convergence and multiple valences of ideas of dignity at work in South African popular thought, with Figlan highlighting that

> Money does not buy dignity because to be a person with dignity you must recognise the dignity of others . . . As poor people we do not live in dignified conditions. In fact when it rains we live like pigs in the mud. Our shacks are always burning. We do not have toilets . . . But poor as we are we achieve our own dignity. Some people achieve dignity in their churches. Some achieve dignity through culture, in something like a choir . . . And we achieve dignity in the togetherness of our struggle. Our struggle gives us dignity now and it also aims to create a world in which land, wealth and political power are shared amongst the people. (Figlan, 2012)

The ideas of dignity used by Zimbabwean interlocutors, and used by Figlan, are similar: Dignity is achieved through togetherness, through access to decent socioeconomic conditions, and through the ability to fulfill rituals such as burial in the "proper" way; to be dignified is to be treated with respect by those around you. In other words, dignity is situational, not intrinsic. This is a far cry from dignity as "intrinsic, incomparable and unconditional" as it appears in the Kantian philosophical roots of rights law (Rosen, 2012: 31).

Dignity as it exists in international law today carries a very different history from ideas of *ubuntu* and *unhu*; one that is based in the individual, not the relational, person. Nonetheless, dignity has become the rallying point for an endorsement of the "localization" of rights discourses: It is in this sense that Deng (2005) argues that African systems of thought, particularly as regards dignity and relational personhood, can be used to enrich ideas of human rights. Deng (2005: 502) asserts that

[There is a] call for a constructive dialogue aimed at a comprehensive approach to human rights . . . the challenge for humanity is to enrich and not impoverish human dignity as an overriding value for all mankind.

Further, he argues that drawing in socioeconomic rights through an "African" understanding of dignity is one means by which such an enrichment could occur. Deng (2005: 502) argues that, historically, in "African traditional systems,"

Rights tended to emphasise cooperative support in the social and economic spheres of life. With the centralization of power in the modern state system, the need to protect individuals and groups against human rights abuses became urgent. This gave rise to the high profile given to civil and political rights. But the modern nation state is also called upon to cater to the welfare of citizens in the social and economic spheres. Drawing a sharp distinction between these sets of rights can therefore be misleading. (ibid.)

Nonetheless, despite the South African state's attempts to encode local ideas such as *ubuntu* (Cornell and Muyangua, 2012), it is exactly such as sharp distinction that is drawn in the Refugee Act. Foucault (1977) reminds us that discourse produces reality in that it affects legitimate ways of interacting in the social world. Direct translations between *unhu*, *ubuntu*, and dignity provide room for frictional encounters between legal discourses and other knowledge systems. Dignity may exist at the level of constitutional law, but where asylum seekers invoke dignity in their relationships with the state it is not a concept that can be heard. Not only is a call on dignity an inadequate means of seeking security of place, but dignity itself is often absent from the relationship between asylum seeker and state. As Moses put it, "Where is the dignity in making me produce a paper like a child producing a sick note for school?" when providing evidence of violation or, in Emmanuel's words, "I have no dignity here. I am made illegal because I am seeking a better life."

Law and Power in the Postcolony

The preceding case study of the use of ideas of rights by Zimbabwean migrants shows that, although "human rights" has emerged as a dominant discourse, it is neither evenly applicable across all contexts nor easily localized. Zimbabwean migrants are drawing on a particular moral cosmology that is partially reflected in South African law but not as it applies to them. The inclusion of what Ramose (1999: 49) posits as "*ubuntu* . . . the wellspring flowing with African ontology and epistemology" in some aspects of law, then, is not legible to the South African state as concerns refugees. Rights discourse hierarchizes some forms of knowledge and makes others entirely invisible. Here, international definitions, based on "Western" ontology and epistemologies, still carry the power. The emergence of multiple systems of meaning making in South African law is limited.

When rights language emerged as the relevant medium for negotiating experience for asylum seekers, "Words mean something different across a divide, even where people agree to speak" (Tsing, 2005: xi). Attempts made by Zimbabweans to use a language of rights to try to seek security of place were ineffective, as the categories being drawn on did not match those that were legible to the state. As Tsing (2009: 13) has noted in a later publication, when words and concepts are tracked from their emergence in the "powerful countries of the global North" through to their dissemination in the global South, it is possible to see how terms may solidify, such that "words are like swords, sometimes becoming so rigid that the words and the practices of power can hardly be separated" (ibid.). The categories provided by rights law have solidified in South Africa: Despite the fact that the South African state has put considerable effort into "localizing" postcolonial and postapartheid law to include ideas such as *Ubuntu*, at the level of asylum seeking such localization is hard to find. On one hand, this internationalism gives rights discourse its legitimacy: Human rights apply to everyone, all of the time, regardless of cultural, political, or economic background and regardless of age, gender, or sexuality. On the other hand, universalizing language can limit the availability of rights to those whose notions of rights are different to such a formulation. The "universal" nature of rights does not unfold so simply when we examine the invocation of rights in practice.

Goodale (2006b) has noted that, within the terms of global rights discourses, universal rights are "believed to be entailed by a common human nature" (Goodale, 2006b: 490). The ethnographic considerations of the uses of rights in this chapter show this underlying assumption to be one that is deeply problematic when we consider that the very construction of that human nature, or of what it means to be a person, is complexly social.

The Situationality of Human Rights

The great value of human rights is that it implies a set of norms whose legitimacy depends on nothing more complicated than the simple fact of common humanness. Political entities (like the nation state) will come and go, but the fact of common humanness, if true, both preexists these entities and will remain after they are gone. That is the real genius of the idea of human rights. It is also its greatest weakness, since it is when such a noble (if essentially speculative) idea is *converted into the language of social and political practice*—as it must necessarily be—that all the problems begin.

Mark Goodale, 2009b: 98 (emphasis mine)

C AN "THE COMMON HUMANNESS" THAT LIES at the heart of discourses of human rights be conceived of as a "simple fact"? In other words, can the assumption of universal applicability that gives rights discourse a great deal of its global symbolic capital (Bourdieu, 1986, 1992) be conceived of as clear cut, or even as accurate? Further, can the set of norms that underlie human rights discourses exist without political entities such as the nation-state, as Goodale rightly argues the discourse assumes?[1] The ethnographic examples and case studies presented in this book illustrate that this is not the case: Although human rights discourse is predicated on an assumed universality and common humanness, this "simple fact" is revealed as deeply complex, politicized and power saturated when one examines the invocation and attempted enactments of human rights in the practices of daily life in Zimbabwe and by Zimbabweans elsewhere. The universal notion of human rights is widely understood to be a political notion in legal studies; this ethnography has provided some examples of the ways in which this unfolds in practice. For example, if personhood is not conceived of in the same way everywhere, then what idea of humanness is upheld as the "common" one? What happens when the laws that are supposed to apply to all persons are in actuality enacted in particular ways that are influenced by political considerations or gendered power imbalances? Rights are social constructions that are used in complexly social environments. As such, they are always political.

Preexisting (and shifting) social categories, modes of thought, and political and moral systems are relevant to understanding the enactment of rights discourses. Nonetheless, as Nyamnjoh (2004: 33) argues,

> Popular and ideological representations of liberal democracy treat its promise of rights and empowerment for the individual as a *fait accompli*. The tendency is to minimize the power of society, social structures and communal and cultural solidarities.

This quotation shows us one of the tendencies of discourses (Foucault, 1977): In reproducing themselves, they present one particular way of knowing the world as the inevitable way of knowing the world. Mignolo (2012) has argued that this is a key trope of coloniality, where monocentric thinking is promoted over multiplicity, thus creating and maintaining the myth of there being one epistemological center from which knowledge emanates. Where a global discourse minimizes the role of social structures in determining its form, and in so doing runs the risk of being naturalized, the value of detailed ethnographic work in tracing its social production becomes apparent.

I began fieldwork with a series of questions about the use of ideas of human rights in postcolonial Southern Africa; these questions were motivated both by academic interest and by my position as a Zimbabwean watching and partaking in (usually unsuccessful) attempts to use ideas of human rights to improve the sociopolitical circumstances of Zimbabweans in the region. These questions were wide ranging—first, under what circumstances were ideas of rights being invoked? Second, were international concepts of human rights being localized, and if so how? How did discourses of rights circulate? How were people's subjective experiences translated into legal categories that reflected the human rights paradigm, and what were the effects of translation? And, finally and centrally, for Zimbabweans, what did discourses of human rights actually do? What material difference has the presence of rights law made to the Zimbabwean sociopolitical crisis? An ethnographic exploration of these questions (and through them of the social and political practice of human rights), such as has been presented here, allows for deeper insight into the complex realities of the "noble idea" of universally shared human rights. In this concluding chapter I draw together the ethnographic and theoretical threads of this book, which has examined the unfolding of human rights discourses within the social realities of daily life in Zimbabwe and South Africa to illustrate the complexities of the emergence of rights in local contexts.

Anthropological approaches to the study of human rights have asserted the need to study rights in practice (Wilson and Mitchell, 2003; Merry, 2005, 2006; Goodale, 2006a, 2006b, 2009a) arguing that detailed ethnographic examination of local contexts can show how supposedly universal ideals become localized. This book furthers these debates by arguing that it is because globalized ideas of rights are, at least as they are used popularly, flexible enough to be open to interpretation that they are able to be considered valid in very disparate contexts. Nonetheless, what localization occurs does so within the terms of human rights discourse itself and is therefore limited, particularly at the level of actual law as compared to the level of popular talk about rights. Furthermore, even though rights talk was prevalent in interlocutors' daily lives, the material presented here has shown that, at the level of implementation, rights rhetoric does not make a great deal of difference to people's lives and livelihoods. "Rights," then, are also limited in their material usefulness.

Human Rights and Law in Postcolonial Zimbabwe

Postcolonial African regimes have not invented what they know of government from scratch. Their knowledge is the product of several cultures, heritages, and traditions of which the features have become entangled over time, to the point where something has emerged that has the look of "custom" without being fully reducible to it, and partakes of "modernity" without fully being a part of it.

Achille Mbembe, 2001: 25

"The post-colonial" does not signal a simple before/after chronological succession. The movement from colonization to post-colonial times does not imply that the problems of colonialism have been resolved, or replaced by some conflict-free era. Rather, the "post-colonial" marks the passage from one historical power configuration or conjuncture to another.[2]

Stuart Hall, 2001a: 213

These quotations reveal some of the complexities that are revealed when examining the emergence of global ideas of rights within postcolonial contexts that are occurring in Zimbabwe today. Both quotations are concerned with temporality and the emergence of historicized patterns of power in the present; both also assume complexity and the enfolding of varied modes of thought and regimes of power in postcolonial contexts. The ethnographic arguments presented in this book have shown that the law (as formally encoded *and* as popularly and discursively invoked) provides a particularly rich site for exploring these entanglements. Through examining law as it is encoded, or in the process of being encoded, as compared to law as it is subsequently enacted or rhetorically invoked, I have been able to contextually examine the multiple interrelationships between local contexts and global discourses, ideologies, and precedents. Let us examine, then, what this book has demonstrated with regard to how the idea of human rights was "converted into the language of social and political practice" (Goodale, 2009b: 98) in Zimbabwe.

The detailed case study of the public debates surrounding the writing of the Zimbabwean constitution demonstrates how human rights, rather than being inalienable, inherent, universal, and indivisible (as they are simplistically presented in the terms of the global discourse), were in fact open to political and politicized interpretation and contestation. The "finished" versions of legal documents such as constitutions and statutes emerge from and are enacted within fields of power and in their turn become constituted as fields of power. The prevalence of a reductionist language of inalienability and inherence within human rights discourse obscures more than it reveals: Though such terminology is invoked as a means of asserting the universal applicability of human rights, it can be dangerous if taken at face value, in that it hides the workings of power in practice. The complexly negotiated process of Constitutional Outreach in Zimbabwe and the gap between the rhetoric of a "people-driven process" versus the realities of the implementation of the process show that the rights that are afforded by documents such as constitutions, for all that they come to be presented as naturalized once encoded, reflect the moment in which they are made.

In Zimbabwe, where such a moment was locally perceived as an instance of democratic performance rather than "actual" democracy in progress, the enormous symbolic, legal, and political capital attached to a constitution carries dangers: Constitutions can as easily limit freedoms as they can support them. In assessing informants' views of democracy as performance in

Zimbabwe, Comaroff and Comaroff's analysis of law as fetish in the post-colony comes to mind:

> Many postcolonies make a fetish of the law, of its ways and means. Even where those ways and means are mocked, mimicked, suspended or sequestered, they are often central to the everyday life of authority and citizenship, to the interaction of states and subjects, to the enactments, displacements and seizures of power. (Comaroff and Comaroff, 2007: 134)

In the Zimbabwean example, such an analysis rings true. Rights-based constitutions are upheld within global transitional justice discourses as central to processes of democratization and the growth of a "culture" of human rights; yet to informants the process of creating a Zimbabwean constitution was one of mimicry rather than substance. To return to the first and broadest question with which I entered the field, then—were discourses of human rights being used in Zimbabwe, and if so in what ways?—here is one answer. Discourses of rights were invoked by multiple players within a political power struggle, all of whom drew on the global lexicon of rights and democratic participation as a means of attempting to encode a constitution that reflected their political interests. This case study also provides a contextualized answer to another of my questions: How are people's relationships to the state configured by the use of rights? In the constitution-writing process in Zimbabwe, we see the combative and protracted setting-in-place of a legal framework that will guide what the state accords to citizens (as well as who can and cannot lay claim to that citizenship) and the responsibilities citizens carry toward others. The contentious nature of the constitution-writing debates encountered in the field reflected the significance of the process. The outcomes of that struggle, which essentially saw the legal encoding of a deeply unsatisfactory constitution despite the opposition of human rights organizations, also go some way toward answering one of the broadest questions with which I entered the field—is the work of human rights discourses actually making much material improvement to people's lives? In this instance, the answer is no; human rights discourses and organizations did not carry sufficient power to challenge the power of the ruling party. Human rights worked as rhetoric but carried little substance.

The constitutional study provides just one (albeit complex) example of how discourses of human rights emerged during fieldwork in Zimbabwe. A consideration of the multiple repertoires of justice being invoked in Harare in

2010 revealed further uses of ideas of human rights and also allowed an ethnographic consideration of the second of my broad questions: Were such ideas of human rights being localized or vernacularized (Merry, 2006) within Zimbabwe, as anthropological literature on rights (Werbner, 1996; Wilson, 1997; Merry, 2006; Shaw and Waldorf, 2010) would suggest, and if so, how? Ideas of justice as I examined them in Harare were called on in light of the failures of the formal legal system to prosecute for political crimes, which lead to a rise of what people, drawing on the global legal lexicon, called a "culture of impunity" in Zimbabwe. This culture of impunity was not all encompassing, however: Fieldwork outside the realm of the formal, state-based legal system revealed intersecting and overlapping justice repertoires at work. As Howell (1997: 11) argues, then, "Within any one society two or more moral discursive practices may coexist and be made operational according to context." Although coloniality may hierarchize knowledge (Mignolo, 2012), it is not possible to shut down all alternative ways of knowing and being in the world.

Some of these "moral, discursive practices" of justice were based on global human rights ideologies, such as the work being done by a local NGO that drew on the paradigm of transitional justice as a means of imagining justice mechanisms in a postconflict Zimbabwe. This case study allowed for an examination of the vernacularization of global transitional justice norms, which emphasize making justice and rights locally relevant and presenting justice within the terms of local moral systems. Nonetheless, the case study illustrated that the comparative global symbolic (and attendant economic) capital of the human rights paradigm ensured that Zimbabwean NGOs largely operated within the constraints of the global norm. Any localization or vernacularization that occurred, then, occurred within the terms of the dominant discourse. This is in keeping with Shaw and Waldorf's (2010) argument that, despite an emphasis within transitional justice discourses on the need to localize, any such adaptation that occurs does so in ways that maintain rather than interrogate the discursive foundations. Again, the effect of global power disparities in constituting the terms of human rights discourses is clear.

Other moral systems of justice, however, not based in and modeled on the human rights paradigm, showed, in the absence of the imposition of the global model of rights, more complex interactions between the local and the global. The Tree of Life, for example, although originating from an international model of "healing circles," was distinctly local in that the model had been adapted to Zimbabwean circumstances by Zimbabweans and drew on local repertoires of social and individual healing. The language used by its practitioners moved between local idioms of conflict resolution, metaphors of nature that drew on a mixture of local cosmology and the global symbolism of healing circles, globally circulating Western psychological ideas of healing, *and* a globally inflected language of violation, democracy, and transitional justice. Human rights were drawn in here, then, as a single set of possibilities among many.

Both of these case studies show that, rather than using "vernacularization" to study the practice of rights in the postcolony, "entanglement," which Mbembe (2001) characterizes as composed of discontinuity, overlay, interpenetration, and envelopment and Nuttall (2009) depicts as a situation of confrontational mutuality, or uneasy intimacy, is more appropriate. Such a model allows for a better examination of the workings of power in the supposed localization of discourses of rights and allows for an examination of when such entanglements are not benign but dangerous—such as is seen when Zimbabwean migrants to South Africa attempt to make use of rights law in their interactions with the state. Before returning to this example, however, let us turn to the next question with which I entered the field: How do such entangled interpenetrations of legal and moral ideas travel and circulate in the Southern African region and beyond?

Human Rights and Law on the Move

Words are always in motion, and as they move across space and time, they inscribe the arcs of our past and present. [We can] consider the relation between words and worlds by tracing the social and political life of words—specific words in specific places at specific times—with an eye to their practical and public effect . . . Words do work in the world, whether organizing, mobilising, inspiring, excluding, suppressing, or covering up . . . they cross cultural borders and become embedded in social and political practices, changing their impact and meaning as they go.

Carol Gluck, 2009: 3

The globe shrinks for those who own it; for the displaced or the dispossessed, the migrant or refugee, no distance is more awesome than the few feet across borders or frontier.

Homi Bhabha, 1992: 88

Rights discourses travel; indeed, Goodale (2009b: 93) asserts that "the eventual transnationality of human rights was implicit in the creation of the postwar human rights system itself," in that the 1948 Universal Declaration of Human Rights aimed to transgress the nation-state's political boundaries by putting a rights architecture based outside individual states in place. Goodale (ibid.) refers to this as the "basic philosophical transnationalism" of human rights; such a transnationalism has been reflected in the spread of human rights discourses around the globe, where "discourse" is composed both of particular systems of language and thought and of accompanying sets of rights-based courses of action and institutions (Foucault, 1972).

How can we trace the movement of human rights discourses? The emergence of multisited ethnography and the shifts that have occurred in anthropology with regard to unit of study (Marcus, 1995) allow for a nuanced consideration of the movement of human rights discourses in practice. Following the discourse, however, as Marcus recommends, entails more than an ethnography based in multiple sites: We also need to conduct ethnographies of interconnection that examine movement *between* sites. In this project, the spaces of new technologies provided one useful avenue by which to do so; the collation of migration histories and participant observation at central nodes of movement such as state borders provided others. Tsing (2009: 14) suggests that in following "words in motion" the scholar must find a "concrete trajectory"; similarly I found that focusing on the movement of specific texts allowed for access to the complex and uneven mobilities that characterize the globalizing world. I thus followed the trajectories of documents out of Zimbabwe. Tsing notes that the (post)modern world contains numerous "projects of imagining and making globality" (Tsing, 2000: 329); although human rights discourse constitutes one of these projects, we need to remember that so too does academic discourse, particularly given the emphasis within social science on an understanding of the world as increasingly globalizing. As scholars, then, in invoking and examining the relationships between the local and the global, we need to take into account what elements of that world we are examining and what characterizes the flows and blockages we find. The ethnographic analyses presented in this book show us that processes of globalization are uneven and can look very different depending on our unit of study and the methodological and analytic starting points we choose. Returning to Nyamnjoh's (2004: 33) critique of popular representations of rights that present them as a fait accompli that disregards sociopolitical realities, then, we can see the value of ethnographic work in uncovering the contestations and refusals of human rights in practice and their uneven application and movement across physical and electronic spaces, but we must also maintain awareness of the positionality that we as social scientists bring to the work we do.

Human Rights, Categories, and Moral Relationships

The final ethnographic example presented in this book allowed further examination of the use of human rights in configuring relationships between individuals and the state. It also allowed examination of the relationship between subjective experiences and legal categories. This chapter considered the experiences of persons who had already moved: Zimbabwean migrants who had crossed the border into South Africa and were now actively using human rights discourse in their attempts to gain refugee status in South Africa. Again, the relationship between the local and the global emerged as key: International human rights instruments had an impact on South African refugee law, and that law in turn delineated the possibilities open to migrants and to the state. However, "local" understandings also emerged as central: During fieldwork, I found that the gap between the law as popularly understood by migrants and the law as it existed on paper and was enacted by the South African state became obvious. "Human rights," then, do not mean the same thing to all people in all contexts—despite the rhetorical insistence on a basic shared humanness and rights' universal applicability. The differences between Zimbabwean migrants' definitions of violation and those encoded in South African refugee law were situated in differing understandings of personhood; what it means to be human, then, is not always a "simple fact" (Goodale, 2009b: 38). An understanding of this allows some insight into why human rights discourses have largely failed as a means of seeking security and asylum for Zimbabweans in South Africa.

Howell (1997: 4) notes that there are multiple overlapping moral domains from which people might operate and "conflicts of premises and values may emerge at the meeting of different moral orders such as, for example, between a modern Western one based on principles of democracy and human rights and Hinduism based on a hierarchical caste system" (Howell, 1997: 4). A process of translation is required for people to speak across those domains, be it translation from one language to another or, even more complex, translation across different ways of seeing and inhabiting the social world (Okazaki, 2003). As Englund (2006) has argued, issues of translation lie at the heart of human rights practice, as the discourse moves across the globe and is inserted into numerous diverse contexts and spaces. He shows, and my work confirms, that this process is not a simple one. Zimbabwean migrants' attempts to use a language of rights to try to seek security of place were often ineffective, as the categories of violation they drew on to describe their reasons for seeking asylum did not match those encoded in South African law. However, human rights terminology was still appealing to migrants: When used popularly, outside of the legal realm, the discourse proved flexible enough to incorporate multiple translations; it was only in bringing those translations to bear on formal rights law that disparities were revealed.

Nyamnjoh (2004: 35) argues that "African societies, through widely shared (even if sometimes contested) ideas of personhood and belonging, could make a contribution towards enriching the current rhetoric of rights": I argue that, at least in terms of popular rhetorical uses, Zimbabweans are attempting to do so. Nonetheless, *formal* rights law as it stands does not (yet?) provide the room for such enrichment. There is thus a need for a social science (such as is presented by Nyamnjoh [2004] and is presented in this book) that accesses "marginalized 'ways of conceiving of human dignity and value'" (Nyamnjoh, ibid., citing Englund, 2000: 580–581)—as is seen in the uneven conversation between Zimbabwean notions of personhood and South African and international refugee law. In ways such as this we can work against the naturalization of the categories that underlie globally circulating discourses of human rights to show the power dynamics at play in their construction. This is necessary so that we might make clear the socially constructed nature of such laws and, in so doing, provide further impetus to enrich the rhetoric of rights.

The language of human rights, for all that it contains contradictions and exists within power-saturated fields, is prevalent within Southern Africa and looks to be here to stay—in trying to understand how political crises such as the one being experienced in Zimbabwe are unfolding, it is worth looking closely at what work is being done by words. The presence of rights discourses within the Zimbabwean crisis has provided a language of resistance, but this has not necessarily resulted in concrete material improvements in people's lives. In the absence of other modes of engagement, rights discourse seems like a good avenue through which to attempt to resolve Zimbabwe's political difficulties, but there is a danger that the international strength of the discourse means that other solutions or forms of justice run the risk of being disregarded. The arguments presented in this book have illustrated that the entanglements of the local and the global in formal and informal rights discourses can provide for sites of rich polyvalence and cultural ingenuity; they can also, however, be less benign.

Reference Matter

Notes

Introduction

1. Robert Mugabe is the president of Zimbabwe and of the political party the Zimbabwe African National Union–Patriotic Front (ZANU-PF). Thabo Mbeki was president of the African National Congress (ANC) and of South Africa at the time of the protest.

2. In Zimbabwean popular speech, the terms *rights* and *human rights* were often used interchangeably, with respondents (including those who work in legal fields) moving between the terms without reflection in daily talk. Legally and academically these two terms are of course distinct. Words as used by people from disparate social positions, then, may have different meanings even when the terms that are used are the same. I explore this further in Chapter 4.

3. Nyamnjoh (2004), Kanyongolo (2004), Johnson and Jacobs (2004), and Halsteen (2004), for example, consider the surfacing of the rhetoric of rights in Botswana, Malawi, South Africa, and Uganda, respectively.

4. Although legal definitions are obviously social constructs and do shift over time, they do so more slowly than popular rights talk and cannot simultaneously stand for a number of ideas as they do outside of courtrooms and statutes.

5. A list of acronyms used in this book is provided at the beginning.

6. Helliker (2013) divides academic understandings of civil society into two categories, the liberal and the radical, and argues that within postcolonial Africa "civil society" has largely been viewed as that which falls under the liberal paradigm. By this, he means forms of civil society that are often driven by international donor or aid money and manifest as nongovernmental organizations, or NGOs. These liberal forms of civil society are the ones that are most likely to promote a discourse of human rights and democratic governance. In Zimbabwe in the 1990s, it is true that such forms of civil society proliferated. But, as Helliker (2013) has argued, "civil society" in Zimbabwe has never been a coherent or homogenous entity, and the sorts of agendas or kinds of rights pushed for within civil society have never been homogenous either. Although the liberal manifestations of civil society pushed for democratic rights and the security of persons, more radical forms of civil society as seen through trade

unions and university students, for example, pushed for socioeconomic rights. The state, in turn, began in the 1990s to strongly promote ideas of "indigenization" (that can still be seen to be occurring in the present), particularly as manifested at that point in the fast track land reform program. Although the state promoted economic restitution in the 1990s through indigenization (and thus a particular form of socioeconomic rights), liberal civil society pushed ideals of rights-based democracy, and radical civil society pushed for socioeconomic and democratic rights. The varied elements of a diverse civil society came together in the late 1990s to push for constitutional reform, as discussed further in Chapter 2, but, although all were speaking in a language of rights, as was the state, they did not necessarily refer to the same thing. It could thus be argued that disputed notions of rights have been entwined in the Zimbabwean crisis since its beginnings in the 1990s.

7. In 1988 ZANU merged with ZAPU to form ZANU-PF.

8. The idea of structural violence stems from the work of Johan Galtung (1969) and refers to the social and economic forces or institutions that constrain or harm individuals by preventing them from meeting their basic needs. The term was popularized in anthropology by Paul Farmer in his 1996 examination of health care in Haiti, in which the poor have no access to basic services. In Zimbabwe, structural violence has its roots in colonial/Rhodesian social and economic structures, which limited the availability of basic services such as health care, education, and access to the economy to nonwhites and gave the black majority fewer rights than the white minority. In postcolonial Zimbabwe, structural violence against the poor has continued, and the rights of citizens have declined since the late 1990s (Harold-Barry, 2004).

9. These two factions are known as MDC-T (MDC-Tsvangirai) and MDC-M (MDC-Mutambara) after the respective leaders of each faction at the time of the split. MDC-M has subsequently, and confusingly, become known as MDC.

10. I use this phrase deliberately because, as is discussed in the following pages, the 2013 elections subsequently became viewed as even more flawed.

11. Where possible, I use *interlocutor* rather than *informant* to refer to research participants as the word better reflects the interactions and negotiations that occur during the research relationship, in which participants and anthropologist together construct particular kinds of knowledge. Devisch (cited in Olukoshi and Nyamnjoh, 2011: 16) refers to this relationship as ideally one of "mutually enriching co-implication." For further discussion, see Morreira 2012a.

12. Ideas of morality surfaced frequently throughout fieldwork.

13. Julia Elyachar's 2005 work in Cairo, for example, illustrates the ways in which neoliberal policies have driven transformations within the markets of Egypt. She argues that decisions made by bankers, social scientists, and economists—by, in other words, members of the knowledge economy—have a strong influence on the daily lives of microentrepreneurs and traders. Instead of, as the language of development suggests, "empowering" people, however, Elyachar argues that the poor are removed from the social systems of exchange that have protected them for generations and

instead become enmeshed in "empowerment debt" that binds them to NGOs and international organizations. Such are the lived effects of hierarchies of knowledge.

14. Appadurai (1996: 34) characterizes ideoscapes as "concatenations of images . . . they are often directly political and frequently have to do with the ideologies of state power or a piece of it. These ideoscapes are composed of elements of the Enlightenment worldview, which consists of a chain of ideas, terms and images, including *freedom, welfare, rights, sovereignty, representation*, and the master term *democracy.*"

15. David Lan's 1985 *Guns and Rain: Guerrillas and Spirit Mediums in Zimbabwe* provides a detailed ethnographic examination of these relationships during the liberation war.

16. This conceptualization of morality echoes Veena Das's (2010) argument that moral wakefulness occurs at the interstices of the human and the nonhuman.

17. Murambatsvina (literally "drive out the filth") was a campaign of violent forced removals conducted against (mainly) urban Zimbabweans following the 2005 elections. See Ncube, 2005; Vambe, 2008; and Morreira 2010a.

18. Using shorthand notions of "rights" outside the realm of the legal, however, does not involve the same process of translation as does using human rights within a legal framework. Merry (2005) has noted the difficulties of translating experiences of violation into legal language. Centrally, this hinges on the sorts of knowledge and evidence that are considered "truth." As Hastrup (2003) shows, there is a difficulty in translating subjective, and possibly unspeakable (see Ross, 2003a, 2003b; and Scarry, 1985), experiences into legal categories. See Chapter 4.

19. As I explore in Chapter 4, and as I have shown in my previous work (Morreira, 2009, 2010b), the South African state's categorization of Zimbabwean immigrants as economic migrants rather than as political refugees has been an area of contention. I am thus conscious that my terming my interlocutors *refugees* reflects my political positioning and am content for it to do so.

Chapter 1

1. Some months after writing this I read a description in (South African constitutional Court Judge) Albie Sachs's *The Strange Alchemy of Life and Law* of the disjunctures he experienced while studying at UCT in the apartheid era between "the beautiful abstraction of norms" (2011: 2) he heard from his professors and the "expressive eyes and mouths of desperately poor [black] people incandescent with determination to give all their energies, even their lives, for justice and freedom" (ibid.). Democracy brought some changes to this dissonance between South African worlds (though poverty remained), but for immigrants to South Africa the disjunctures seem not dissimilar to those encountered in the present. In some ways, then, the figure of the immigrant in present-day South Africa echoes the figure of the black man or woman in apartheid South Africa, with papers instead of pass laws and international borders instead of Bantustans.

2. As was explored in Chapter 1, when referring to rights practice or rights praxis I invoke the realm of both talk *and* other forms of behavioral action; when a distinction

between talking about rights and enacting those rights has been necessary, I refer to "rights talk" and "the performance of rights," respectively. In keeping with a Foucauldian view of discourse (Foucault, 1972; Hall, 2001b), then, I assume that discourses of rights consist of both talk and enactment.

3. The slogan "bread and roses" is historically linked to the labor movement; drawn from a poem by James Oppenheim that was used during a textile strike in Massachusetts in 1912, it has subsequently been used all over the world to call for both fair wages ("bread") and decent working conditions ("roses") (Watson, 2005).

4. The policy was spearheaded by Mbeki and resulted in the South African state according legitimacy on a number of occasions to increasingly undemocratic electoral processes in Zimbabwe (see Bond, 2005). For reasons such as this, international commentators called Mbeki's actions "unconscionable" (*The Economist*, April 17, 2008), whereas political opponents in the Democratic Alliance questioned Mbeki's "curious silence" (Peta, 2007) on the Zimbabwean issue, and local commentators positioned Mbeki's stance on Zimbabwe as the "low moral ground" and as his "moral blindspot" (*Cape Business News*, 2005). Interestingly, many participants in my research also viewed South Africa's stance on Zimbabwe as a *moral* (as well as political) issue.

5. And even then, much of the deal happened on the party's own terms; see Matyszak and Reeler, 2011.

6. As elsewhere, names are changed. I have called this interlocutor Tarisai as it translates from Shona as "here it is," "look at this," or "everybody see this," and Tarisai was determined, at considerable emotional cost to herself, to expose the use of rape as a political weapon in Zimbabwe.

7. I have also briefly pointed to a third key trope of rights discourses, that of dignity, but return to this in Chapter 4.

8. Mugabe's rhetoric has positioned Zimbabwe against what he broadly characterizes as "the West"—as exemplified by Britain, America, and any other nation-state that has criticized his political stance and the happenings in Zimbabwe. In using this term, then, I am not assuming that there necessarily is any such monolith as "the West" but am rather invoking the rhetoric of the Zimbabwean state.

9. Even at the time, before the outcome of the 2013 elections, it was clear that whether Zimbabwe could be said to be in transition was debatable, as was what it might be transitioning toward. Academic voices throughout Murithi and Mawadza's 2011 edited volume *Zimbabwe in Transition: A View from Within*, for example, were divided as to what transition might even mean in the context of Zimbabwe, let alone whether it was happening.

10. Protected by Article 20(1) of the UDHR and Article 22 of the ICCPR.

11. Article 18 of the UDHR and Article 18 of the ICCPR.

12. Article 20(1) of the UDHR and Article 21 of the ICCPR.

13. Article 19 of the UDHR and Article 19 of the ICCPR.

14. In the case of this particular arrest, ZLHR were able to successfully use the Lancaster House Constitution to argue against the charges of "intentionally engaging in a disorderly or riotous conduct as defined in section 41(a) of the Criminal Law

Codification and Reform Act" by arguing the activists' arrest infringed on their right to freedom of expression and freedom of assembly.

15. I return to a consideration of the different emphasis accorded to political and socioeconomic rights in Chapter 4, where I examine the notions of violation at work in Zimbabwean applications for refugee status.

16. I use autochthony ("of the soil") deliberately here in that ZANU-PF rhetoric has, in the last fifteen years, made use of an imagined relationship to land as a political and rhetorical tool. Seen most strongly during the land invasions, where rhetoric went hand in hand with violent action, calls on land as a marker of belonging and identity have surfaced frequently since. Geschiere (2009) has argued that moments of economic and political change and uncertainty influenced the similar invocations of a primordial autochthony that have occurred in the otherwise very different contexts of Cameroon and the Netherlands. As such, he categorizes autochthony as the flip side of globalization.

17. Here he was referencing a statement attributed to both Mugabe and to Jonathan Moyo (one of the core architects of POSA) during the latter's tenure as minister of information.

Chapter 2

1. Although interlocutors characterized the culture of impunity here as a feature of the present moment, similar conversations around impunity and the failures of justice in Zimbabwe occurred in the 1980s and 1990s—see Bhebhe and Ranger, 1995; Reeler, 1998; and Werbner, 1998.

2. See, for example, Speed and Collier (2000); Speed (2002); Cowan et al., 2006; Merry (2006); and Inda and Rosaldo (2008).

3. This is particularly the case in discourses of transitional justice.

4. The legal system consists of the Legislature, with legislative authority vested in the president and in a bicameral Parliament, case law and precedent, and customary law and common law. The justice system is comprised of the Supreme Court, the High Court, the Administrative Court, and the Magistrates' Courts; and the Office of the Attorney General and public prosecutors. The judiciary consists of the chief justice, judges of the Supreme Court, and judges of the High Court. At the level of law enforcement, the Zimbabwe Republic Police (ZRP), headed by a commissioner, is provided for under Article 93 of the (Lancaster House) Constitution for the purposes of internal security and the maintenance of law and order (see Human Rights Watch, 2008; Saki et al., 2011).

5. Gluck and Tsing (2009: 1) characterize such circulating global terms as "words in motion."

6. Mbuya Nehanda (literally, Grandmother Nehanda) or Nehanda Charwe Nyakasikana (1840–1898) is an iconic figure of the struggle against colonialism. A spirit medium, she channeled the ancestral spirit/*mhondoro* Nehanda and inspired rebellion against the British colonists. She was hanged by the British in 1898.

7. Though I categorize these reasons as economic here for reasons of expediency, their underlying cause can be said to be political, in that hyperinflation and economic collapse was the result of political decision making on the part of ZANU-PF; see Chapter 4.

8. Mugabe's version of national reconciliation as displayed here is a modernist one, from which the "traditional" means of reconciliation are excluded. It is for reasons such as this that Mugabe's refusal to visit rain shrines to conduct cleansing ceremonies for the land and the people in the wake of the liberation war was criticized by spiritual leaders (see Lan, 1985).

9. As Anderson (1983) has noted, nations are imagined communities, whereas Chatterjee (1983) has explored the gendering of such imagined nations. The masculine bias in the preceding quotation shows a clear gendering of the nationalist discourse in Zimbabwe.

10. This shows a particular geographical positioning vis-à-vis the past—in Matabeleland, postindependence politics unfolded slightly differently, in that ZANU, not the Ndebele-supported ZAPU, came to power. Although ZAPU politician Joshua Nkomo was made deputy president in the 1980s, there was little acknowledgment beyond this of the role Matabeleland played in liberation.

11. Nor has the process of citizenship been as simple as it is presented in this speech, and many Zimbabweans (those of white descent, Mozambican descent, or Ndebele descent, for example) do not feel they bear the same "national interest, loyalty, rights, and duties," as do others.

12. A somewhat disturbing moniker in light of the masculinization of Zimbabwean political discourse.

13. The idea of "transition" within transitional justice discourse invokes a linear temporality based on an assumed progression from one particular form to another; in the case of transitional justice discourse, the ideal political form that nation-states should transition *to* is that of democracy, with attendant moral adherence to international human rights standards. The small word *transition* is thus freighted with a great many assumptions.

14. The Research and Advocacy Unit is directed and staffed by Zimbabweans.

15. Formed in 2002, the ZANU-PF youth militia undergo training at camps across the country before being deployed and are notorious for inflicting violence on local populations (Mashingaidze, 2010).

16. Epworth's status as a Methodist Mission under the British and Rhodesian dispensations partially protected its inhabitants from the violence of the colonial state.

17. *Falanga* is a form of torture in which the soles of the feet are beaten. It has been used extensively in Zimbabwe.

18. It was while I was writing up my fieldnotes in Epworth that I realized that I, like my interlocutors, was using *elections* as shorthand for political violence. This raises an interesting ambiguity: *Elections* refers to both the possibilities of democracy and to the fierce opposition to that.

19. Similar processes have emerged in other contexts: Kayser (2005) has examined one such in post-TRC South Africa, Forcier (2010) presents an ethnographic study of a similar process in Rwanda, and Curling (2005) has examined a Namibian workshop from the point of view of clinical psychology. The model studied by Forcier was strongly influenced by Healing of the Memories (HoM) workshops run in South Africa and studied by Kayser. HoM was a civil society response to the TRC, and its premises have become part of the process of vernacularizing transitional justice paradigms.

20. The binary of "victim" and "perpetrator," which stems from rights discourse and the terminology associated with clinical psychology, was recognized as too simplistic by many of the Zimbabweans with whom I worked; despite this, however, it was frequently invoked.

21. Kinship groupings at the level of clan share totems: Members of the same totem are assumed to be descended from a common ancestor.

22. In 2009, the Tree of Life carried out research into the effectiveness of the method using pre- and postpsychiatric screening measuring depression and anxiety and a self-reported response on the effectiveness of the workshop. The study, although small, found that 36 percent of the sample showed clinical improvement, and 56 percent reported coping better (Reeler et al., 2009).

23. Cf. the RAU workshops as previously described, where legal accountability was also emphasized.

24. There is also an emphasis on extending that healing from individuals to families and from families to communities. Transitional justice models also link narration and ideas of social healing, but in this model it is occurring on a smaller scale, in face-to-face settings aimed at restoring relationships on a more intimate scale than that afforded by nationwide truth commissions.

25. Although the intimate entanglement of ideas at play in the Tree of Life example is not one of resistance and unease, this is not always the case. I return to Nuttall's stance on uneasy entanglements in Chapter 4 in considering the (mis)translations of violations that occur in Zimbabwean asylum seeking cases.

26. This quotation is taken from a second article about *ngozi* that followed a week later and was written by Tirivangana himself (Tirivangana, 2010).

Chapter 3

1. He conceptualizes it as a "dilemma" because people must mediate between the dangers and opportunities of such potentially hegemonic yet also potentially liberatory discourses, whereas the social theorist must further mediate between academic critiques of such discourses and the enthusiasm with which they may be embraced by interlocutors.

2. Women of Zimbabwe Arise and the Women's Coalition of Zimbabwe, respectively.

3. I discuss the construction of such terms as *monitor* within rights discourse in the following discussion.

4. Tarisai was introduced in Chapter 1: Employed by a rights advocacy organization, she is a Shona woman with a law degree and a fierce moral compass concerning the rights of Zimbabwean women.

5. Note the use of language here: "Women's human rights violations" is intended to mean violations against women, as can be seen from the emphasis later in the paragraph; the phrasing, however, is ambiguous and could be read as violations enacted *by* women. The fact that the authors do not feel the ambiguity worth correcting or clarifying reflects the emphasis within the discourse on women as victim.

6. I am indebted to Fiona Ross for her insightful commentary around this issue.

7. Although I attended the focus groups, I was not involved in the report writing.

8. Any act by which severe pain or suffering, whether physical or mental, is intentionally inflicted on a person for such purposes as obtaining from him or a third person information or a confession, punishing him for an act he or a third person has committed or is suspected of having committed, or intimidating or coercing him or a third person, or for any reason based on discrimination of any kind, when such pain or suffering is inflicted by or at the instigation of or with the consent or acquiescence of a public official or other person acting in an official capacity. (UN Convention against Torture, 1984: Article 1)

9. The statistical data collected by rights group thus carried relevance for the women, even without the inclusion of more qualitative data: Such numerical data do carry weight.

10. A blog, a word shortened from *weblog*, is an often personal online journal with entries intended for public consumption.

Chapter 4

Excerpts of an earlier version of this chapter have been published previously in the *Anthropology Matters* online journal (Morreira, 2011). The material presented here has been substantially revised.

1. Such persons may be illegally resident in the country or may be temporarily legally resident and seeking more permanent legal status: asylum-seeking papers, for example, although giving a person legal status in the country, have a time limit.

2. The temporary Zimbabwean Dispensation Project (ZDP) aimed to regularize undocumented Zimbabwean migrancy to South Africa by allowing Zimbabweans to apply for Special Dispensation Permits to work in South Africa. To apply for a ZDP permit, one needed a passport and a letter from an employer; this cut off the option from many migrants. Permits were issued for a maximum of four years, and a ZDP permit holder would be considered an economic migrant and had to give up asylum-seeking papers they might hold (PASSOP, 2011). Refugee status, on the other hand, is based on political asylum status (see the following discussion) and can be indefinitely renewed for as long as the situation in the home country is deemed by the South African state to endanger the holder of such status.

3. The number of Refugee Reception Offices in South Africa has been steadily lessening as the state attempts to centralize the process. When I began research, there were offices in Musina, Durban, Cape Town, Port Elizabeth, and Pretoria; this has

now shrunk to Pretoria, Musina, and Durban, despite court orders to reopen the offices in Port Elizabeth and Cape Town (Chennells, 2012).

4. Hammar and Raftopoulos, 2003; Hough and Du Plessis, 2004; Kamete, 2008; Taundi, 2009; Sachikonye, 2011.

5. I will return to the importance of being able to go home occasionally when discussing how interlocutors translated local notions of personhood and dignity into a language of human rights.

6. Throughout this book, when referring to rights practice or rights praxis I invoke the broad realm of both talk and other forms of behavioral action; when a distinction between talking about rights and enacting those rights has been necessary, I refer to "rights talk" and "the performance of rights" respectively. Both talk and performance form part of the discourses of rights.

7. Though Betts (2010) would see those categories expanded as the regime is stretched, his formulation still relies on this framework of using categories legible to the state—though the discourse may stretch, its terms do not change entirely.

8. *Sadza* refers to maize meal, a Zimbabwean (and Southern African, though under other names) staple. During hyperinflation food was often unavailable for purchase even if money was available, and many Zimbabweans were reliant on such food as they could grow (see Morreira, 2009, Chapter 3, for an analysis of an urban household's survival techniques in 2007).

9. Engelke (1999), in a discussion of rights and homosexuality in Zimbabwe, notes that ideas of human rights at play in Zimbabwe in the late 1990s also drew on ideas of the rights of the social person. Interestingly, Engelke shows how, in the context of homosexuality, the importance of social relationships as the bedrock of a shared humanity was used as an argument *against* basic rights in 1990s Zimbabwe: Homosexuals, in the arguments presented by the state, did not fulfill their familial obligations as they did not have "proper" marriage or relationships, and as such homosexuality should not be legal. Once again, the situationality of rights talk is apparent.

10. Nyamnjoh (2004) has noted similar contradictions at work in Botswana, which—despite the coexistence of "what may be termed its impressive record at institutionalizing liberal democracy" (2004: 36) *and* of a communal rather than individual concept of personhood—continues to draw more closely on the global, individualized notion of rights rather than expanding its rights framework to include local ideas.

Conclusion

1. Such as where, for example, human rights are conceptualized as inalienable and inherent; here, the role of the state in realizing rights is obfuscated.

2. I would amend this conceptualization to the plural: There is no single all-encompassing historical power configuration at play in postcolonial Zimbabwe and postapartheid South Africa but rather interacting sets of power configurations and conjunctures.

Bibliography

Abu-Lughod, Lila. 2010. "Against Universals: The Dialectics of (Women's) Human Rights and Human Capabilities," pp 69–94 in M. Molina and D. Swearer, eds., *Rethinking the Human*. Cambridge, MA: Harvard University Press.

Africa Community Publishing and Development Trust. 2009. *A People's Guide to Constitutional Debate*. Harare: Africa Community Publishing and Development Trust.

Africa Community Publishing and Development Trust. 2014. "About Us." Retrieved in January 2014 from www.acpdt.org.

Africa Community Publishing and Development Trust and Zimbabwe Human Rights NGO Forum. 2009b. *A People's Guide to Transitional Justice: An Introduction*. Harare: Africa Community Publishing and Development Trust.

Akokpari, John, and Daniel Shea Zimbler, eds. 2008. *Africa's Human Rights Architecture*. Johannesburg: Centre for Conflict Resolution and Jacana.

Anderson, Benedict. 1983. *Imagined Communities: Reflections on the Origin and Spread of Nationalism*. London: Verso.

Anzaldúa, Gloria. 1999. *Borderlands/La Frontera: The New Mestiza* (2nd edition). San Francisco: Aunt Lute Press.

Appadurai, Arjun, ed. 1986. *The Social Life of Things: Commodities in Cultural Perspective*. Cambridge, UK: Cambridge University Press.

———. 1996. "Disjuncture and Difference in the Global Cultural Economy," pp. 27–47 in *Modernity at Large: Cultural Dimensions of Globalization*. Minneapolis: University of Minnesota Press.

Bakhtin, Mikhael. 1981. *The Dialogical Imagination*, C. Emerson and M. Holquist, trans. Austin: University of Texas Press.

———. 1984. *Problems of Dostoevsky's Poetics*. Caryl Emerson, ed. and trans. Minneapolis: University of Minnesota Press.

BBC News. November 19, 1999. "Zimbabwe Constitution: Just a Bit of Paper?" Retrieved on October 1, 2011, from http://news.bbc.co.uk/2/hi/africa/528137.stm.

——. September 18, 2008. "Deal a Humiliation, says Mugabe." Retrieved on September 30, 2011, from http://news.bbc.co.uk/2/hi/africa/7622495.stm.

Betts, Alexander. 2010. "Survival Migration: A New Protection Framework." *Global Governance: A Review of Multilateralism and International Organizations* 16(3): 361–382.

Betts, Alexander, and Esra Kaytaz. 2009. "National and International Responses to the Zimbabwean Exodus: Implications for the Refugee Protection Regime," in *New Issues in Refugee Research: Research Paper No. 175*. Geneva: UN High Commission for Refugees (UNHCR) Policy Development and Evaluation Service.

Bhabha, Homi. 1992. "Double Visions." *Art Forum* 88.

——. 1994. *The Location of Culture.* New York: Routledge.

Bhebhe, Ngwabi, and Terence Ranger, eds. 1995. *Soldiers in Zimbabwe's Liberation War*, Vol. 1. Oxford, UK: James Currey.

——. 2001. *The Historical Dimensions of Democracy and Human Rights in Zimbabwe. Volume One: Precolonial and Colonial Legacies.* Harare: University of Zimbabwe Publications.

Bloch, Alice. 2008. "Gaps in Protection: Undocumented Zimbabwean Migrants in South Africa." Migration Studies Working Paper Series No. 38, Forced Migration Studies Program, University of the Witwatersrand. Available online at http://cormsa.org.za/wp-content/uploads/Research/SADC/38_BlochZim.pdf.

Bond, Patrick. May 23, 2005. "Anti-(sub) imperial solidarity: The Case of SA-Zimbabwe." *ZNet Daily Commentaries.* Retrieved in June 2008 from www.zcommunications.org/anti-sub-imperial-solidarity-the-case-of-sa-zimbabwe-by-patrick-bond.

Bourdieu, Pierre. 1986. "The Forms of Capital," pp. 241–258 in J. Richardson, ed., *Handbook of Theory and Research for the Sociology of Education.* New York: Greenwood.

——. 1992. *The Logic of Practice*, trans. R. Nice. Stanford, CA: Stanford University Press.

Bourdillon, Michael. 1987. *The Shona Peoples* (3rd edition). Gweru: Mambo Press.

Bourgois, Phillipe. 2006. "Foreword," pp. ix–xii in *Engaged Observer: Anthropology, Advocacy and Activism.* Victoria Sanford and Asale Angel-Ajani, Asale. New Brunswick, NJ: Rutgers University Press.

Cape Business News. July 2005. "Pres Mbeki's Moral Low Ground." Retrieved on September 30, 2011, from www.cbn.co.za/viewg.php?id=1433.

CCJP (Catholic Commission for Justice and Peace in Zimbabwe). 1997. *Breaking the Silence: Report on the 1980s Atrocities in Matabeleland and the Midlands.* Zimbabwe: CCJP.

Channock, Martin. 1985. *Law, Custom and Social Order: The Colonial Experience in Malawi and Zambia.* New York: Cambridge University Press.

Chatterjee, Partha. 1983. *The Nationalist Resolution of the Women's Question*. Calcutta: Centre for Studies in Social Science.

Chennells, Rebecca. 2012. "High Court Order the Department of Home Affairs to Abide by Interim Order to Accept New Asylum Seekers at the Cape Town Refugee Office." Retrieved in January 2013 from www.cormsa.org.za/2012/09/06/high-court-orders-the-department-of-home-affairs-to-abide-by-interim-order-to-accept-new-asylum-seekers-at-the-cape-town-refugee-office/.

Chimuka, Tarisayi. 2001. "Ethics among the Shona." *Zambesia*, 28(i): 23–37.

Clarke, Kamani. 2007 "Global Justice, Local Controversies: The International Criminal Court and the sovereignty of victims." In M.-B. Dembour and T. Kelly, eds., *Paths to International Justice: Social and Legal Perspectives*. Cambridge, UK: Cambridge University Press.

Clifford, James. 1988. *The Predicament Of Culture: Twentieth-Century Ethnography, Literature, and Art*. Cambridge, MA: Harvard University Press.

Cole, Jennifer. 2001. *Forget Colonialism? Sacrifice and the Art of Forgetting in Madagascar*. Berkeley and Los Angeles: University of California Press.

Comaroff, John, and Jean Comaroff. 2001. "On Personhood: An Anthropological Perspective from Africa." *Social Identities* 7(2): 267–283.

———. 2004. "Criminal Justice, Cultural Justice: The Limits of Liberalism and the Pragmatics of Difference in the New South Africa." *American Ethnologist* 31(2): 188–204.

———. 2007. "Law and Disorder in the Postcolony." *Social Anthropology* 15(2): 133–152.

Conklin, Beth, and Lynn Morgan. 1996. "Babies, Bodies, and the Production of Personhood in North America and a Native Amazonian Society." *Ethos*, 24(4): 657–694.

CORMSA (Consortium for Refugees in South Africa). 2012. "How to Apply for Asylum in South Africa." Retrieved in October 2012 from www.cormsa.org.za/applying-for-refugee-status-in-south-africa/#4.

Cornell, Drucilla, and Muvangua, Nyoka. 2012. *Ubuntu and the Law: African Ideals and Postapartheid Jurisprudence*. Bronx, NY: Fordham University Press.

Cowan, Jane. 2006. "Culture and Rights after *Culture and Rights*." *American Anthropologist* 108(1): 9–24.

Cowan, Jane, Marie-Benedicte Dembour, and Richard A. Wilson, Richard A., eds. 2001. *Culture and Rights: Anthropological Perspectives*. Cambridge, UK: Cambridge University Press.

Crisis in Zimbabwe Coalition. May 18, 2011. "Zimbabwe Briefing." Harare.

———. December 10, 2012. "Government Has Responsibility to Create Jobs: DPM Khupe." Retrieved in December 2012 from www.crisiszimbabwe.org/index

.php?option=com_content&view=article&id=1684:govt-has-responsibility-to-create-jobs--dpm-khupe&catid=47:news.

Curling, Penelope. 2005. "The Effectiveness of Empowerment Workshops with Torture Survivors.' *Torture* 15(1): 9–15.

Das, Veena. 2010. "The Life of Humans and the Life of Roaming Spirits," pp. 31–49 in Michelle Moline and Donald Swearer, eds., *Rethinking the Human.* Cambridge, MA: Harvard University Press.

Deng, Francis. 2005. "Chapter 41: Human Rights in the African Context." In Kwasi Wiredu, ed., *A Companion to African Philosophy.* Malden, MA: Blackwell.

Dube, Jennipher. 2011. "Chokuda Case: Avenging Spirits Exact Justice?" *The Standard,* October 30. Retrieved on October 30, 2011, from www.thestandard.co .zw/2011/10/30/chokuda-case-avenging-spirits-exact-justice.

Dudai, Ron. 2009. "'Can You Describe This?' Human Rights Reports and What They Tell Us about the Human Rights movement," in R. Wilson and R. Brown, eds., *Humanitarianism and Suffering: The Mobilisation of Empathy.* Cambridge, UK: Cambridge University Press.

Dzinesa, Gwinyayi. 2012. "Zimbabwe's Constitutional Reform Process: Challenges and Prospects." Cape Town: Institute for Justice and Reconcilisation. Available online at www.ijr.org.za/publications/pdfs/IJR%20Zimbabwe%20Constitutional %20Reform%20OP%20WEB.pdf.

The Economist. April 17, 2008. "Zimbabwe: Africa's Shame. South African President Has Prolonged Zimbabwe's Agony." Retrieved on September 10, 2011, from www.economist.com/node/11052889.

Electoral Institute for the Sustainability of Democracy in Africa (EISA). *EISA Zimbabwe: Election Archive.* Retrieved in June 2012 from www.eisa.org.za/WEP/ zimelectarchive.htm.

Elphick, Rosalind, and Ronnie Amit. 2012. "Border Justice. Migration, Access to Justice and the Experiences of Unaccompanied Minors and Survivors of Sexual and Gender-Based Violence in Musina." Johannesburg: African Centre for Migration and Society Research Retrieved in December 2012 from www.migration .org.za/sites/default/files/border_justice_migration_access_to_justice_and_ the_experience_of_unaccompanied_minors_and_sgbv.pdf.

Elyachar, Julia. 2005. *Markets of Dispossession: NGOs, Economic Development and the State in Cairo.* Durham, NC: Duke University Press.

Engelke, Matthew. 1999. "'We Wondered What Human Rights He Was Talking About': Human Rights, Homosexuality and the Zimbabwe International Book Fair." *Critique of Anthropology* 19(3): 289–314.

Englund, Harri. 2000. "The Dead Hand of Human Rights: Contrasting Christianities in Post-Transition Malawi." *The Journal of Modern African Studies* 38(4): 579–603.

———. 2004. "Introduction: Recognising Identities, Imagining Alternatives," in Francis Nyamnjoh and Harri Englund, eds., *Rights and the Politics of Recognition in Africa*. London: Zed Books.

———. 2006. *Prisoners of Freedom: Human Rights and the African Poor*. Berkeley and London: University of California Press.

Englund, Harri, and Nyamnjoh, Francis, eds. 2004. *Rights and the Politics of Recognition in Africa*. London: Zed Books.

Eriksen, Thomas Hyland. 1997. "Multiculturalism, Individualism and Human Rights," in Richard Wilson, ed., *Human Rights, Culture and Context*. London: Pluto.

Escobar, Arturo. 1997 [1995]. "The Making and the Unmaking of the Third World through Development," pp. 85–93 in M. Rahnema and V. Bawtree, eds., *The Post-Development Reader*. Cape Town: David Philip.

Essof, Shereen. 2005. "She-Murenga: Challenges, Opportunities and Setbacks of the Women's Movement in Zimbabwe." *Feminist Africa* 4: 29–45.

———. 2006. *Zimbabwean Women in Movement*. Durban: Centre for Civil Society, University of KwaZulu Natal.

Farmer, Paul. 1996. "On Suffering and Structural Violence: A View from Below." *Issues on Social Suffering—Journal of American Academy of Arts and Sciences* 125 (1): 261–276.

Feltoe, Geoffrey. 2003. *Repression Camouflaged as Law in Zimbabwe*. Paper produced for "Civil Society and Justice in Zimbabwe" Symposium, Johannesburg, South Africa, August 2003.

———. 2004. "The Onslaught against Democracy and the Rule of Law in Zimbabwe in 2000." In David Harold- Barry, ed., *Zimbabwe: The Past Is the Future*. Harare: Weaver Press.

Ferguson , James. 1990. *The Anti-Politics Machine: "Development," Depoliticisation and Bureaucratic Power in Lesotho*. Cambridge, UK: Cambridge University Press.

Figlan, Lindela. 2012. "The politics of human dignity." Reproduced in *Pambazuka News*, 606. Available online at http://pambazuka.org/en/category/features/85441.

FMSP (Forced Migration Studies Program). 2009a "National Survey of the Refugee Reception and Status Determination System in South Africa." Johannesburg: FMSP, University of Witwatersrand. Retrieved in April 2010 from cormsa.org .za/wp-content/uploads/Research/Asylum/FMSPMRMPRefugeeReception Report.pdf.

———. 2009b. "Zimbabwean Migration into South Africa: New Trends and Responses." Johannesburg: FMSP, University of Witwatersrand.

———. 2010. "Population Movements in and to South Africa." *Migration Fact Sheet 1.* Johannesburg: FMSP, University of Witwatersrand.

Forcier, Angela. 2010. *"If You Keep Your Problems in Your Stomach the Dogs Cannot Steal Them." Trauma, Forgiveness and Conviviality in Rwanda: An Ethnographic Study Following the Healing and Rebuilding Our Communities (HROC) Project in Gisenyi, Rwanda.* Unpublished Master's Dissertation, Department of Social Anthropology, University of Cape Town.

Foucault, Michel. 1970. *The Order of Discourse.* Inaugural Lecture at the College de France, given December 2, 1970. Reproduced in Robert Young,. 1981. *Untying the Text: A Post-Structuralist Reader.* Boston: Routledge and Kegan Paul.

———. 1972. *The Archaeology of Knowledge.* London: Tavistock.

———. 1977. *Language, Counter-Memory, Practice: Selected Essays and Interviews.* Ithaca, NY: Cornell University Press.

———. 1991. "Governmentality," In G. Burchell, C. Gordon, and P. Miller, eds., *The Foucault Effect: Studies in Governmentality.* London: Harvester Wheatsheaf.

Galtung, Johan. 1969. "Violence, Peace and Peace Research." *Journal of Peace Research* 6(3): 167–191.

Gaonkar, Dilip Parameshwar, ed. 2001. *Alternative Modernities.* Durham, NC: Duke University Press.

Geertz, Clifford. 1983. *Local Knowledge: Further Essays in Interpretive Anthropology.* New York: Basic Books.

Gelfand, Michael. 1970. "Unhu: The Personality of the Shona." *Studies in Comparative Religion* 4(1); available online at www.studiesincomparativereligion.com/ Public/articles/UNHU%E2%80%94The_Personality_of_the_Shona.aspx.

Geschiere, Peter. 2009. *The Perils of Belonging: Autochthony, Citizenship and Exclusion in Africa and Europe.* Chicago: University of Chicago Press.

Gluck, Carol. 2009. "Introduction: Words in Motion," in Carol Gluck and Anna Lowenhaupt Tsing, eds., *Words in Motion: Toward a Global Lexicon.* Durham, NC, and London: Duke University Press.

Gluck, Carol, and Anna Lowenhaupt Tsing, eds. 2009. *Words in Motion: Toward a Global Lexicon.* Durham, NC, and London: Duke University Press.

Goodale, Mark. 2002. "Legal Ethnography in an Era of Globalization: The Arrival of Western Human Rights Discourse to Rural Bolivia," pp. 50–71 in Mark Goodale and June Starr, *Practicing Ethnography in Law: New Dialogues, Enduring Methods.* New York: Palgrave Macmillan.

———. 2006a. "Introduction to Anthropology and Human Rights in a New Key." *American Anthropologist* 108(1): 1–8.

———. 2006b. "Toward a Critical Anthropology of Human Rights." *Current Anthropology* 47 (3): 485–511.

———. 2009a. *Dilemmas of Modernity: Bolivian Encounters with Law and Liberalism.* Stanford, CA: Stanford University Press.

———. 2009b. *Surrendering to Utopia: An Anthropology of Human Rights.* Stanford, CA: Stanford University Press.

Goodale, Mark, and June Starr, eds. 2002. *Practising Ethnography in Law: New Dialogues, Enduring Methods.* New York: Palgrave Macmillan.

Gready, Paul. 2011. *The Era of Transitional Justice: The Aftermath of the Truth and Reconciliation Commission in South Africa and Beyond.* Oxford, UK: Routledge.

Guma, Lance. August 30, 2010. "Problems in Masvingo as Outreach Meetings Abandoned." SW Radio Africa News. Retrieved on October 5, 2010, from www .swradioafrica.com/news300810/problems300810.htm.

Guyer, Jane, Naveeda Khan, Juan Obarrio, Caroline Bledsoe, Julie Chu, Souleymane Bachir Diagne, Keith Hart, Paul Kockelman, Jean Lave, Caroline McLoughlin, Bill Maurer, Federico Neiburg, Diane Nelson, Charles Stafford, and Helen Verran. 2010 "Introduction: Number as an Inventive Frontier." *Anthropological Theory* 10(1–2): 36–61.

Haas, Michael. 2008. *International Human Rights: A Comprehensive Introduction.* London: Routledge.

Hafner-Burton, Emilie, and Kiyoteru Tsutsui. 2005. "Human Rights in a Globalizing World: The Paradox of Empty Promises." *American Journal of Sociology* 110(5): 1373–1411.

Hall, Stuart. 2001a. "Chapter 10: Conclusion: The Multi-Cultural Question," in B. Hesse, ed., *Un/Settled Multiculturalisms: Diasporas, Entanglements,'Transruptions.'* New York and London: Zed Books.

———. 2001b. "Foucault: Power, Knowledge, and Discourse," In M. Wetherall, S. Taylor, and S. Yates, eds., *Discourse Theory and Practice: A Reader.* London and New Delhi: Sage.

Halsteen, Ulrik. 2004. "Taking Rights Talk Seriously: Reflections on Ugandan Political Discourse," Chapter 4 in *Rights and the Politics of Recognition in Africa*, Harri Englund and Francis Nyamnjoh, eds. London: Zed Books.

Hammar, Amanda, and Brian Raftopoulos. 2003. *Zimbabwe's Unfinished Business: Rethinking Land, State and Nation in the Context of Crisis.* Harare: Weaver Press.

Hanke, Steve. December 22, 2008. "The Printing Press." *Forbes Magazine.* Retrieved in January 2009 from www.forbes.com/forbes/2008/1222/106.html.

Hannerz, Ulf. 1998. "Transnational Research." In H. Russell Bernard, ed., *Handbook of Methods in Anthropology.* Walnut Creek, CA: Altamira Press.

Harold-Barry, David, ed. 2004. *Zimbabwe: The Past Is the Future.* Harare: Weaver Press.

Hassim, Shireen, Tawana Kupe, and Eric Worby. 2008. *Go Home or Die Here: Violence, Xenophobia and the Reinvention of Difference in South Africa*. Johannesburg: Wits University Press.

Hastrup, Kirsten. 1993. "Hunger and the Hardness of Facts." *Man* 28: 727–739.

———. 2001. "Representing the Common Good: The Limits of Legal Language," in Jon Mitchell, ed., *Human Rights in Global Perspective: Anthropological Studies of Rights, Claims and Entitlements*. London and New York: Routledge.

———. 2003. "Violence, Suffering and Human Rights: An Anthropological Perspective." *Anthropological Theory* 3(3): 309–323.

Helliker, Kirk. 2013. "Civil Society and State Centred Struggles," in David Moore, Norma Kriger, and Brian Raftopoulos, eds., *Progress in Zimbabwe: The Past and Present of a Concept and a Country*. London: Routledge.

Hough, Michael, and Anton Du Plessis, eds. 2004. *State Failure: The Case of Zimbabwe*. Pretoria: University of Pretoria, Institute for Strategic Studies.

Howell, Signe (ed.). 1997. *The Ethnography of Moralities*. London: Routledge.

Human Rights Watch, 2006. "'You Will Be Thoroughly Beaten': The Brutal Suppression of Dissent in Zimbabwe." *Human Rights Watch*, 18 (10A).

———. 2008. *"Our Hands Are Tied": Erosion of the Rule of Law in Zimbabwe*. New York: Human Rights Watch.

Ignatieff, Michael. 1996. "Articles of Faith." *Index on Censorship* 5: 110–122.

Iliff, Andrew. 2012. "The Coming Elections in Zimbabwe: Hysterical Headlines and Happy Losers." The Social Science Research Council (SSRC). Retrieved in July 2012 from www.possible-futures.org/2012/06/15/coming-elections-zimbabwe-hysterical-headlines-happy-losers/.

Inda, Jonathan, and Renato Rosaldo. 2002. "Introduction: A World in Motion," in Jonathan Inda and Renato Rosaldo, eds., *The Anthropology of Globalization: A Reader*. Melrose, MA, and Oxford, UK: Blackwell.

———. 2008. "Chapter 1: Tracking Global Flows," pp. 3–46 in Jonathan Inda and Renato Rosaldo, eds., *The Anthropology of Globalization: A Reader* (2nd edition). Melrose, MA, and Oxford, UK: Blackwell Publishing.

Institute for Democracy in South Africa (IDASA). 2012. "Home." Retrieved on January 30, 2012, from www.idasa.org.

International Centre for Transitional Justice (ICTJ). 2012. "About Us." Retrieved on January 30, 2012, from www.ictj.org/about.

International Crisis Group. 2008. "Zimbabwe: Prospects from a Flawed Election." *Africa Report* 138 (March 20).

Jackson, Michael. 2005. "Storytelling Events, Violence, and the Appearance of the Past." *Anthropological Quarterly* 78(2): 355–375.

Johnson, Krista, and Sean Jacobs. 2004. "Democratisation and the Rhetoric of Rights: Contradictions and Debate in Post-Apartheid South Africa," Chapter 3 in

H. Englund and F. Nyamnjoh, eds. *Rights and the Politics of Recognition in Africa*. London: Zed Books.

Jones, Pip, Shaun Le Boutillier, and Liz Bradbury. 2011. *Introducing Social Theory* (2nd edition). Cambridge, UK: Polity Press.

Kamete, Amin. 2008. "Planning versus Youth: Stamping out Spatial Unruliness in Harare." *Geoforum* 39: 1721–1733.

Kanyongolo, Fidelis. 2004. "The Rhetoric of Human Rights in Malawi: Individualization and Judicilization," Chapter 2 in H. Englund and F. Nyamnjoh, eds., *Rights and the Politics of Recognition in Africa*. London: Zed Books.

Kaulemu, David, ed. 2010. *Political Participation in Zimbabwe*. Harare: African Forum for Catholic Social Teachings.

Kawadza, Sydney. 2008. "Zimbabwe Will Never Be a Colony Again." *The Herald*, April 18.

Kayser, Undine. 2005. *Imagined Communities, Divided Realities: Engaging the Apartheid Past through "Healing of Memories" in a Post-TRC South Africa*. Unpublished PhD thesis, Department of Social Anthropology. University of Cape Town, 2005.

Khan, Fatima, Rebecca Chennells, and Annabel Heaney. 2009, September 30. "Persecuted at Home, Rejected in SA." *The Cape Argus*.

Kihato, Catherine. 2004 "NEPAD, the City and the Immigrant." *Development Update* 5(1): "The City and Its Future? The Eternal Question": 267–286.

Kleinman, Arthur. 1997. "The Violences of Everyday life: The Multiple Forms and Dynamics of Social Violence," in V. Das, A. Kleinman, M. Ramphele, and P. Reynolds, eds., *Violence and Subjectivity*. Berkeley: University of California Press.

Koptyoff, Igor. 1986. "The Cultural Biography of Things: Commoditization as process," In Arjun Appadurai, ed., *The Social Life of Things: Commodities in Cultural Perspective*. Cambridge, UK: Cambridge University Press.

Lan, David. 1985. *Guns and Rain: Guerrillas and Spirit Mediums in Zimbabwe*. London: James Currey.

Magaisa, Alex. 2009. *The Politics of Constitution-Making in Zimbabwe*. Blog posted on the New Zimbabwe Blog on March 26, 2009. Retrieved in September 2011 from www.newzimbabwe.com/blog/index.php/2009/03/amagaisa/the-politics-of-Constitution-making-in-zimbabwe/.

Mamdani, Mamoud, ed. 2000. *Beyond Rights Talk and Culture Talk: Comparative Essays on the Politics of Rights and Culture*. Cape Town: David Philip.

Marcus, George. 1995. "Ethnography in/of the World System: The Emergence of Multi-Sited Ethnography." *Annual Review of Anthropology* 24: 95–117.

Martinez, Jenny. 2012. *The Slave Trade and the Origins of International Human Rights Law*. Oxford, UK: Oxford University Press.

Marwizi, Walter. May 23, 2010. *"Ngozi*: Primitive Superstition or Reality?" *The Standard: Zimbabwe's Leading Sunday Newspaper.* Retrieved in June 2012 from www.thestandard.co.zw/local/24789-ngozi-primitive-superstition-or-reality.html.

Mashingaidze, Terence. 2010. "'Guardians of the Nation or Unruly Disciples?' A Critique of Youth Participation in Post-Colonial Zimbabwe's Contested Political Spaces." *Understanding Africa's Contemporary Conflicts: Origins, Challenges and Peacebuilding.* Retrieved in December 2012 from www.humansecuritygateway.com/documents/ISS_UnderstandingAfricas ContemporaryConflicts_Origins ChallengesandPeacebuilding.pdf#page=140>.

Masunungure, Eldred, ed. 2009. *Defying the Winds of Change: Zimbabwe's 2008 Elections.* Harare: Weaver Press and Konrad Adenauer-Stiftung.

Matyszak, Derek. 2010. *Law, Politics and Zimbabwe's "Unity" Government.* Harare: The Konrad-Adenauer-Stiftung in association with The Research and Advocacy Unit.

——. 2013. "Human Rights and Zimbabwe's Draft Constitution." Harare: Report released by the Research and Advocacy Unit (RAU).

Matyszak, Derek, and Tony Reeler. 2011. "Articles of Faith: Assessing Zimbabwe's GPA as a Mechanism for Change: A Legal Perspective." Harare: The Research and Advocacy Unit.

Mawere, Munyaradzi. 2010. "On Pursuit of the Purpose of Life: The Shona Metaphysical Perspective." *The Journal of Pan African Studies* 3(6): 269–284. Available online at www.jpanafrican.com/docs/vol3no6/3.5OnPursuit.pdf.

Mbembe, Achille. 2001. *On the Postcolony.* Berkeley: University of California Press.

——. 2003. "Necropolitics." *Public Culture* 15(1): 11–40.

Mbire, Moreblessing. 2011. "Seeking Reconciliation and National Healing in Zimbabwe: Case of the Organ on National Healing, Reconciliation and Integration (ONHRI)." Unpublished research paper, International Institute of Social Studies. Retrieved on July 1, 2012, from http://oaithesis.eur.nl/ir/repub/asset/10814/MOREBLESSING_MBIRE_RP_16NOV_2011.pdf.

Mbiti, John. 1969. *African Religions and Philosophy.* Oxford, UK: Heinemann.

McFadden, Patricia. 2000. "Issues of Gender and Development from an African Feminist Perspective." Lecture presented in honor of Dame Nita Barrow, at the Center for Gender and Development Studies, University of the West Indies, Bridgetown, Barbados, November 2000. Retrieved in December 2012 from www.wworld.org/programs/regions/africa/patricia_mcfadden4.htm.

McGreal, Chris. 2008. "Mugabe's Men Bring Rape and Torture to Harare's Suburbs." *The Guardian.* June 21, 2008. Retrieve on July 1, 2012, from www.guardian.co.uk/world/2008/jun/21/zimbabwe.

MDC Today. August 31, 2010. "ZANU-PF Setting up Militia Bases ahead of Copac Meetings." Retrieved in October 2010 from www.sokwanele.com/thisis
zimbabwe/archives/5984.

Merry, Sally Engle. 1988. "Legal Pluralism." *Law and Society Review.* 22: 869–896.

———. 2005. "Anthropology and Activism: Researching Human Rights across Porous
Boundaries." *Political and Legal Anthropology Review (PoLAR)* 28(2): 240–257.

———. 2006. "Transnational Human Rights and Local Activism: Mapping the Mid-
dle." *American Anthropologist* 108(1): 38–51.

Merry, Sally Engle, and Mark Goodale, eds. 2007. *The Practice of Human Rights:
Tracking Law between the Global and the Local.* Cambridge, UK: Cambridge
University Press.

Messer, Deborah. 1993. "Anthropology and Human Rights." *Annual Review of Anthropology* 22: 221–249.

Mhiripiri, Dominic. 2011. *Amid Lack of Freedom, Zimbabwe Reaches Independence Milestone.* Global Conversation. Retrieved in June 2011 from www
.globalconversation.org/2011/04/22/amid-lack-freedom-zimbabwe-reaches-
independence-milestone.

Mignolo, W. 2012. *The Darker Side of Western Modernity: Global Futures, Decolonial
Options.* Durham, NC: Duke University Press.

Morreira, Shannon. 2009. "Seeking Solidarity. Categorisation and the Politics of
Alienism in the Migration of Zimbabweans to South Africa." Unpublished
master's thesis, University of Cape Town.

———. 2010a. "Living with Uncertainty: Disappearing Modernities and Polluted Ur-
banity in Harare, 2007." *Social Dynamics: A Journal of African Studies* 36(2):
352–365.

———. 2010b. "Seeking Solidarity: Zimbabwean Undocumented Migrants in Cape
Town, 2007." *Journal of Southern African Studies* 36(2): 433–488.

———. 2011. "Framing Harm: Legal, Local and Anthropological Knowledge in the
Context of Forced Migration.' *Anthropology Matters* 13(1): 1–13. Available online at www.anthropologymatters.com/index.php/anth_matters/article/view/
221/377.

———. 2012a. "'Anthropological Futures?': Thoughts on Social Research and the Ethics of Engagement." *Anthropology Southern Africa* 35 (3 & 4): 100–105.

———. 2012b. "Book Review: Zimbabwe in Transition: A View from Within." *Social
Dynamics: A Journal of African Studies,* 38(1): 152–154.

———. 2015a. "'Making a Plan': Responses amongst the Wealthy to Declining Socioeconomic Conditions in Suburban Harare." *Social Dynamics* 41(2).

———. 2015b. "'You Can't Just Step from One Place to Another': The Socio-Politics of
Illegality in Migration from Zimbabwe to South Africa." *Migration Letters* 14:
67–78.

Mugabe, Robert. September 3, 2002. Speech at the Earth Summit, Johannesburg. Quoted in John Battersby and Andrew Grice, "Anti-West Anger at Summit as Mugabe Rounds on Blair," *The Independent*, 1.

———. December 6, 2003. Speech to ZANU-PF Congress. Reported in Michael White and Andrew Meldrum, "Commonwealth leaders delay decision on defiant Mugabe," *The Guardian*.

———. September 26, 2007. Speech to the UN General Assembly. Retrieved on 15 December 15, 2015, from connection.ebscohost.com/c/speeches/27424050/mugabe-let-mr-bush-read-history-correctly.

Mupinda, M. 1997. "Loss and Grief among the Shona: The Meaning of Disappearances." *Legal Forum* 9: 41–49.

Muponde, Robert. 2004. Chapter 10: "The Worm and the Hoe: Cultural Politics and Reconciliation after the Third Chimurenga," Chapter 10, pp. 176–192, in Brian Raftopoulos and Tyrone Savage, eds., *Zimbabwe: Injustice and Political Reconciliation*. Cape Town: Institute for Justice and Reconciliation.

Murithi, Tim, and Aquilina Mawadza, eds. 2011. *Zimbabwe in Transition: A View from within*. Cape Town: Fanele/Jacana Media and The Institute for Justice and Reconciliation.

Musarandega, Reuben. 2009. "Integrated Human Rights and Poverty Eradication Strategy: The Case of Civil Registration Rights in Zimbabwe." *International Social Science Journal (ISSJ)* 60(197–198): 389–402.

Musiyiwa, Mickias. 2008. "Eschatology, Magic, Nature and Politics: The Responses of the People of Epworth to the Tragedy of Operation Murambatsvina," pp. 65–73 in M. Vambe, ed., *The Hidden Dimensions of Operation Murambatsvina in Zimbabwe*. Pretoria: Weaver Press.

Mutambirwa, Jane. 1989. "Health Problems in Rural Communities." *Social Science and Medicine* 26(8): 927–932.

National Constitutional Assembly of Zimbabwe (NCA). 2007. "About the NCA." Retrieved in April 2010 from www.ncazimbabwe.info/index.php?option=com_content&task=view&id=9&Itemid=14.

———. April 15, 2009. *The Shortcomings of the Kariba Draft Constitution*. Harare: NCA.

Ncube, Pius. 2005. "State in Fear: Zimbabwe's Tragedy Is Africa's Shame: A Report on Operation Murambatsvina—"Operation Drive Out the Filth"—and Its Implications." Retrieved on September 27, 2005, from www.fightingmalaria.org/pdfs/state_in_fear.pdf.

Ncube, Welshman. 2001. "The Courts of Law in Rhodesia and Zimbabwe: Guardians of Civilisation, Human Rights and Justice or Purveyors of Repression, Injustice and Oppression?," pp. 99–123 in Ngwabi Bhebhe and Terence Ranger, eds., *The Historical Dimensions of Democracy and Human Rights in Zimbabwe*.

Volume One: Precolonial and Colonial Legacies. Harare: University of Zimbabwe Publications.

Ndlovu, Mary. 2012. "Zimbabwe: Political Paralysis of Coalition Government Stalls Nation." *Pambazuka News,* 589 (June 13); retrieved in September 2012 from www.pambazuka.org/en/category/features/82894.

Ndlovu-Gatsheni, Sabelo. 2008. "Who Ruled by the Spear? Rethinking the Form of Governance in the Ndebele State." *African Studies Quarterly* 10, 2 & 3 (Fall 2008). Retrieved in December 2012 from http://africa.ufl.edu/asq/v10/v10i2a4 .htm.

———. 2013. *Empire, Global Coloniality and African Subjectivity.* New York and Oxford, UK: Berghahn Books.

Nelson, Diane. 2010. "Reckoning the After/Math of War in Guatemala." *Anthropological Theory* 10(1–2): 87–95.

New African. 2009. "Tsvangirai's Boycott a Strategic Move." Retrieved on October 20, 2009, from www.africasia.com/services/news/newsitem.php?area=africa&item =091017011615.2qq8borb.php.

NewsDay. August 31, 2010a. "Donors Dump COPAC." Retrieved on October 5, 2005, from www.newsday.co.zw/2010/08/31/2010-08-31-donors-dump-copac/.

Nkrumah, Kwame. 1961. *Speak of Freedom: A Statement of African Ideology.* London Heinemann.

Nuttall, Sarah. 2009. *Entanglement: Literary and Cultural Reflections on Post-Apartheid.* Johannesburg: Wits University Press.

Nyamnjoh, Francis. 2004. "Reconciling 'the Rhetoric of Rights' with Competing Notions of Personhood and Agency in Botswana," Chapter 1 in H. Englund and F. Nyamnjoh, eds., *Rights and the Politics of Recognition in Africa.* London: Zed Books.

———. 2012a. "Blinded by Sight: Divining the Future of Anthropology in Africa." *Africa Spectrum* 47(2–3): 63–92.

———. 2012b. "Potted Plants in Greenhouses: A Critical Reflection on the Resilience of Colonial Education in Africa." *Journal of Asian and African Studies* 47(2): 129–154.

Nyerere, Julius. 1968. *Essays in Socialism.* Oxford: Oxford University Press.

Okazaki, Akira. 2003. "Making Sense of the Foreign : Translating Gamk Notions of Dream, Self and Body," in T. Maranhao and B. Streck, eds., *Translation and Ethnography: The Anthropological Challenge of Intercultural Understanding.* Tucson: University of Arizona Press.

Olukoshi, Adebayo, and Francis Nyamnjoh. 2011. "The Postcolonial Turn: An Introduction," pp. 1–26 in R. Devisch and f. Nyamnjoh, eds., *The Postcolonial Turn: Re-Imagining Anthropology and Africa.* Cameroon: Langaa Research and Publishing Common Initiative Group.

Orner, Peter, and Annie Holmes, eds. 2010. *Hope Deferred: Narratives of Zimbabwean Lives*. San Francisco: Voice of Witness and McSweeney's Books,

Ortner, Sherri. 1973. "On Key Symbols." *American Anthropologist* 75(5): 1338–1346.

PASSOP (People Against Suffering, Oppression and Poverty). 2011. "The Road to Documentation: Asylum-Seekers' Access to Cape Town's Refugee Reception Centre." Monitoring Report. Retrieved in November 2012 from www.passop .co.za/publications/reports.

Peta, Basildon. March 9, 2007. "Zimbabwe: Mbeki, Mugabe Finally Discuss Zimbabwe Crisis." *Independant Online (IOL)*. Retrieved on September 11, 2011, from www.afrika.no/Detailed/13697.html.

Quijano, Anibal. 1999. "Coloniality and Modernity/Rationality." In Goran Therborn, ed., *Globalizations and Modernities*. Stockholm: FRN.

Raftopoulos, Brian. 2004. "Current Politics in Zimbabwe: Confronting the Crisis," in D. Harold-Barry, ed., *Zimbabwe: The Past Is the Future*. Harare: Weaver Press.

Raftopoulos, Brian, and Alois Mlambo, eds. 2009. *Becoming Zimbabwe: A History from the Pre-Colonial Period to 2008*. Johannesburg: Jacana.

Rahnema, Majid. 1997. "Afterword: Towards Post-Development: Searching for Signposts, a New Language and New Paradigms," pp. 377–403 in M. Rahnema and V. Bawtree, eds., *The Post-Development Reader*. London: Zed Books.

Ramose, Mogobe B. 1999. *African Philosophy through Ubuntu*. Harare: Mond Books.

Ranchod-Nilsson, Sita. 2006. "Gender Politics and the Pendulum of Political and Social Transformation on Zimbabwe." *Journal of Southern African Studies* 32(1): 49–67.

Ranger, Terence. 2001. "Democracy and Traditional Political Structures in Zimbabwe, 1890–1999," pp. 31–52 in Ngwabi Bhebhe and Terence Ranger, eds., *The Historical Dimensions of Democracy and Human Rights in Zimbabwe. Volume One: Precolonial and Colonial Legacies*. Harare: University of Zimbabwe Publications.

Reeler, Anthony. 1998. "Compensation for Gross Human Rights Violations: Torture and the War Victims Compensation Act." *Legal Forum* 10(2): 6–21.

Reeler, Anthony, Kudakwashe Chitsike, Fungisai Maizva, and Bev Reeler. 2009. "The Tree of Life: A Community Approach to Empowering and Healing the Survivors of Torture in Zimbabwe." *Torture* 19(3): 180–193.

Research and Advocacy Unit (RAU) and Zimbabwe Association of Doctors for Human Rights (ZADHR), 2010a. *No Hiding Place: Politically Motivated Rape of Women in Zimbabwe*. Harare: RAU.

———. 2010b. *"When the Going Gets Tough, the Man Gets Going!": Zimbabwean Women's Views on Politics, Governance, Political Violence, and Transitional Justice*. Harare: Report produced by the Research and Advocacy Unit [RAU], Idasa

[Institute for Democracy in Africa], and the International Center for Transitional Justice [ICTJ].

———. 2010c. *Women, Politics and the Zimbabwe Crisis.* Harare: IDASA, the International Centre for Transitional justice(ICTJ), RAU, and the Women's Coalition of Zimbabwe (WCoZ).

Robertson, Geoffrey. 2006. *Crimes against Humanity: The Struggle for Global Justice* (3rd edition). London: Penguin.

Robins, Steven. 2008a. *From Revolution to Rights in South Africa: Social Movements, NGOs and Popular Politics after Apartheid.* South Africa: University of Kwa-Zulu-Natal Press.

———. 2008b. "Rights," pp. 182–194 in N. Shepherd and S. Robins, S., eds., *New South African Keywords.* Johannesburg: Jacana.

Rosen, Michael. 2012. *Dignity: Its History and Meaning.* Cambridge, MA, and London: Harvard University Press.

Ross, Fiona C. 2003a. *Bearing Witness: Women and the Truth and Reconciliation Commission in South Africa.* London: Pluto Press.

———. 2003b. "On Having Voice and Being Heard: Some After-Effects of the South African Truth and Reconciliation Committee." *Anthropological Theory* 3: 325–341.

———. 2003c. "Using Rights to Measure Wrongs: A Case Study of Method and Moral in the Work of the South Africa Truth and Reconciliation Commission," pp. 163–182 in R/ Wilson and J. Mitchell, eds., *Human Rights in Global Perspective: Anthropological Studies of Rights, Claims and Entitlements.* London and New York: Routledge.

———. 2010. "An Acknowledged Failure:Women, Voice, Violence and the South African Truth and Reconciliation Commission." In R. Shaw and L. Waldorf, eds., *Localizing Transitional Justice: Interventions and Priorities after Mass Violence.* Stanford, CA: Stanford University Press.

Sachikonye, Lloyd. 2011. *When a State Turns on Its Citizens: Institutionalized Violence and Political Culture.* Johannesburg: Jacana.

Sachs, Albie. 2009. *The Strange Alchemy of Life and Law.* Oxford, UK, New York, and Cape Town: Oxford University Press.

Saki, Otto, Tatenda Chiware, Jimcall Pfumorodze, and Emma Chitsove. 2011. "Update: The Law in Zimbabwe." New York: GlobaLex/Hauser Global Law School Program. Retrieved in March 2012 from www.nyulawglobal.org/Globalex/Zimbabwe1.htm.

Samkange, Stanlake, and Tommie Samkange. 1980. *Hunhuism or Ubuntuism: A Zimbabwe Indigenous Political Philosophy.* Salisbury, Rhodesia: Graham Publishing.

Scarry, Elaine. 1985. *The Body in Pain: The Making and Unmaking of the World*. New York: Oxford University Press.

Schmidt, Elizabeth. 1992. *Peasants, Traders and Wives: Shona Women in the History of Zimbabwe, 1870–1939*. Harare: Baobab Books.

Scott, James. 1998. *Seeing Like a State: How Certain Schemes to Improve the Human Condition Have Failed*. New Haven, CT: Yale University Press.

Scott, Joan. 1991. "The Evidence of Experience." *Critical Enquiry* 17: 773–797.

Scully, Pamela, and Diana Paton. 2005. *Gender and Slave Emancipation in the Atlantic World*. Durham, NC: Duke University Press.

Senghor, Leopold. 1964. *On African Socialism*. New York: Praeger.

Shaw, Rosalind, and Lars Waldorf. 2010. "Introduction: Localizing Transitional Justice," in R. Shaw and L. Waldorf, eds., *Localizing Transitional Justice: Interventions and Priorities after Mass Violence*. Stanford, CA: Stanford University Press.

Sifile, Vusumuzi. 2010. "High Drama as Ngozi Fears Hit Gokwe." *The Standard*, March 7. Retrieved on October 1, 2011, from www.zimbabwesituation.org/?p=9699.

Sisterhood Is Global Institute. 1999. Urgent Action Alert. June 30. Retrieved on July 22, 2011, from www.africa.upenn.edu/Urgent_Action/apic_71499.html.

Slaughter, Joseph. 2007. *Human Rights, Inc.: The World Novel, Narrative Form and International Law*. New York: Fordham University Press.

Sokwanele. 2012. "Zimbabwe Inclusive Government Watch: The Most Breached Clauses of the Global Political Agreement." Sokwanele, December 16, 2012. Retrieved on December 17, 2012, from www.sokwanele.com/zimbabwe-inclusive-government-watch-most-breached-clauses-global-political-agreement/16122012.

South Africa. *Refugees Act 1998*. Retrieved on April 2, 2012, from www.gov.za/sites/www.gov.za/files/a130-98_0.pdf.

Speed, Shannon. 2002. "Global Discourses on the Local Terrain: Human Rights and Indigenous Identity in the Chiapas." *Cultural Dynamics* 14(2): 205–228.

Speed, Shannon, and Jane Collier. 2000. "Limiting Indigenous Autonomy in Chiapas, Mexico: The State Government's Use of Right." *Human Rights Quarterly* 22: 877–905.

Stearns, Peter. 2012. *Human Rights in World History*. London and New York: Routledge.

Steinberg, Jonny. 2008. "South Africa's Xenophobic Eruption." *Institute for Security Studies (ISS)*. Paper 169.

Stewart, Julie. 1990. "The Legal Situation of Women in Zimbabwe," pp. 195–222 in J. Stewart and A. Armstrong, eds., *Women and Law in Southern Africa*. Harare: University of Zimbabwe Publications.

STOPVAW/The Advocates for Human Rights. 2003. "Investigation and Documentation of Women's Human Rights Violations." Retrieved on October 22, 2012, from www.stopvaw.org/investigation_and_documentation_of_women_s_human_rights_violations.

Tamale, Sylvia. 2008. "The Right to Culture and the Culture of Rights: A Critical Perspective on Women's Sexual Rights in Africa." *Feminist Legal Studies* 16(1): 47–69.

Taundi, Josiah. 2009. "The Pro-Democracy Movement in Zimbabwe (1998–Present)." International Centre on Non-Violent Conflict. Retrieved on October 1, 2011, from www.nonviolent-conflict.org/index.php/movements-and-campaigns/movements-and-campaigns-summaries?sobi2Task=sobi2Details&sobi2Id=12.

Tirivangana, Augustine. 2010. "The Metaphysical Scope of Ngozi." *The Standard*, May 29. Retrieved on October 1, 2011, from www.thestandard.co.zw/opinion/24857-the-metaphysical-scope-ofngozi-.html.

Tsing, Anna Lowenhaupt. 2000. "The Global Situation." *Cultural Anthropology* 15(3): 327–360.

———. 2005. *Friction: An Ethnography of Global Connection*. Princeton, NJ: Princeton University Press.

———. 2009. "Worlds in Motion," in Carol Gluck and Anna Lowenhaupt Tsing, eds., *Words in Motion: Toward a Global Lexicon*. Durham, NC, and London: Duke University Press.

Turner, Victor. 1969. *The Ritual Process: Structure and Anti-Structure*. London: Routledge.

Twiss, Sumner B. 2004. "History, Human Rights, and Globalisation." *Journal of Religious Ethics* 32(1): 39–70.

United Nations. 1948. United Nations Declaration of Human Rights (UNDHR). Available online at www.un.org/en/universal-declaration-human-rights/.

United Nations. 1984. "United Nations Convention Against Torture." Geneva: United Nations. Retrieved on January 30, 2012, from www.un.org/documents/ga/res/39/a39r046.htm.

United Nations Office of the High Commissioner for Human Rights (UN OHCR). 2001. "Training Manual on Human Rights Monitoring." Professional Training Series No. 7. United Nations: New York and Geneva.

Vambe, Maurice. 2008. "Introduction: Rethinking Citizen and Subject in Zimbabwe," in M. Vambe, ed., *The Hidden Dimensions of Operation Murambatsvina in Zimbabwe*. Pretoria: Weaver Press.

Van Gennep, Arnold. 1960. *The Rites of Passage*. London: Routledge.

Watson, Bruce. 2005. *Bread and Roses: Mills, Migrants and the Struggle for the American Dream*. New York: Viking.

Weinstein, Harvey, Laurel Fletcher, Patrick Vinck, and Phuong Pham. 2010. "Stay the Hand of Justice: Whose Priorities Take Priority?" In R. Shaw and L. Waldorf, eds., *Localizing Transitional Justice: Interventions and Priorities after Mass Violence*. Stanford, CA: Stanford University Press.

Werbner, Richard. 1996 "Human Rights and Moral Knowledge: Arguments of Accountability in Zimbabwe," in M. Strathern, ed., *Shifting Contexts*. London and New York: Routledge.

———. 1998. "Smoke from the Barrel of a Gun: Postwars of the Dead, Memory and Reinscription in Zimbabwe," pp. 71–104 in R. P. Werbner, ed., *Memory and the Postcolony: African Anthropology and the Critique of Power*. London: Zed Books.

Wilson, Richard, ed. 1997. *Human Rights, Culture and Context*. London: Pluto.

———. 2006. "Afterword to 'Anthropology and Human Rights in a New Key': The Social Life of Human Rights." *American Anthropologist* 108(1): 77–83.

Wilson, Richard, and Richard Brown, eds. 2009. *Humanitarianism and Suffering: The Mobilisation of Empathy*. Cambridge, UK: Cambridge University Press.

Wilson, Richard, and Jon Mitchell, eds. 2003. *Human Rights in Global Perspective: Anthropological Studies of Rights, Claims and Entitlements*. London and New York: Routledge.

Women's Coalition of Zimbabwe (WCoZ). 2012. "About Us." Retrieved on January 30, 2012, from www.wcoz.org/about-wcoz-.html.

Worby, Eric, Shireen Hassim, and Tawana Kupe. 2008. "Introduction," pp. 1–26 in Shireen Hassim, Tawana Kupe, and Eric Worby, *Go Home or Die Here: Violence, Xenophobia and the Reinvention of Difference in South Africa*. Johannesburg: Wits University Press.

Zimbabwe Central Statistic Office, 2002. "Census 2002:National Report." Harare: Zimbabwe Central Statistic Office.

ZCC (Zimbabwe Council of Churches). 2009, April. "Pastoral Letter to the Nation." Harare: ZCC.

Zimbabwe Human Rights NGO Forum. 2001. *Enforcing the Rule of Law in Zimbabwe*. Harare: Zimbabwe Human Rights NGO Forum. Retrieved in April 2009 from http://archive.niza.nl/docs/200406111512063324.pdf.

———. 2011. *Transitional Justice National Survey: A Report on the People's Perceptions and Recommendations*. Harare: Zimbabwe Human Rights NGO Forum. Retrieved on July 1, 2012, from www.hrforumzim.org/wp-content/uploads/2012/02/TJ_Survey_July_20111.pdf.

ZIMSTAT (Zimbabwe National Statistic Agency) and IOM (the International Organisation for Migration). 2010. "Migration in Zimbabwe: A Country Profile." Retrieved in September 2012 from www.publications.iom.int/bookstore/free/mp_zimbabwe.pdf.

The Zimbabwean. August 16, 2010. "COPAC Meeting Abandoned after Violence." Retrieved on August 20, 2010, from www.thezimbabwean.co.uk/human-rights/33459/-copac-meeting-abandoned-after-violence.html.

ZZZICOMP (ZESN [Zimbabwe Electoral Support Network]/ZPP [Zimbabwe Peace project]/ZLHR [Zimbabwe Lawyer's for Human Rights] Independent Constitution Monitoring Project). September 20, 2010. "Chaos and Violence Mars COPAC Meetings as Residents Deprived on Right to Participate on Racial Grounds." Harare.

Index

OAU. *See* Organisation of African Unity

Okazaki, Akira, 147

ONHRI. *See* Organ on National Healing, Reconciliation, and Integration

Operation *Murambatsvina*: in Epworth, 74, 75; as government punishment of opposition, 74; and justification of violence against citizens, 17–18

The Order of Discourse (Foucault), 10

Organisation of African Unity (OAU), and definition of human rights, 9

Organ on National Healing, Reconciliation, and Integration (ONHRI): creation of, 63; entanglement of diverse justice repertoires and, 86–87; and international influence on reconciliation process, 66; limited impact of, 66–67; and localized justice mechanisms, 87; transitional justice model of, 63, 66

Orner, Peter, 6

Ortner, Sherri, 2

overlay, entanglement and, 82

participant-observer model, 1–2, 21, 22–23

PASSOP. *See* People Against Suffering Oppression and Poverty

Paton, Diana, 14

People Against Suffering Oppression and Poverty (PASSOP), 22–23, 25–26, 122

A People's Guide to Constitutional Debate (African Community Publishing and Development Trust), 40–42, 53

personhood: as anthropological concept, 128; conflicting concepts of, and universal human rights, 128–29, 136–37, 140, 147–48; in South Africa, *Ubuntu* and, 131; Western concept of, 128

personhood in Zimbabwean culture: conflict with personhood in international human rights law, 128–29, 136–37, 140, 147–48; as relationship-based, 127–29, 130; *unhu/hunhu* as characteristic of, 130–31

police in Zimbabwe: constitutional provision for, 155n4; as instrument of government rule, 58, 60, 61, 62

political crime in Zimbabwe: and culture of impunity, 57–58, 60–62, 61, 144; danger of speaking about, 57, 58, 60; increase in after 2000–2001, 61–62; *ngozi* (avenging spirits) as punishers of, 57–58, 58–59, 83–87; profound impact of, 62; violence surrounding elections, 58, 60, 61, 73, 74–75, 93, 156n18; as widespread, 61

political power: impact on localization of human rights, 4, 55; of Zimbabwean presidency, expansion of, 30–31, 34, 35, 38, 61

politics: conduits of exchange and circulation and, 107; many forms of meaning making in, 114; of Zimbabwe, rift in since independence, 47–48

polyphony, Tree of Life healing model and, 81

POSA. *See* Public Order and Security Act of 2002

postcolonial Africa: conception of time in, 16–17, 71–72; dominance of liberal civil society in, 151n6; rhetoric of rights in, 2

postcolonial state: colonial carryovers into, 4, 10–11, 141–42; and colonial influence on human rights discourse, 4, 10–11, 12–13, 17–18; fetishism of law in, 18–19, 143; increasing importance of human rights discourse in, 114

postdevelopment theory, 11–12

power, production of reality by, 95

Practicing Ethnography in Law (Goodale and Starr), 21–23

presidential powers in Zimbabwe, expansion of, 30–31, 34, 35, 38, 61

prosecution for human rights violations, second-generation rights and, 15

Public Order and Security Act of 2002 (POSA) [Zimbabwe], 18, 41–42, 48

Quijano, Anibal, 10, 11

Raftopoulos, Brian, 5, 6, 47–48

Rahnema, Majid, 11

Worby, Eric, 7
work, access to, Zimbabwean perception
of as human right, 124–25
World War II, and human rights discourse, 14
WOZA. *See* Women of Zimbabwe Arise

youth militia of ZANU-PF, 54, 73, 101,
108, 156n15

Zambia, human rights in, 49, 53
ZANU-PF. *See* Zimbabwe African National Union-Patriotic Front
ZAPU. *See* Zimbabwe African People's
Union
ZCC. *See* Zimbabwe Council of Churches
Zimbabwe: choice of as locus of study,
20–21; colonial, 5, 90; history of, 5–9;
independence for (1980), 5; indigenization programs in, 152n6. *See also other
specific topics*
Zimbabwe African National Union-
Patriotic Front (ZANU-PF): autochthony rhetoric of, 46, 49, 155n16;
and constitutional reform process of
1990s, 32–35; and Constitution of 2013,
37–38; and election of 1980, 5; and
election of 2013, 9; on freedom as freedom from Western influence, 50–52;
and Global Political Agreement, 8, 29;
ignoring of popular calls for reform
in 1990s, 35; and politicization of
reconciliation process, 65; and public
consultations on constitution of 2013,
37–38, 50–52, 54; public dissatisfaction with government of, 6; punishment
of opposition supporters by, 74–75,
84–85, 86; undermining of rule of law
by, 61, 62
Zimbabwe African People's Union
(ZAPU), 5, 152n7, 156n10
Zimbabwean constitutional court, weakening of through constitutional amendments, 31
Zimbabwean constitution of 1979. *See*
Lancaster House Constitution

Zimbabwean constitution of 2013: ap-
proval of by national referendum, 27,
54; and human rights guarantees, failure to include, 54–55; limitations of, 27
Zimbabwean constitution of 2013, writing
of: Article VI provisions for, 35–37; and
constitution concept as Western intrusion, 52; debate surrounding, 27, 37–38;
as democratic performance rather than
actual democracy, 142–43; GPA stipula-
tion of, 30; and human rights in theory
vs. real-world application, 142–43; human rights stakes in, 37–38; as "people
driven" process, 35–36, 40, 142; and
politicized conditions, influence of, 38;
public skepticism about process, 37; and
struggle between liberal civil society
and autocratic Kariba Draft, 36–38, 54.
See also Global Political Agreement,
Article VI; Select Constitutional Parliamentary Committee (COPAC)
Zimbabwean Dispensation Project, 115,
119, 158n2
Zimbabwean migrants: and citizenship as
issue in constitution of 2013, 45; desti-
nations for, 113; volume of, 113
Zimbabwean migrants in South Africa:
experience of as analogous to apartheid,
153n1; fear of returning home, 8; majority of as undocumented, 113; number
of, 113; overwhelming of Reception
Centres by, 115, 123; reasons for migration, 5, 136; reasons for migration as
inadequate for asylum status, 115–16,
117–19, 120–26; refugee status, efforts to obtain, 6–7, 115, 122–23; undocumented, high number of, 113; and
xenophobic violence, 8. *See also* South
African asylum process
Zimbabwean migrants in South Africa,
and human rights: economic decline in
Zimbabwe and, 7; insistence on validity
of socioeconomic rights, 122, 123–27;
language of, as central to their experience, 3; localized version of human
rights discourse in, 3–4, 124–27, 127–29,

Values in Translation: Human Rights and the Culture of the World Bank
Galit A. Sarfaty
2012

Disquieting Gifts: Humanitarianism in New Delhi
Erica Bornstein
2012

Stones of Hope: How African Activists Reclaim Human Rights to Challenge Global Poverty
Edited by Lucie E. White and Jeremy Perelman
2011

Judging War, Judging History: Behind Truth and Reconciliation
Pierre Hazan
2010

Localizing Transitional Justice: Interventions and Priorities after Mass Violence
Edited by Rosalind Shaw and Lars Waldorf, with Pierre Hazan
2010

Surrendering to Utopia: An Anthropology of Human Rights
Mark Goodale
2009

Human Rights for the 21st Century: Sovereignty, Civil Society, Culture
Helen M. Stacy
2009

Human Rights Matters: Local Politics and National Human Rights Institutions
Julie A. Mertus
2009